CROOM HELM
CLASSICAL STUDIES

PRIAPEA: POEMS FOR A PHALLIC GOD

Introduced, translated and edited, with notes
and commentary
by
W. H. PARKER

CROOM HELM
London & Sydney

© 1988 W.H. Parker
Croom Helm Ltd, Provident House,
Burrell Row, Beckenham, Kent BR3 1AT
Croom Helm Australia, 44–50 Waterloo Road,
North Ryde, 2113, New South Wales

Published in the USA by
Croom Helm
in association with Methuen, Inc.
29 West 35th Street
New York, NY 10001

British Library Cataloguing in Publication Data

Priapea : poems for a phallic god.
    1. Latin poetry 2. Latin poetry—
Translations into English 3. English
poetry—Translations from Latin
I. Parker, W.H.
871'.01'08   PA6121.A7

ISBN 0–7099–4099–8

Printed and bound in Great Britain by
Biddles Ltd, Guildford and King's Lynn

Contents

Contents

Illustrations

1a. Red-figure *kylix*: young man carving a herm of Priapus. Late 6th cent. BC.

1b. Attic cup. Woman worshipping a herm of Priapus.

2. Attic *krater* (bell bowl). Pan chasing a shepherd; statue of Priapus.

3. Boeotian *skyphos*: the hero Cephalus sacrifices to Priapus. 5th cent. BC.

4a. Carnelian gemstone: Priapus and two Cupids, one playing the double flute, the other sacrificing at an altar. 2nd/3rd cent. AD.

4b. Carnelian gemstone: a satyr sacrifices to Priapus. 1st cent. AD.

Preface

Two radical changes in Western society have made possible new perceptions of classical literature, leading to unprecedented opportunities for study and debate. The first revolution has been the dissolution of the Judaeo-Christian sexual ethic, and the resulting partial lifting of taboos on the literary use of erotic material and explicit language. This has made possible, for the first time, an unblinkered look at vital aspects of the ancient world of letters. A superb example of the potential of this new freedom to illuminate previously neglected and misunderstood themes, is Amy Richlin's *The Garden of Priapus* (Yale University Press, 1982). Vincenz Buchheit has demonstrated beyond doubt the credentials of the *Priapea* to be regarded as a literary work of the first class (*Zetemata* 28, 1962). Richlin's book provides the psychological background.

The second revolution has been the transformation in the status and activities of women. As a result classical studies have seen an influx of female scholars, again bringing a fresh approach to the literature, and questioning some of the assumptions that have hitherto underlain its study. Richlin's book illustrates the value of this for Latin studies, as does Eva Keuls' *The Reign of the Phallus* (New York: Harper, 1985) for Greek.

Such contributions smooth the path for a new edition of the *Priapea*. We acknowledge our indebtedness to all who have laboured for a greater understanding of the work, and not least to the authors of two recent doctoral dissertations: Richard Clairmont: *Carmina Priapea* (Loyola University Chicago, 1983) and Eugene O'Connor: *Dominant themes in Graeco-Roman priapic poetry* (University of California Santa Barbara, 1984).

W.H. Parker

Note to the Reader

NAMES AND NUMBERS

The corpus of 80 or so poems about Priapus, previously included among the minor works of Virgil, were entitled *Priapea* in most manuscripts, and until recently, in the printed editions. In the twentieth century, when it became customary — without any manuscript authority — to detach the three priapic epigrams found at the beginning of the *Catalepton* and give them also the title *Priapea*, the larger body often came to be distinguished as the *Carmina Priapea* or the *corpus Priapeorum*. We have retained the traditional title *Priapea* for the 80 poems, using *priapea* to denote other such poems, including those of the *Catalepton*.

References to the *Priapea* by number are made in bold type thus: **19**; other priapic poems, enumerated in the tables on pp. 3 and 11, are referred to by numbers in italic type, e.g. *20*.

Priapea: poems about Priapus

Priapea are poems written about the phallic god Priapus, or addressed to him, or spoken by him, or invoking him.[1] Strabo (c. 64 BC–AD 19) tells us that the Alexandrian poet Euphronius of Chersonnese (3rd cent. BC) wrote Greek *priapea*, and this kind of writing may be older still, for Athenaeus (11 473) quotes from a book entitled *Priapos* by Xenarchos, who lived in the fourth century BC. According to Suetonius (AD ?70–?130), Virgil wrote *priapea* in Latin. They were clearly regarded as a distinct kind of verse, and were often written in their own metre, the priapean (double glyconic). The three lines of Euphronius' *priapea* — and the one line of Virgil's — that have survived, were in this metre.[2]

Priapus was distinguished by his large erect member or phallus. The phallus itself had long been carried about as an apotropaic averter of evil, and venerated in special ceremonies as a symbol of nature's generative power. For, as Diodorus of Sicily (1st cent. BC) wrote, "it is right for that part of the body which is the origin of procreation, the prime begetter of all animal life, so to be honoured" (1 88 1). It was a short step to the erection of figures in human shape who would themselves bear and display it and claim to exercise its powers. These figures were at first herms: plain columns of wood with nothing more than a carved head and an erect penis, but subsequently iphyphallic statues, more completely human in their appearance, were developed and worshipped in the names of Priapus and other similar divinities.

Priapus himself seems to have originated in Asia Minor, where the Hellespontiac region, especially the city of Lampsacus, was held to be the source of his cult, whence it spread to Greece and the rest of the Mediterranean world. A Greek inscription found at the Aegean island city of Thera, reads, "I, Priapus, came to this city of Thera from Lampsacus, and brought enduring prosperity. I came to aid and succour you all, both citizens and strangers" (*IG* 12 3 421). Another, from Thyrreum in Acarnania, although only fragmentary, is clearly in praise of his sexual prowess.[3] He was, with his father Bacchus, especially popular in Alexandria.

GREEK PRIAPEA

The earliest surviving complete *priapea* are those by Hedylus

(*11*),* Leonidas (*14, 28, 37*) and Theocritus (*12, 13*), all from the third century BC. The 37 surviving Greek *priapea* are drawn from many centuries, stretching from the third BC to the sixth AD, although most of them cannot be precisely dated. Date has remarkably little significance, however, as their approach to their subject remains much the same throughout.

They fall into four groups. The first is dedicatory, twelve in number, in which Priapus is presented with or promised gifts; either the dedicator himself addresses the god or a third person describes the offering. The dedicators are fishermen (*4, 5, 7, 8*), horticulturalists (*2, 3, 6, 9*), courtesans (*1, 11*), a catamite (*10*) and a goatherd (*13*). Objects dedicated include animals (*13*), fish and fishing implements (*5, 7, 8*), a stool (*4*), finery (*1, 10, 11*). In two of the epigrams (*3, 9*) no reason is given for the gift and it is accompanied by no request or condition, e.g. *3*:

> The pomegranate ripe; in its first bloom, the quince;
> The fig with wrinkled skin — a navel in its midst;
> The purple bunch of grapes — a cluster rich with wine;
> The walnut fresh, without its peeled-off pale green rind;
> Priapus crude, carved from a single block, to thee
> The orchard-keeper dedicates these fruits of tree.

In *9* Priapus shares with Pan a gift of some fine delicacies.

In four instances the offerings are dedicated by the old, presumably in gratitude for a lifetime's favour. In *7* and *8*, aged fishermen, Phintylus and Damaetas, dedicate their equipment, while in *2* a landsman gives his tools in thankfulness:

> The tool that broke the thirsty earth — his spade,
> That cut his ready crops — his bow-shaped blade,
> His worn-out coat — so useful when it rained,
> His sturdy boots of hide — old, tough and stained;
> His aid in planting out — his dibble round
> That eased his seedlings into the soft ground;
> The hoe that saw he never was without
> Some irrigation through the summer drought:
> All these, Potamon, rich from harvest fine,
> O god Priapus, wills to make them thine.

---

*The *priapea* of the Greek Anthology will henceforth be referred to by the numbers on the left-hand side of the table on page 3.

Table of Priapea in the Greek Anthology (AP)

No.	AP Ref.		Author	Date	Type	Length
1	5	200	Anon.	?	dedicatory	4
2	6	21	Anon.	?	dedicatory	10
3	6	22	Anon.	?	dedicatory	6
4	6	33	Maecius	BC/AD	dedicatory	8
5	6	89	Maecius	BC/AD	dedicatory	8
6	6	102	Philippus	2nd cent.AD	dedicatory	8
7	6	192	Archias	1st cent. BC	dedicatory	8
8	6	193	Philaecus?	?	dedicatory	6
9	6	232	Crinagoras	BC/AD	dedicatory	8
10	6	254	Myrinus	1st cent. AD	dedicatory	8
11	6	292	Hedylus	3rd cent. BC	dedicatory	6
12	9	338	Theocritus	3rd cent. BC	erotic	6
13	9	437	Theocritus	3rd cent. BC	dedicatory	18
14	10	1	Leonidas of Tarentum	3rd cent. BC	marine	8
15	10	2	Antipater of Sidon	BC/AD	marine	8
16	10	4	Marcus Argentarius	BC/AD	marine	8
17	10	5	Thyillus	?	marine	8
18	10	6	Satyrus	?	marine	8
19	10	7	Archias	1st cent.BC	marine	8
20	10	8	Archias	1st cent. BC	marine	8
21	10	9	Anon.	?	marine	6
22	10	14	Agathias Scholasticus	6th cent. AD	marine	10
23	10	15	Paulus Silentarius	6th cent. AD	marine	8
24	10	16	Theaetetus Scholasticus	?	marine	14
25	10	17	Antiphilus	1st cent. AD	marine	6
26	11	224	Antipater	[BC/AD]	erotic	2
27	16	86	Anon.	?	watchman	6
28	16	236	Leonidas of Tarentum	3rd cent. BC	watchman	4
29	16	237	Tymnes	?	watchman	4
30	16	238	Lucian	2nd cent.AD	watchman	4
31	16	239	Apollonides	1st cent. AD	erotic	4
32	16	240	Philippus	2nd cent. AD	watchman	8
33	16	241	Marcus Argentarius	BC/AD	watchman	6
34	16	242	Erycius	1st cent. BC	erotic	8
35	16	243	Antistius	BC/AD	watchman	6
36	16	260	Anon.	?	watchman	4
37	16	261	Leonidas of Tarentum	3rd cent. BC	watchman	4

The fourth gratitude-on-retirement dedication is *10*, in which an old male prostitute offers up his finery and his flute.

It did not always take a lifetime's benevolence to earn Priapus such gifts. In *4*, fishermen, delighted with a rich haul, offer him a stool on which he may rest, and a bowl and glass from which he may refresh himself. And in perhaps the oldest *priapeum* extant, *11*, a girl, probably a courtesan, dedicates a fawn skin and a

3

golden jug to Priapus "who was the judge in the beauty competition". *1* may also be a gratitude dedication:

> Alexo's yellow dress, her sea-green ivy crown,
> That still retains the scent of myrrh, her head-dress too,
> She gives Priapus with the girlish squinting eyes,
> Commemorating his nocturnal sacred rites.

Alexo is probably a hetaera who did well out of the festivities and wishes to thank the god; one is reminded of **34*** (pp. 122–3) in which a prostitute makes an offering because she has done so well "during the night . . . at the salacious god's holy festival".

One may well be surprised that Priapus, renowned for his imposing masculinity, should be described as looking 'girlish'. Yet in paintings, statuary, etc., there is often an hermaphroditic contrast between his prominent male genitalia and his female figure with soft, rounded features. It has been said of such portrayals that, but for his *membrum virile*, he would have been taken for the goddess Pomona.[4] This concept of combining the male or impregnating aspect of reproduction with the female or conceptual, within one symbolic figure, was oriental in origin.

Offerings are also made in anticipation of favours to come, with the hoped-for boon sometimes expressed in a prayer (*do ut des*). Paris, a poor fisherman, in an epigram by Maecius (*5*), does not have much to give, but he does not expect much in return:

> Priapus, thou who lov'st the coastal caves,
> The islet rocks, and cliffs worn by the waves,
> To thee does Paris, fisher poor, donate
> This shell-fish he has been so fortunate
> To catch, but, after roasting, has devoured
> With his bad teeth, leaving the shell, well-scoured,
> To thee. So grant no greater boon, but let
> Him ease his pangs with fish caught in his net.

And in *6*, by Philippus, the gardener Lamon gives fine fruit, praying for good harvest and good health.

In only one instance the gift to the god is made conditional upon a boon being granted. This is in an idyll by Theocritus (*13*), the longest of the Greek *priapea*. A goatherd intends to sacrifice a

---

*Numerals in bold type refer to the eighty poems of the *Carmina Priapea*.

4

kid immediately, praying to be cured of his love for the beautiful boy Daphnis, but if the prayer is granted, he will further sacrifice a heifer, a fat lamb and a billy goat.

In the second group, which also numbers twelve, Priapus appears as the god of harbours, encouraging mariners to set sail, and promising them his protection. Most have a common theme — that spring has arrived, the storms of winter are passed, the season for sailing has arrived, and Priapus, the seamen's god, will favour their endeavours (*14, 15, 16, 17, 18, 23*). Others refer to his worship by fishermen and other seafarers, and to the grateful offerings they place upon his altars (*19, 21, 22*). These two motifs are combined in *22* and *24*, the second of which is freely rendered below:

Summer is here; the flowered field
Doth now the budding roses yield.
On cypress branch the paths along
The cicada sings its soothing song;
The house-martin beneath the thatch
Has built her nest, and rears a batch
Of young. The sea's at rest. No more
The angry waves beat on the shore.
So, sailor, for Priapus roast
Fish, for he's master of the coast.
Thou then may'st without dread proceed
Across th'Ionian Sea with speed.

A fresh motif is introduced in *19* and *20*: that of a Priapus who is a talking statue 'set up' by humans rather than a remote and potent divinity. In *19* Priapus tells that sailors who had called upon him in distress, had set him up on a wave-lashed rock to guard the straits. In *20* he refers to his unprepossessing shape, excusing it on the grounds that he was carved by untutored fisherfolk. But although a rough-hewn statue, he still claims godlike powers:

Yet should one of them call to me in need,
I hasten to him with a godlike speed,

and concludes:

The deep-sea fish are ruled by me alone;
By deeds and not by shape we gods are known.

And in *21*, although only "a little Priapus under a bush", he claims to have been responsible for a fine haul by having shown the fishers where the shoals were. In *25* one Archelaus asks the "god of the harbour's" blessing on his voyage.

A feature of the *priapea* surveyed so far is their pious tone. They are concerned with worship and divinity, with altars and sacrifices, with dedication and prayer. But in the third group (of nine poems), where Priapus appears as garden guardian or orchard watchman, as a crudely-made deterrent to thieves and birds, much less is heard about religious observance, and much more about the physical nature and weaknesses of the images themselves: the countryman's Priapus is altogether on a lower plane than the mariner's. The latter is, perhaps, because of his struggle with natural phenomena, given to a more religious turn of mind than the crude peasant whose coarse humour and earthy outlook inevitably colour his *priapea*.

The rural Priapus makes clear, more than any fisherman's, that he has a 'master' who has 'set him up' and to whom he owes fealty; he speaks and behaves more like a dog than a god, a faithful one usually, but often dirty as well; for, seeing his main function now as the protection of his lord's fruit and vegetables, he menaces potential thieves with his chief attribute, his phallus, which means, in effect, with anal rape. So that, although his great member is seldom directly mentioned, it and its threatened use lie implicit in all these poems. The maritime epigrams, by contrast, make no reference whatever to his phallus. And so the rustic Priapus of the Greek epigram brings obscenity into the *priapeum*, though to nothing like the degree reached in the Latin *Carmina Priapea*. Thus, in *28*, Leonidas refers to the god's extended and expanded weapon (see p. 107). *32* and *33* purport to be dialogues between Priapus and a trespasser, and turn about the double meaning of 'fig', which could signify, not only the edible fruit, but the vagina or anus — in these two instances the latter. In both conversations the lewd god — for that is what he now is — offers to allow the wayfarer to take figs from the orchard if he will give his 'fig' (see p. 75).

There is always an element of jest in the peasant's view of his Priapus — the threat of buggery is not meant seriously; it is a coarse joke of the countryside. This jocular element often finds expression in the mocking attitude of passers-by or intruders towards the wooden home-made god. Priapus himself sometimes admits that he is mocked, but warns the scoffer that, should he steal, he will laugh on the other side of his face. Thus Antistius in *35*:

> I am the watchman of the farm;
> I guard our Phricon's plants and hall;
> And this is what I say to all:
> "Laugh at my tool — but do no harm".
> For, should you to temptation fall,
> Your bearded face — that you're a male,
> Will be to you of no avail:
> 'Tis known I penetrate them all.

Lucian makes a Priapus tell how one Eutychides has set him up just for the sake of appearances, for the vineyard he is in is barren, and there is nothing to steal but himself (*30*).

Priapus realizes the inconsistency in being a god on the one hand and behaving so obscenely on the other — but he cannot help it: that's what he's been set up for by his master. So, in *29* he says he behaves "like Priapus to all thieves without distinction, and if anyone should tell him that it is wrong for him to say this, he would agree, but he will go on saying it just the same". And the similar *36* runs something like this:

> Hey, thief! Not to go near to the kail have a care!
> Or I, a Priapus, will strip you off bare.
> You'll say for a god so to do's a disgrace:
> You're right; but that's why I was put in this place.

As with herms of Mercury, statues of Priapus were placed at crossroads or road forks, his erect member combining the functions of pointer for the wayfarer and warning for the marauder, e.g. *37*:

> I, Priapus, watch well the meeting of the ways:
> My lower trunk a full-extended club displays.
> 'Twas Theocritus set me up. So do not thieve,
> Or else this swollen part of me thou wilt receive.

The final group of Greek *priapea* consists of four epigrams which are primarily concerned with the god's sensuality. The earliest is a warning to the beautiful young Daphnis that he is being pursued by Priapus and Pan "with a single purpose" (*12*). The

reader may surmise what this is. Next comes a remarkable
epigram by Ericius (*34*) who accuses the god of indecent exposure
in his home town of Lampsacus.

> How heavy, Priapus, that tool of yours, and stout,
>   That from your groin, all of it, sticks out!
> Get married, friend, if women you so much desire.
>   Your heart is swollen too, and all afire!
> You must relieve your thrust-out cock of its distress,
>   Or hide it 'neath some flower-patterned dress.
> You're not upon some mountain top where none can see,
>   But here in Lampsacus-upon-the-Sea.

In complete contrast is Antipater's couplet on a god who finds
himself humiliated by a better-endowed mortal (*26* — see p. 195).
And besides a sexually-humiliated Priapus we find a sexually
exhausted one — brought to his knees by the close proximity of a
lovely female statue — in *31*:

> The wise Anaxagoras placed me here to be
> His garden Priapus, but as you well can see,
> My knees are on the ground — indeed, a sorry sight.
> Yet blame not Phylomachus, my maker, for my plight.
> My neighbour, fair Charito, look on if you please;
> You then will understand why I'm found on my knees.

Anaxagoras (5th cent. BC) was a philosopher who fled to
Lampsacus from Athens after Cleon had attacked him for stating
the sun to be a ball of fire. Phylomachus was one of the famous
sculptors of Pergamon. An old bronze engraving of a kneeling
Priapus survives.[5]

Of the 37 extant Greek *priapea*, all but five say something about
the god besides the mere mention of his name. There is
conflicting evidence about his appearance. On the one hand he is
described as "sweet and girlish" (*1*) with a "beautiful head" (*12*)
and "fine horns" (*9*), while on the other he is roughly made out of
figwood "with the bark left on" (*13*), with no ears (*13*) and no feet
(*20*), and not polished or properly carved (*27*). Once he is called
"little" (*31*). Yet his "weapon" is "weighty" and "tightly
stretched" (*28*); it is a club that juts straight out (*37*). With it he is
able to perform "Venus's procreative task" (*13*). Little is said

about dress — or lack of it, but for a wreath of saffron-coloured ivy on his head (*12*).

Where is the Priapus of the Greek Anthology to be found? Usually, "on the beach" (*15, 17, 22*), or "on a sea-lashed rock" (*19*). But he is under a bush in *21* and "on a garden wall" in *28*. As for his functions, most references are to his marine powers: "lord of the ocean" (*24*), "god of the harbour" (*14, 18, 25*), "provider of good harbours" (*24*), "faithful to ships" (*23*); but he is also "keeper of the kitchen garden" (*27*), "watchman over the figs" (*33*), and the "gardener" (*2*). And, like Paris, he judges a beauty contest (*11*). There are also references to his character and behaviour: he delights in the wave-lashed rocks (*5*), takes care of sailors (*17, 20*, etc.), befriends the wayfarer (*6*) — unless he is after the figs, is very observant and alert as a watchman (*28, 33*), loves dancing and wine (*4, 9*); but, alas, he chases the young lad Daphnis (*13*), for "he behaves like Priapus to all" (*29*), or, putting it more bluntly, "knows how to penetrate all" (*35*).

GREEK-LATIN PRIAPEUM

Appropriate to our transition from Greek to Latin *priapea* is an inscription discovered at Acireale near Catania in 1921.[6] It begins with five or six lines of Greek — a language still widely used in Sicily in the third century, the likely date of the lettering — and ends with three lines of Latin. Further, it appears to have gone with a bi-frontal statue — a Priapus who looked both ways. Unfortunately the top and both sides of the stone on which it was inscribed have been broken off, and the first and last words of each line have been lost. Intelligent guesswork has provided reconstructions, but there are several of these and each tells a rather different story. One of them is translated below:

Greek   Rubrius of Samos set me up to look
This way and that, and he commands
Those from the city to refrain
And those from the country to abstain
From theft of fruit, and so to thieves
My huge erect organ I am to show.

Latin   The Samian put me here, looking both ways,
To display this enormous organ.
Rubrius son of Samos.

LATIN PRIAPEA

Outside of the 80 epigrams of the *corpus Priapeorum*, Latin has only about 15 *priapea* — the number is imprecise because it is sometimes arguable whether a poem is a *priapeum* or not. One is the long hymn found as an inscription near Tivoli (*60*). Three are the dedicatory type of epigram, five the rustic-watchman type, while three combine the watchman motif with the dedicatory. Two are 'erotic' — i.e. concerned with Priapus' sexual proclivities. One is unique in that it refers to Priapus in his surprising but well-attested function as guardian of the dead.[7]

Of the dedicatory *priapea* two are plain dedications (*38, 39*), one is anticipatory (*do ut des*) (*46*), and one is conditional on the god granting the accompanying prayer (*48*): in two, Priapus expresses himself obliged by the attentions he receives to take care of the dedicators and their property (*40, 41*). The dedicators include the poet Catullus, Encolpius of the *Satyricon*, a civil servant, and various peasants. Among the objects dedicated are a temple (*44*), a grove (*38*), ears of wheat, fruit, vegetables, flowers, vine shoots, barley stalks, milk and cake. Goats, a calf and a piglet are sacrificed. Of those with the watchman motif, three (*40, 44, 51*) contain a threat to thieves, and two of these hint that the penalty for stealing will be anal rape; in two there is, instead, a polite request not to steal (*41, 53*). Usually it is a garden or orchard that Priapus has to guard, but in *54* it is a wood.

Although these 15 *priapea* make up only 173 lines, there is a further body of verse, amounting to 277 lines, which, though not strictly speaking *priapea*, may be termed priapic poetry. There are four complete poems, two of them spoken in whole or in part by Priapus (*42, 43*), the third addressed initially to the god, but thereafter ceasing to be concerned with him (*45*). The rest are parts of longer poems which, however, could stand on their own as *priapea*. There are, besides, many other isolated lines of verse referring to the large-membered god, and several more references to him in Latin literature. Many of these are cited in the pages that follow.

There is little information in the Latin poetry about the god's appearance, apart from the material he is made of: just wood in *39*, the trunk of some old tree (*49*), useless firewood (*42*), poplar (*40*), oak (*41*), the best cypress (*51, 53*), and pastry (*56*); but in *46* and *47* he is "ruddy", in *43* his beard is rough and his hair unkempt, while in *44* he wears a wreath upon his head. His member stands erect in *42* and *51*, and it is variously described as red (*42*, *45*), unsheathed (*59*), and *trux* or "grim" in *40*.

Latin priapic poetry differs from the Greek in various ways. There is less serious religious poetry (if *60* is parody, scarcely any), but more that is mocking or facetious. There is no mention whatever of Priapus as a sailors' god, but he is once portrayed as guardian of the grave (*59*). Except for one extreme instance (*45*), there is not notably more obscenity.

Table of Latin Priapea and priapic poetry (excluding the Carmina Priapea)

No.	Author	Date	Ref.	Type	Length
*38**	Catullus	c.84–c.54 BC	*fr.* 1	dedicatory	4
*39**	Virgil (?)	70–19 BC	*catalepton* 1a	dedicatory	4
*40**	Virgil (?)	70–19 BC	*catalepton* 2a	watchman/dedicatory	21
*41**	Virgil (?)	70–19 BC	*catalepton* 3a	watchman/dedicatory	21
42	Horace	65–8 BC	*sat.* 1 8	narrative	50
43	Tibullus	c.60–19 BC	1 4	erotic	84
*44**	Tibullus (?)	c.60–19 BC	*CIL* 5 2805	watchman/dedicatory	6
45	?	?	*app. virg.*	erotic	45
46	Ovid	43 BC–AD 18	*fast.* 1 391–440	narrative	50
47	Ovid	43 BC–AD 18	*fast.* 6 319–346	narrative	28
*48**	Petronius	?–AD 65	*sat.* 133	dedicatory	17
49	Columella	1st cent. AD	*r.r.* 10 29–34	watchman	6
*50**	Martial	c.AD 40–104	6 16	watchman	4
*51**	Martial	c.AD 40–104	6 49	watchman	11
*52**	Martial	c.AD 40–104	6 72	watchman	6
*53**	Martial	c.AD 40–104	6 73	watchman	10
*54**	Martial	c.AD 40–104	7 91	erotic	4
*55**	Martial	c.AD 40–104	8 40	watchman	6
56	Martial	c.AD 40–104	14 70	erotic (?)	2
57	Prudentius	4th cent. AD	*symm.* 1 102–13	historical	14
*58**	Anon.	?	*anth. lat.* 885	erotic	5
*59**	Anon.	?	*CIL* 6 3708	funerary	2
*60**	Anon.	?	*CIL* 6 3565	hymn	52

* = priapeum

The earliest surviving reference to Priapus in Latin is a fragment attributed to the comic writer Afranius (b. c.150 BC): "What people say about me, that I was born of a long-eared parent [i.e. an ass], simply isn't true". In some lines by Furius Bibaculus (b. 103 BC) on Valerius Cato, a poet who lived out his old age in penury, we have the first mention in Latin of Priapus as the garden god:

If you, by chance, should see my Cato's lair,
    Its shingles painted with red lead,
Its garden in Priapus' watchful care,
    You'd wonder by what art he came
To school himself into such wisdom rare,
    That just three greens, a little flour,
Of grapes two bunches — such a diet spare
    Could nourish him to ripe old age.

Catullus' first fragment (*38*) is, in fact, almost a complete
priapeum, missing only a two-syllable word in line 2, and perhaps
a concluding couplet. It takes us back to the origins of the phallic
god at the Hellespontiac city of Lampsacus:

I dedicate and consecrate this grove, Priapus lord, to thee
At Lampsacus, where thine abode and sacred rites are
        known to be;
For in her towns and harbours, of thy worship principally
        boasts
The Hellespontiac shore — more oyster rich than any other
        coasts.

The second fragment has only a few words: "I have a mind to
have a bite myself", and is thought to have formed part of a
priapeum in which the god warns thieves that, if they taste the
fruit, then so will he, with the suggestion of *irrumatio*. Both
fragments are in the priapean metre. In his 47, Catullus calls Piso
'Priapus', meaning that he is a lecherous fellow.

There are three *priapea* at the beginning of the *Catalepton*, a
collection of epigrams in the Virgilian *Appendix*. The first (our *39*)
has been more readily conceded to be possibly by Virgil than the
other two, which editors before Lachmann (1825) assigned to
Catullus as his 20 and 19. Some manuscripts and the early editors
placed them after the *Priapea*. The modern practice has been to
give them the separate heading of *Priapea* in the Virgilian
Appendix, on the assumption that they are the Virgilian book of
Priapea referred to by Suetonius.

Critics disagree about these three poems: they are all by a
single author (Vollmer, Rand), they are by different authors
(Schanz); they are by Virgil (Vollmer, Bird, Rand), they are by
Ovid (Radford), they are by Martial (Herrmann); they are late
Republican or Augustan in date (Birt, Sommer), they belong to

the last quarter of the first century AD (Galletier); they are shot
through with Virgilianisms (Galletier), yet full of non-Virgilian
words (Fairclough); they are "stiff and awkward" (Klingmer),
but "graceful and sprightly" (Rand); the style is poor and
unworthy of a great poet (Cali), and "of the finest workmanship"
(Birt).[8]

They are rich in allusions to rural life, all three refer to the
god's being made of wood, and all three introduce the four
seasons of the year. In each, Priapus is the speaker and in each he
boasts of the honour done him by the country people, although in
the first he doubts whether their religious fervour would survive a
cold winter:

> Spring roses, autumn fruit, and summer grain
>   I get; but winter brings me pain,
> Lest, as a god who's made of wood, I stoke
>   The fires of ignorant country folk.

In the second (*40*), the god's member (*mentula*) appears, not,
however, as threatening *pedicatio*, but to be used by the farm
bailiff as a cudgel, a rather odd conclusion to a poem in which the
god boasts of honours done to him:

> Wayfarer, 'tis I, made from poplar tree
> By rustic hand, who guards the house you see,
> The garden too, this field upon the left —
> A poor man's property — from evil theft.
>
> In spring, with garlands gay they do me crown;
> In summer hot, they bring me wheat ears brown;
> In fall, on me vine shoots and grapes they lay;
> In winter harsh, they come with olives gray.
>
> The frisky she-goat, from our pastures fetched,
> Bears to the town her milk-rich udders stretched;
> A fat lamb, ta'en to market from the fold,
> Sends us back home with right hand full of gold;
> A calf so young — and while its mother moans —
> Pours out its blood upon the altar stones.
>
> So traveller, do respect our divine powers:
> Be wise, and keep your hands off what is ours.
> Else our blunt prick the punishment will be.

"I'd like . . .", you say. But now the farmer, see
He comes, and with his muscled arm removes
My tool that in his hand a truncheon proves.

If the *velim pol* . . . ("By Pollux, I'd like . . .") in the third line from
the end is an aposiopesis, it could have continued: ". . . to see you
do it!" or ". . . to have some figs", or even ". . . to feel the
punishment". But whatever the intruder meant to reply, the
sudden arrival on the scene of Priapus' 'no-nonsense' master
breaks off the conversation. The 21 lines of the original are
written in pure iambics.

In the third (*41*), again 21 lines long in the original, and written
in the priapean metre, it is again Priapus who speaks, but instead
of threatening marauders, he tries to persuade them to go to the
neighbour's:

It's I, my lads, who guard this earth-built shack,
The roof of which is wov'n of rush and sedge;
I who was carved by rustic axe from oak.

And may they prosper more and more each year —
My masters — for they worship me right well,
Father and son, poor peasants though they are:
The one works hard to clear the brambles from
My shrine, the nettles too; the other brings
With generous hand all kinds of little things.

In spring, they place the flowered garlands and
The stalks of barley green with tender shoots,
The wild flowers bright with colours gay,
And vegetables, and such sweet-tasting fruits;
My altar they anoint — don't tell a soul —
With blood of bearded and horn-hooved goats.

So all these honours Priapus oblige
Good care to take of orchard and of field.
So, boys, steal nothing here. The neighbour's rich,
Neglectful his Priapus of his charge:
This very path will take you to his place.

Elsewhere in the Virgilian *Appendix*, in *Copa*, there is a brief
reference to the god (line 23) as "the guardian of the bower,
armed with willow sickle". The *copa* is hostess at a roadside public

14

house who uses her blandishments to lure in the traveller. No
need, she says, to worry about the figure standing outside with
wooden hook — "nor to be frightened by his huge member".

Virgil introduces Priapus in his Georgics (4 109–11): "May
gardens exhaling the fragrance of flowers attract them [bees], and
may the warden, with his willow scythe, guard them from thieves
and birds with the protection of Hellespontiac Priapus". And in
the Eclogues (7 33–6) Priapus is told that all he can expect in the
way of an offering each year is a little milk and some cakes, for
"thou lookest after a poor man's garden". Nevertheless, he is no
wooden Priapus, but of marble, and the shepherd Thyrsis tells
him: "If our flock multiplies thou shalt be of gold". The
incongruity of a poor man's Priapus being of marble, let alone of
gold, has not gone unnoticed.[9]

One of Horace's Satires (1 8) is spoken by Priapus. The god
introduces himself in the first seven lines, which combine several
motifs common to priapic poetry — his wooden manufacture, his
watchman/scarecrow function, his red and minatory member, his
harundo, which conveys the double meaning of a wreath worn by a
deity and a trap for birds made of limed twigs:

> A fig tree once I was, which useless wood
> The carpenter in doubt was if he should
> To a priapus turn, or to a chair.
> He chose the god, and so my job's to scare
> Away the thieves with penis painted red
> From loins erect; the wreath upon my head,
> From gardens new deters the birds.

These new gardens were an extension of the gardens of Maecenas
on the Esquiline hill in Rome, where they had recently
incorporated a cemetery area, most of which had been used for
the burial of slaves and paupers, and of bankrupts like the
Pantolabus and Nomentanus mentioned in line 11. But all the
tombstones had not gone: one remained to record the dimensions
of the land (line 12), and to make clear that no permanent rights
of burial attached to the heirs of those buried there, while the
moon was able to hide behind another (lines 35–6):

> Before,
> From meanest slums the corpses of the poor
> Were borne in coffin cheap by wretched slave

15

To this the bankrupt's, pauper's common grave.
Pantolabus, Nomentanus are there.
Lines on a stone the boundary declare,
Warning no burial right goes to the heir.
And now the Esquilines can take the air,
And walk the sunny path, where once were found
The whitened bones of mortals on the ground.

Priapus goes on to say that it is not so much thieves and birds that trouble him as the witches who resort there at night to scratch up bones and perform their horrid rites. Two are particularly revolting: Canidia, who makes a woollen doll which burns on the fire a smaller waxen one, representing someone she hopes to destroy, and the howling Sagana:

Nor are the thieves and birds my chief concern,
But plaints the witches wail, the brews they burn
To torture human souls. Of these I do complain.
There seems no way to rid me of this bane.
Let but the moon show forth her face severe,
And they to gather bones and herbs appear.
I've looked upon these howling sorceresses,
Black-coated bare-foot Canidia with loose tresses,
And th'elder Sagana — the pair a match
For pallid horror. I have seen them scratch
A runnel in the earth to take the gore
From a black lamb that with their teeth they tore,
That they might secrets learn from dead man's shade;
And effigies of wool and wax, one made:
The woollen was the greater, that it might
The lesser, waxen, kill, which showed its plight
In servile stance. They called on Hecate
And on Tisiphone. You seemed to see
The snakes and dogs of hell. The blushing moon
By this affrighted, hid behind a tomb.

Priapus is describing a scene so unbelievably horrible that he invites excrement, not only from birds, but from such disreputable characters as Pediatia and Voranus, if he is not telling the truth:

May birds whiten my head if 'tis not true,

And may Pediatia, Julius and Voranus too,
Befoul me if I lie. But why say more
Of moans that Sagan' and the spirits pour
Into each other's ears, and shrieks so weird?
Beneath the ground they hide away the beard
Of wolf with serpent's tooth and, unrestrained,
The fire burns up the wax.

However, Priapus gets his own back: he lets out a loud fart:

Like bladder bursting, out of fear,
I farted loud and split my fig-wood rear.
They fled to town, and as they ran, let fall
Canidia's teeth, Sagana's head-dress tall;
They dropped their herbs and magic trappings. Oh!
With laughter you'd have roared to see them go.

Horace's Priapus is a watchman, not over garden or orchard, but over a cemetery. An inscription found near a grave in Rome provides further evidence of the association of this god of the life force with death: "I, who with unsheathed member guard this grave, Priapus am, seat of both death and life" (*59*). Another funerary inscription in Verona (*CIL* 5 3634) refers to "a place reserved for a memorial with a shrine of Priapus".

Horace's poem, with its references to excrement and breaking wind, is rather scatologically indecent than sexually obscene, something rare in priapic poetry. And whereas we usually meet the god out in the country, here he is in Rome itself and in the gardens of Maecenas, where Horace would have made his acquaintance.[10] In his second Epode, Horace tells how Priapus is honoured with the fruits of the season.

Tibullus addressed one of his elegies (1 4) to Priapus. It is a didactic parody, and with 84 lines is the longest of the priapic poems. It begins with a *do ut des* dedicatory promise: of much-needed shelter from the elements in return for advice on how to win the affection of fair boys, with the poet wondering how such a rough, shaggy and weather-worn object should himself be so successful in attracting them:

Priapus, thou shalt have a shady stead
Where neither sun nor snow may harm thy head.
Just tell me how thou charm'st the handsome youth:

Thy beard is rough, thine hair is kept uncouth;
Cold winter's fog all naked thou dost greet,
And naked bring'st thou in dry summer's heat.

The next 64 lines give the god's counsel:*

Don't sulk if at the first try he says "No":
With time his neck under the yoke will go.
Lions, with time, to men obedience pay;
With time soft water eats hard rocks away.
The year matures the grapes on sunny slopes.
Surely the year fulfils each season's hopes.

Fear not to swear. The winds will sweep
Love's perjuries o'er land and ocean deep.
Proclaimed it was by Jupiter above:
"That oath means nothing that was sworn in love".
Swear by Diana's arrows — she won't mind;
Swear by Minerva's locks — no harm you'll find.

Time passes: you err if you refrain;
The day of harvest will not come again.
How soon the autumn loses gold and brown!
How soon the poplar sheds its beauteous crown!
The horse laid low by weak old age's fate,
Once strainëd eager at the starting gate.

Persuade your boy with what he much desires,
For often will a gift arouse love's fires.
He wants a walk — your company then yield,
Though long the way and heat scorching the field,
Even if the sky, with aspect black and sour,
Tells that the south-east wind will bring a shower.

Should he desire upon the waves to roam,
Then row the boat yourself across the foam;
Such arduous labour you must not regret,
Although the toil your unused hand may fret.
And if he seeks in valleys beasts to snare,
Carry his nets upon your shoulders bare.

*For the sake of brevity 32 lines have been omitted. A full translation
may be found in Lee, G, *Tibullus: Elegies*, 2nd edn 1982.

If he inclines to fight, then you join in;
Arrange it often that the boy shall win. ·
Then he'll be kind; now you may steal a kiss.
At first he'll struggle — yet allow your bliss.
At first a theft, it next becomes a grace;
And in the end himself desires embrace.

Although this poem begins with a promissory dedication, and
brings in the motif of Priapus exposed to the elements, its main
theme is his exercise of his function of counsellor in erotic
matters. Its appeal for help in the unrequited love of a boy recalls
the Greek idyll of Theocritus (*13*), where the goatherd asks for
help in his hopeless love for Daphnis.[11] There is also a brief
reference to the god in the first elegy (1 1 17f.):

Amidst the orchard's fruit the ruddy guard they stand,
That with his hook he may afright the birds from off the
land.

The next *priapeum* (*44*) is a dedication-without-prayer (*do ut des*)
epigram in three elegiac distichs. It was assigned to Tibullus by
Scaliger in the sixteenth century, an attribution rejected by
Mommsen, who, however, wrote: "none will deny that the poem
is worthy of an excellent poet of the Augustan age" (trans.).[12]
According to Bembus it was found near Padua engraved on
stone, but Baehrens and others have questioned its antiquity as
an inscription:[13]

I was a civil servant once, but now I farm some land.
Priapus, god, I vow to thee this temple grand!
And in return, if you see fit, I hope you'll promise me
That of my little farm a zealous guard you'll be.
And if some rascal thief should trespass on my plot, then
you . . .
No need to say: you know, I think, just what to do.

The aposiopesis neatly preserves the epigram from any overt
obscenity.

Scaliger also assigned *45* to Tibullus; this was challenged by
Von Broekhuyzen (1649–1707) on metrical grounds.[14] In fact, it
is found in many manuscripts as part of the Virgilian *Appendix*.
Until the Baehrens edition of 1879, it was placed with the

Carmina Priapea as 82 or 83. It is a long, jocular, obscene, yet elegant poem in which the author, stricken by impotence, heaps abuse, first on Priapus for such an ungrateful response to the attentions that have been paid him, and then upon his own member:

> What have we here? Why do the gods annoy?
> At dead of night there lay a beauteous boy
> In bed with me, close in my warm embrace.
> My sex lay still, unmanly 'twas and base,
> And, senile, could not raise its drooping head.

The poet then rounds on the god, and the next 13 lines could be said, by themselves to constitute a *priapeum*:

> This is thy doing, who, in shady stead,
> Priapus, we have crowned with vine shoots thick,
> As thou satst ruddy-faced with scarlet prick.
> How oft, Triphallus, we with flowers fair
> Have bound and garlanded thy sacred hair!
> How oft, also, we've scared off with a roar
> Some aged crow, some pertinacious daw
> That sought to peck thy head with beak of horn!
> Priapus, farewell then: thou'st earned my scorn;
> Farewell, thou bad betrayer of manly pride;
> I'll hurl thy carcase to the fields outside;
> On thee shall urinate the savage dog,
> Shall rub thy trunk with filth the wild hog.

With this maledictory dismissal, the priapic part of the poem ends, and the author turns to his own penis:

> Accursed cock! I'll make you pay for this:
> Deserved punishment you'll sure not miss.
> No use complaining now: no tender boy
> On groaning bed will give you any joy,
> Assisting you with ever-moving bum,
> Nor playful girl, caressing, help you come,
> Pressing against you with her soft smooth thighs;
> Instead, for you an old hag ready lies,
> Amidst whose filthy groin there is set
> A hole, in front of which you'll hang and fret,

The poem continues with a revolting description of the penance to be done. Such invective against an old hag's disgusting genitalia is a motif found elsewhere, e.g. in Horace *Epodes* 8 and 12, and in **12**. The poet's threats appear to have some effect, giving the poet hope that he will be able to indulge in copulation until his dying hour. Joseph Scaliger so delighted in this poem that he translated it into Greek iambics.

Ovid's Priapus is more in the Greek tradition and more rooted in mythology than that of other Roman poets. Two books of the *Fasti* (1 and 6), which describe and account for the festivals and sacred rites of the Roman calendar, contain long passages about the god. Both end with an incident to explain why the ass was sacrificed to Priapus at Lampsacus. The first story begins: "An ass is slain for the rigid guardian of the countryside", applying rigid, of course, to his hard erect member. There follows a description of a Bacchic feast (the subject of a painting by Bellini). It was attended by the Fauns and amorous young Satyrs, as well as by beautiful Naiads. The old and lewd Silenus had come on his ass, and also "the ruddy one who scares off the birds with his penis". The wine flowed, and Priapus lusts after the nymph Lotis:

> Now night it was; drowsy with wine are all.
> Some here, some there, o'ercome by sleep they fall.
> At last on to the grass drops Lotis; she,
> Weary, finds rest beneath a maple tree.

> Up gets her lover, holds his breath, and goes
> With stealthy careful step, upon his toes,
> And when he finds the drowsy nymph, so fair,
> Lest he the slightest sound should make, takes care.

> But now he's there, stands ready on the grass:
> Quite unaware sleeps on the beauteous lass.
> With joy he snatched the coat 'neath which she lay,
> To satisfy his lust was on his way.

> When to the most untimely bray, gave vent
> Silenus' ass: its sound the stillness rent.
> The nymph awoke; she with Priapus strove,
> And fleeing, shrieked, arousing the whole grove.

> The moon his readiness for th'act revealed:
> At his sad plight the woods with laughter pealed.

He straightway slew the ass who made the row:
That's why an ass is welcome victim now.

Welcome, that is, to Priapus upon his altars. There is another version of this story in the *Metamorphoses* (9 331–48): Dryope picks flowers to amuse her baby son, but drops of blood fall from them, for the flower she picks is in fact Lotis, who has hidden in the guise of a lotus tree from Priapus' intended outrage. A very similar story occurs in *47*, but instead of Lotis, the goddess Vesta is the prospective victim. Cybele gives a banquet for the other gods and goddesses. Again the satyrs and nymphs are there, and again Silenus comes on his ass:

Priapus ruddy, shall I tell thy grief?
Or no? The tale is funny, and 'tis brief.
She whose height by turrets is increased, [Cybele]
Asked the gods immortal to a feast,
And satyrs wild, and rustic nymphs so fair;
And tho' unasked, Silenus too was there.

Too long 'twould take to tell how the gods dine,
Unlawful too. All night there flowed the wine.
Some through Ida's shady vales they pass,
Or lying, stretch their limbs on the soft grass.
Some play, some sleep, some arm in arm are seen
To dance swift-footed on the verdure green.

There Vesta rested careless on the ground;
Her head was pillowed on a turfy mound.
But the red garden guard runs to and fro,
And eyes the goddess nymphs as by they go.
He Vesta saw, but whether he knew 'twas she
Or just a nymph, he could not tell, says he.

His lust gained hope, and stealthily the god,
With throbbing heart on tiptoe softly trod.
Now, by a quiet stream, Silenus hoar
Had left the ass which on its back him bore.
The Hellespontiac god was almost there,
When th'ass let forth a bray into the air.

With fright Vesta awoke, and called for aid;
Priapus fled, by hostile hands assayed.

And so at Lampsacus they sacrifice an ass, saying:
"To fire we give th'entrails of this tell-tale beast, for
   braying."

Ovid links Lampsacus to the god also in *Tristia* 1 10 26,
addressing the city as "thee, Lampsacus, protected by the rural
god". In *Metamorphoses* 14 (637ff.) the nymph Pomona is
pursued by "that god who scares off thieves with his scythe or his
penis". There is also a reference in the *Amores* (2 4 32): Ovid says
that he is so exposed to temptation by the luscious girls about him
that, in his place, even Hippolytus, renowned for his sexual
frigidity, would become like Priapus.

The next *priapeum* (*48*), by Petronius Arbiter, is, like *45*
concerned with male sexual impotence. Encolpius, the hero of the
Satyricon, is smitten with this calamity, and like the author of *45*,
he vilifies and curses his flaccid member (132). He is taken for
cure to Proselenos, an old witch, who marks his forehead,
incanting:

While there's life there's hope! Thou rustic guard,
   Priapus, hither come and make him hard![15]

This fails, so he decides upon a direct approach to the god. He
addresses him in verse, and to curry favour, heaps all kinds of
titles and extravagant apostrophes upon him:

O friend of nymphs and Bacchus, whom Dione[1] fair
As godhead to the woodland spirits gave, and whom
Renowned Lesbos[2] and green Thasos[2] both obey,
For whom a temple in their town the Lydians[3] made,
Be here, thou guard of Bacchus, Dryads' darling, and
My timid prayers receive, for bloodstained come I not.

[1] a goddess reputed to be the mother of Venus.   [2] islands in the
Aegean Sea.   [3] inhabitants of Lydia in Asia Minor.

But he has first to excuse his own desecration of a Priapus shrine
earlier in the tale:

It was not with ill intent thy temple I defiled,
But pressed by want unwillingly I did the deed:
Whoever sins from need is less to blame, and so
Relieve my mind, I beg; forgive my little sin.

23

He promises a reward should the boon be granted, making this a
dedicatory *priapeum* of the conditional kind:

> If fortune smiles again on me, thy glory shall
> Be honourably crowned; O god, the horned goat,
> The father of the flock, shall to thine altar go;
> As sacrifice also, the babe of squealing sow.
> And this year's wine in bowl shall foam; the merry youth
> Shall three times dance triumphant round and round thy
> > shrine.

Far from placating the god, however, Encolpius makes matters
much worse by accidentally killing one of his sacred geese. His
prayer to Priapus is, of course, a parody.[16] In fact, the *Satyricon*
itself is obviously (*pace* Marchesi and Baldwin) a parody of the
Odyssey, of the adventures of Ulysses as victim of Neptune's ire:
the *ira Priapi* is the driving force, and Encolpius the driven victim.
This is confirmed by the verses he recites towards the end (139):
"I am not the only one", he cries, "to have been pursued by a god
and fate implacable". He gives examples from mythology, ending
with Neptune's blows against Ulysses.[17] And then this final
couplet:

> So too, throughout the land, the ocean and the sea,
> Hellespontiac Priapus' stern ire follows me.

The fifth-century Sidonius Apollinaris (23 257) called Petronius
"the equal of Hellespontiac Priapus".

Our next priapic verse (*49*) is six lines from Columella, who, as a
writer on the Italian countryside, could hardly ignore the rustic
god (for translation see p. 83). He uses motifs common to
priapea: the statue's coarse manufacture, and the orchard watch-
man's dual threat to thieves after fruit, employing his two
weapons. In comparing the peasants' workmanship with that of
famous sculptors, he anticipates **10**. In a passage on aphrodisiac
herbs (10 158–9), he implies that planting them near the god's
statue will enhance their efficaciousness. Of the rocket or
colewort, *Brassica eruca*, he says:

> Which, if beside Priapus, who brings fruit, you sow its seed,
> 'Twill stimulate reluctant husbands to the amorous deed.

This reference to Priapus' importance in marriage was re-echoed some 400 years later by Martianus Capella (7 725 17ff.); he advises the married to worship Priapus before all others.

Martial's first *priapeum* (*50*) parodies the traditional prayer to a god. He is offered no more than the hope that, instead of arresting adult thieves, he may be lucky enough to catch a boy or girl:[18]

> Thou, who with prick the men, with sickle queers dost
> scare,
> Of acres few, in plot apart, take care.
> So may no thieves — if old — into this orchard dare:
> Only a boy and long-haired maiden fair.

In *51* Priapus himself speaks, but instead of, as is customary, describing himself as rough hewn from inferior wood, he boasts that he has been made of the finest cypress. Surprisingly, he says that this tree will yield the thieves a fig — for *ficus* can also mean an ulcer, or — in the context of the threatened anal rape — piles:

> That member of mine that stands up so bold
> Is not made of elm or any old wood,
> But from the best cypress — not very old.
> And if any rascal, up to no good,
> Should even the tiniest bunch of grapes hold
> In his thieving hand, let it be understood,
> Piles from the cypress in him you'll behold.

In *53* again we find Priapus boasting that he is of the finest workmanship and of the best wood. But gone the obscene threat — just a polite request to the neighbours! As in most *priapea* of the watchman genre, Priapus has a master: he is Hilarus, a wealthy landowner from the Caere district:

> No boorish peasant with his axe made me:
> A steward's noble work you see.
> The richest man in Caere[1] farms this land
> And owns these hills and acres grand.
> That I'm of wood you'd be surprised to learn,
> Or that my prick as fuel would burn,
> For 'tis of lasting cypress: proud it stands
> As if 'twere made by Phidias'[2] hands.
> Honour Priapus, friends: take my advice,
> And spare these acres seven-twice.[3]

[1] named as Hilarus in the original.   [2] a famous Athenian sculptor.   [3] *bis septenis* = twice seven or fourteen.

The next Martial *priapeum* (*52*) is one of those in which Priapus is shown as ineffectual, and not feared, but mocked by the thief:

> Fabullus mine, I tell thee of Cilix,[1]
> A well-known thief who would a garden rob.
> Although 'twas large, the garden empty was,
> Save for Priapus lone, of marble made.
> But rather than go empty-handed off,
> He took Priapus with him as he went.

[1] the name means Cilicean. Cilicean pirates were notorious in antiquity.

The incongruity of a marble priapus in a poor garden follows Virgil (*ecl.* 7 35); Lucian's epigram (*30*) had another derelict garden where there was "nothing to steal but me, the watchman".

In *54* the poet plays upon the fact that *nux*, a 'nut', and *pomum*, a 'fruit' or 'apple', can also mean 'jests' and 'erotic favours' respectively. Martial gives his friends humorous verses; Priapus gives the girls sexual pleasures:

> Eloquent Juvenal, to thee our friend,
> Behold these Saturnalian nuts we send.
> The guardian god's gross member has assigned
> To wanton girls fruits of another kind.

In *55* there is a veiled threat to a priapus by its master, inspired no doubt by *39* (p. 13). The god's statue is reminded that it is combustible:

> Of neither fruitful orchard nor of blessed vine,
> But of a copse, Priapus, custody is thine,
> 'Twas from its wood thou wast — and could'st again — be
>   made.
> So take good care no thieving hands on it are laid:
> Protect it so that it can fuel thy master's grate,
> For should'st thou fail, that thou art wood will seal thy fate.

Willenberg regards *56* also as a *priapeum*:

26

If you wish to have enough, eat up Priapus, and none waste:
  You can even eat his prick — you'll still be chaste.

That is, you can eat up the whole of a pastry priapus, taking the
phallus into your mouth, without committing an impure act
(*fellatio*), because it is only made of flour. A pastry priapus stood
on the table at Trimalchion's feast (Petronius *sat.* 60); such
objects were probably among the 'unmentionables' carried in the
Athenian ceremonies, held in June, in honour of Aphrodite and
which, incidentally, explain line 8 of Martial 3 68 (see p. 78).[19]
In the next two lines of the same poem (3 68), Martial describes
Priapus as:

That which the farmer's man sets up to guard his land,
  Which lest she see, the maid puts up her hand.

There are references to Priapus in several other Martial
epigrams. The last line of 1 35 runs: "Nothing is worse than a
Gallic [i.e. castrated] Priapus". This sums up the argument of the
poem: to take salaciousness from his verse would be to cast-
rate it. In 3 58, a long poem, the poet contrasts the villa farm
with the suburban garden where "you are secure, for your
Priapus fears no thief". In 11 18 Martial describes his tiny
window garden where "there is not half enough room for a
Priapus, even without his sickle and penis". 11 51 tells of a man
with a penis as large as the god's, just as was Cimon's in *26*, and
the poet's in **79**. Priapus is referred to obliquely by the mention of
Lampsacus:

The column that hangs from Titius is as great
As that which Lampsacian girls all celebrate.
Not even all alone in the big pool
Has Titius room enough to wash his tool.

The point of 11 72 is very similar, bearing in mind that Gallus
also means a castrated priest:

Though Natta calls her athlete's prick quite small,
Compared with it Priapus looks a Gaul!

Ovid saw Priapus as a chaser of nymphs, and in Martial 10 92 11 "the tender Flora" flees into a laurel grove with Priapus in hot pursuit.

The god of priapic poetry is portrayed almost wholly as a rustic deity in a rural setting. Only occasionally do we glimpse those secret orgiastic rites in which he was worshipped by frenzied women in the city, and which had developed from his cult as a fertility god. One such is the passage in Juvenal (6 314–17) which tells of the maenads of Priapus, excited by dancing, music and wine. Later in the same satire, Juvenal refers to the "god of the vine and the garden" (375), while at 2 95 someone "drinks from a Priapus glass" — i.e. from a vessel shaped like the god.

An anonymous *priapeum* from the Latin Anthology *(58)* exploits the double meaning of *hortus*, 'garden' — as does **5**:

> Sabellus, your girl's garden's yet more ploughed
> Than was the garden of th'Hesperides.
> But that is no surprise, Sabellus dear!
> Priapus, garden god, himself it digs,
> And every day he waters it as well.

The long hymn that follows *(60)* was found inscribed on a herm-pillar at Tivoli, and is extravagant in its adulation of the god. Buchheit believes it to be a parody, but Kleinknecht asks, "why shouldn't Priapus, at some time in the Antonine age, have been regarded as an omnigod?" (trans.). An inscription of AD 235 from the province of Dacia (*CIL* 3 1139) is dedicated to "Priapus the omnigod". And Fischer thinks that the poem points to "a genuine worship of this godhead among the people".[20]

> Priapus, of all things holy father, hail!
> Give me of blooming youth the well-loved joys,
> That I may pleasing be to girls and boys
> With virile member; also that I may
> With them amusing games for ever play;
> And from my mind those cares and worries keep
> That are the mortal enemies of sleep;
> And let me not of old age live in dread,
> Nor fear because one day I shall be dead
> And carried off in coffin or in urn,
> To there from whence no traveller may return.
> Hail, hail, Priapus, holy father, hail!

Come all you nymphs, how many you may be,
Whether you dwell in sacred grove or, free,
Among the holy waters have your seat,
Here congregate, and with your voices sweet,
Fair blandishments pray to Priapus give,
The holy father of all things that live!
A thousand kisses on his privates plant,
And fragrant garlands to his member grant;
And all of you again to him then sing:
Priapus, father, god of everything!

He undertakes these woods around to guard,
Ensuring peace and quiet are not marred,
By wild or wicked men who lack restraint;
He takes care too, lest evil men should taint
The sacred waters, and their calm demean
By walking through them with their feet unclean,
Who take it on themselves to wash their hands
Without first honouring you, girl-goddess bands.
Now all, with seemly grace, to him then sing:
Priapus, father, god of everything!

Priapus lord, for virile force so famed,
Preferest thou the father to be named
Of all the world? Or called great Pan?
Indeed, without thy vigour no one can
Imagine life on earth, in air, in sea.
Priapus holy, greetings then to thee!

At thy caprice great Jove will leave alone
His awesome thunderbolts, and from his throne
Resplendent hasten down, drawn by desire;
And Venus bright, and Cupid full of fire,
And those sisters fair, the Graces three,
And Bacchus who brings joy — all cherish thee!
Without thy power, Venus and all the rest —
The Graces, Cupid, Bacchus — lose their zest.
Priapus lord, of potency the friend,
To whom chaste maidens fervent prayers do send
That girdles, too long fastened, be untied.
To thee prays too the newly-wedded bride
Her husband's manliness may never fail.
Hail, hail, Priapus, holy father, hail!

From the very beginning Priapus was both god procreator, the god who presided over reproduction in the plant and animal world, and god protector, the shield — through his very obscenity — from evil, whether in the form of invisible malignant influences or in the more tangible shape of thieving intruders into the orchard. In the Latin *priapea*, generally, it is most often in his role of god protector that we see him; but in the Tivoli hymn he is the god procreator, and as such a very god of gods — that is, if we take the hymn seriously.

Our final piece is by Prudentius, a fourth-century Christian writer. With its potted account of the god, his Greekness, his origins, his strong libido, his coming to Italy, his rites and rustic guardian duties, his 'club', it would serve better as introduction than conclusion, which, chronologically, it has to be:

You see that Greek, of bronze a shining sight,
Among the gods on Numa's august height?
A good and sturdy farmer once he was,
Renowned for his sheep, but he, alas,
Became a fornicator: lecherously he raced
After the country wenches, whom he chased
Into the bushes, bedding them with zest.
The hot blood in his veins gave him no rest;
Untamed his lust, aye ready for the deed.
This famous god of Hellespontine breed
T'Italian gardens came, and brought his rude
Observances, his rites and ritual lewd,
Where he receives the offerings that they make
Each year: a bowl of milk, a piece of cake.
And he protects the vines in Sabine yard,
Though shameful 'tis to see his club so hard.

REFERENCES

1. For a more restrictive definition, see Herrmann, L. *Latomus* 22 (1963), 31.

2. Strabo 8 6 24; Suetonius *de poetis: virg.* 17; Powell, J.U. *Collectanea Alexandrina* (Oxford, 1925), 176; Keil, H. *Grammatici Latini* (Leipzig, 1857), 512.

3. Herter, H. *De Priapo* (Giessen, 1932), 224.

4. Braun, E. *Bull.Inst.Corr.Arch.* 1 (1843), 51; Michaelis, A. *Arch. Epigr.Mitt.Oest.* 1 (1877), 88–9; Anthes, E. *Westdeutsche Zeitschr.* 13 (1894), 24.

5. Reinach, S. *Répertoire de la statuaire* 2 (1897), 77 (6).

6. Casagrandi, V. *Archivio storico Sicilia orientale* 18 (1921), 185–90; Libertini, G. *Atti R.Acad.Lincei* 19 (1922), 491–9; Sabbadini, R. *Boll.fil. class.* 30 (1923), 19–20; Ribezzo, F. *Riv.Indo-Greco-Ital.Fil.Ling.Antiq.* 9 (1925), 65–6; Hondius, J. *Supp.Epigr.Gr.* 2 (1925), 95–6.

7. Especially archaeologically, e.g. Priapus depicted on a sarcophagus, Gnirs, A. *Pola* (1915), 155, 157; figure of Priapus in a female tomb at Nimes, Espérandieu, E. *Bul.Achaéol.* (1926), clv.

8. For the *priapea* of the Catalepton, see Baehrens, E. *N.Jahrb.Class. Phil.* 21 (1875), 149; Ellis. R. *Appendix Vergiliana* (Oxford, 1907); Vollmer, F. *Sitz.Bayer.Akad.* (1907), 335–74; Birt, T. *Jugendverse und Heimatspoesie Vergils* (Leipzig, 1910); Rand E.K. *Harv.Stud.* 30 (1919), 104–32; Galletier, E. *Vergilii Maronis Epigrammata et Priapea* (Paris, 1920); Kleinknecht, H. *Die Gebetsparodie* (Stuttgart, 1937), 194–5; Richmond, J.A. *Hermes* 102 (1974), 301–4; for another verse translation, see Mooney, J.J. *The minor poems of Virgil* (Birmingham, 1916).

9. Leach, E.W. *Vergil's Eclogues* (Ithaca, 1974), 198–201.

10. See also Hallett, J.P. *Rh.Mus.* 124 (1981), 341–7; Anderson, W.S. *Essays in Roman satire* (Princeton, N.J., 1982), 74–8; O'Connor, E.M. *Dominant themes in Greco-Roman priapic poetry* (diss. Univ. of Calif. Santa Barbara, 1984), 27.

11. See also Luck, G. *The Latin love elegy*, 2nd edn (London, 1969), 83–97; Ball, R.J. *Tibullus the elegist* (Göttingen, 1983), 67–76.

12. Bembus, P. *Ad Herculem Strotum* (Venice, 1530), b1a–b1b; Scaliger, J. *In appendicem P. Virgilii Maronis* (Leyden, 1595), 209–10; Broukhusius, J. *Albii Tibulli* (Amsterdam, 1708), 406–7; Mommsen, T. *CIL* 5 2803.

13. Baehrens, E. *N.Jahb.Class.Phil.* 29 (1883), 860–2.

14. Broukhusius, *Albii Tibulli*, 407.

15. The first four words of this incantation are found in **80**, where the poet also is asking Priapus to cure his impotence.

16. Raith, O. *Stud.Class.* 13 (1971), 109–25.

17. For Priapus and the *Satyricon*, see Marchesi, C. *Petronio* (Milan, 1921), 42; Rankin, H.D. *Class.Med.* 27 (1966) 225–42; Sullivan, J.P. *The 'Satyricon' of Petronius* (London, 1968), 41–2, 70–3; Gill, C. *Class.Phil.* 68 (1973), 294–6; Richlin, A. *The garden of Priapus* (New Haven, 1983), 192.

18. For a pentrating analysis of Martial's *priapea*, see Willenberg, K. *Hermes* 101 (1973), 320–51.

19. Schilling, R. *ÉtudesComm.* 112 (1979), 149–53.

20. Buchheit, V. *Zetemata* 28 (1962), 70–1; Kleinknecht, *Die Gebetsparodie*, 5 n.2; Fischer *Priapea* (1969), 125.

The Priapea: introduction

AUTHORSHIP

We do not know who wrote the *Priapea*, nor whether there was just one author, two or three, or many. We first hear of *Priapea* in Suetonius (c. AD 130), who says that Virgil, when he was but 16, wrote "*Catalepton* and *Priapea* and *Epigrammata* and *Dirae* and also *Ciris* and *Culex*". This list was repeated, with modifications, by the fourth-century grammarians Donatus and Servius.[1] Confirmation that the youthful Virgil wrote scabrous matter comes from the younger Pliny (AD 105), who claimed that Virgil was "pre-eminent" among those who wrote unchaste verse (*epist.* 5 3 2–6), and from another late grammarian, Diomedes, who quotes a lascivious line from a lost Virgilian *priapeum* which, he says, was among the poet's early works.[2]

Whether the *Priapea* referred to by Suetonius and others are the 80 *Carmina Priapea* is not certain, and it is a big leap to the conclusion that Pliny's words leave no doubt that "the whole licentious corpus of the *Priapea* lay before him, and was accepted by him as Vergilian".[3] Nevertheless, this corpus is invariably ascribed in the manuscripts to Virgil, any exceptions resulting from later alterations. The manuscripts are all late fourteenth- and fifteenth-century, but that this attribution goes back a long way is evident from the ninth-century catalogue of the Murbach monastery library. It lists a volume of Virgil's minor works which includes *Priapea*.[4] Thus there is a tradition, from the second century through to the fifteenth, that Virgil wrote *Priapea*. The first printed editions of Virgil's works, beginning with that of Rome 1469, also included the 80 *Priapea*, and early editors and commentators for the most part accepted the Virgilian attribution.

In the oldest known surviving manuscript to contain the *Carmina Priapea*, the original title with Virgil's name has been erased, and a second inscription superimposed: DIVERSORVM AVCTORVM PRIAPEIA — "Priapea by various authors". Renaissance humanists could not believe that Virgil, whom they regarded as the most virtuous of poets, could have written verse of this kind. Pomponio Leto (1425–98) of Rome was one of the first to dissent from the Virgilian attribution and embrace the idea of multi-authorship:

I agree with those who do not believe that the book of
Priapea is by Virgil. For what could be more wanton than
these poems? . . . Most likely to be right are those who think
that all these verses were composed in fun by a group of
poets who were friends among themselves; a good many of
them they assign to Ovid. And, since Ovid was not a friend
of Virgil, they say that none of the poems in the book are by
Virgil.[5]

Others, like Floridus Sabinus in 1530, thought Virgil a contribu-
tor (of the more innocent poems), along with Ovid and others,
and that this explained the attribution to Virgil.[6] Aldus,
introducing his 1517 edition, wrote: "and it is possible that Virgil
wrote some of them, especially as there are several not to be
surpassed in elegance and polish. But though we do not deny this,
we must emphasize that no one poet could have written them
all".

In 1573 Scaliger lent his weighty authority to the view that
Virgil was too moral a poet to have written them, but that they
were composed by Catullus, Tibullus, Ovid and Petronius, and
put together by the author of the two introductory epigrams.
Scioppius (1606) agreed, and gave an explanation as to how
various poets may have come together to write the collection:

They have been attributed by some to Virgil, but I think
this unlikely; in fact, I dare swear by Jove that not a single
one is by Virgil. It seems to me that, as there was said to be
a shrine to Priapus in Maecenas' garden, some of these
poets who daily visited Maecenas, wrote jesting verses on
the walls. Later, Petronius, Martial and others wrote many
more in imitation of these, and they were all finally
gathered together in a single book by him who placed the
poem *To the reader* as a preface.

Although Scioppius is generally credited with introducing this
fanciful account of their origin, it had been suggested half a
century before by Baptistus Pius and by Gyraldus. The latter
wrote: "in these gardens [of Maecenas] there was a Priapus
shrine . . . poets meeting there hung up appropriate verses,
which, because they were collected by Virgil, are now published
under his name".[7] Barthius opined (1624) that many of the
poems were so indecent that they could not have been written by

Virgil, by Ovid, nor by any good, or even tolerable poet; but there were "about ten", he thought, that were good enough to be by Martial.[8]

For more than three centuries after Scaliger, the multi-authorship theory was accepted without question. In 1874 Lucius Mueller prefaced his text of the *Priapea* with such assertions as "this collection cries out that it is by several authors" and "even a child can tell that it is by many authors".[9] In 1918 Pascal claimed: "that the *carmina Priapea* were composed by different authors and then collected by a certain man of antiquity who affected such jests, is now universally agreed by scholars".[10] Buecheler (1863) maintained that the poems had mostly originated as inscriptions on Priapus statues and shrines.[11] Baehrens, in 1879, reverted to the 'Maecenas' gardens' theory of origin.[12] Vollmer, in 1923, suggested that the collection could well have been put together by Martial.[13] Rand (1919) argued that it was made up of two collections combined, one consisting of the hendecasyllabic epigrams, the other of those in elegiac couplets, with the introductory poems to each placed together at the beginning.[14] Maggi (1923) likewise supported the idea of two or more collections, with **1**, **2**, and also **49** as their prefatory pieces.

The multi-authorship theory was first challenged in the twentieth century by R.S. Radford (1921); he argued that the 80 *Priapea*, and indeed the whole Virgilian *Appendix*, are by a single author and that he is Ovid: "the astounding language of the two prefaces, the diction and *schemata* of all the poems, the unity of the refined metrical art revealed by innumerable details, confirm at every point" — he claims — his single-author thesis.[15] Thomason (1931) agreed, but R. Steele (1932), while not disputing the arguments for single authorship, went far to demolish those for Ovidian parentage of all the poems.[16] Nevertheless, G. Baligan reasserted Ovidian authorship in his *Appendix ovidiana* (Bari, 1955). Actually, Angelus Politianus had stated his belief that Ovid was the author as long ago as 1489.[17] He based this on a passage in Seneca, who has one Scaurus say *inepta loci* and call it *Ovidianum illud* — "that phrase of Ovid's" (*contr.* 1 2 22). As these two words are found together only in **3**, and in the same context as their quotation by Scaurus, this is very strong evidence indeed that **3** is by Ovid. And if you assume a single author, as Politianus did, then Ovid would have to have written all the *Priapea*.

No one has claimed again that Virgil was the sole author of the

80 Priapea, but it has become fashionable to regard the three *priapea* at the beginning of the *Catalepton* (also part of the Virgilian *Appendix*) as the *Priapea* referred to·by Suetonius and the fourth-century grammarians. As these three poems are quite inoffensive — apart from a naughty word (used twice) in the second — they provide an excuse for excluding the 80 from the *Appendix*, and so making the possible attribution of the whole *Appendix* to Virgil easier. This view found expression in Ellis's 1907 edition. He detaches the three *priapea* from the *Catalepton*, and prints them separately with their own heading. Birt (1910) quite justifiably commented: "we have no reason and no right to place the title Catalepton that comes before the *Priapea* after iiia, as Ellis does, but have to recognise that the *Priapea* have belonged to this collection from the beginning".[18] Vollmer (1907) and Rand (1919) also accepted that the *Priapea* referred to by Suetonius were the three at the beginning of the *Catalepton*. For when he had written *Deinde catalepton et priapea et epigrammata et diras*, he had meant *Deinde catalepton (et priapea et epigrammata) et diras*: "Then [he wrote] the Catalepton (the Priapea and the Epigrams) and Dirae".[19] However, it seems most unlikely that Suetonius would have used two *ets* in this way within a string of *ets* meaning just 'and', but would have used *id est* or *scilicet* after *catalepton*. Nor did Servius accept this interpretation: he says Virgil wrote "seven or eight books", whereas if two of them had made up a third, there would have been only four or five. Radford was right to call the suggestion "most forced and unnatural".[20]

Single authorship by Martial had been conjectured by Paul Melissus (15th cent.) on the ground that the initials V.M. found in some mss., and normally assumed to be Virgilius Maro, had, in fact, stood for Valerius Martialis. Jan Gruterus (1560–1627) claimed that they were Martial's fifteenth book. The chief modern proponent of Martial's authorship has been L. Herrmann.[21] There are other possibilities. Menagius wrote in 1690: "I am not of the opinion of M. Guiet, who believes Domitius Marsus was the sole author of the Priapea".[22] Marsus enjoyed high repute as an Augustan writer of epigrams, but his work has not survived. Guyetus (1575–1655), by choosing him, finds both an author for the *Priapea* and epigrams for Marsus.

The most detailed and powerful case for a single author was made by Buchheit (1962).[23] He demonstrates the probability that **1** and **2** are by the same hand, and points out that in **2** the author states quite clearly *haec carmina . . . scripsi*, "I have written these poems", and later, *notavi* — that he has inscribed them. This he could not have done had he made a collection of poems known to be by others. He emphasizes the remarkable uniformity, consistency and purity of the metrical style; only three metres are used, which would be unlikely for an anthology — although, as O'Connor observes, the *Musa Puerilis* (*AP* 12), which contains poems by several authors, uses only one metre.[24] Furthermore, there are numerous similarities and repetitions linking many of the poems together, and also several 'cycles' in which the author tries out variations on a single motif. Finally, there is the manuscript tradition of a single author. Most of Buchheit's points had already been made by Radford in 1921, but had little impact because they were associated with his discredited argument for Ovidian authorship. Buchheit's case has swayed modern opinion, and most scholars who have since written on the subject have accepted it, including Kytzler and Fischer (1969), Cartelle (1981) and Goodyear (1982).[25] Kenney, reviewing Buchheit's monograph, wrote: "His arguments are clear, concise and persuasive, and I can only say that in the main I find them completely convincing".[26] On the other hand, O'Connor concludes that we are dealing with an anthology put together by "a poet who is also a skilful editor and who, very possibly, wrote several of these Priapea himself".[27] But if it is an anthology why are there no attributions of individual poems to their authors, real or supposed? An editor must have known who some of them were.

The chief obstacle to the single-author theory is the evidence from Seneca that **3** is by Ovid — unless you are prepared to concede Ovid as author of them all. Buchheit has no real answer to this, other than to suggest that Seneca's quotation refers to an Ovid poem that has been lost, adding that it is unlikely that the supposed collector, having in **2** claimed authorship of all the poems, would then at once introduce as **3** a poem known to be by Ovid. On the other hand the quotation of just the last two words of a line, *inepta loci*, is odd, because they are not syntactically linked but thrown together by the exigency of the metre. The problem of authorship is clearly insoluble.

DATE

The date of the *Priapea* is also a matter for conjecture. Some, believing that they were written by the Augustan poets who frequented the gardens of Maecenas, have assumed them to belong to the Augustan age. Buecheler placed them "at the end of the Ovidian age, neither earlier nor later".[28] Vollmer thought that, although Martial had collected them, "the poems them- selves are scarcely later than Ovid [43 BC – AD 18]".[29] But many of those who believe them to be a collection would extend the period of their composition to the end of the first century to make room for the influence of, or contributions by, Petronius and Martial — e.g. Galletier in 1920 and O'Connor in 1984.[30]

A third view is to place them all at the end of the first century AD or later. In the seventeenth century, Barthius wrote: "few of them are older than Martial's time, for before then less care was taken over metre, especially the phalaecian hendecasyllables, in which this work rigidly follows the rules, as did Martial himself so strictly".[31] Buchheit argues for their being after Martial (AD 40– 104) on the grounds that Martial's *priapea* compare so badly in richness and variation of motif, that Martial could not have written his as he did had he known them. But Buchheit perhaps exaggerates the difference in quality between Martial's *priapea* and those of the corpus. He believes too that their author was influenced by Strato of Sardes, whom he places in the reign of Nero (AD 54–68). He concludes that the most likely date would be soon after Martial.[32] Citroni has suggested after Martial's Book 1, and Cali even as late as the fourth century.[33] The question of date is complicated by two Pompeian inscriptions which appear to echo lines from the *Priapea*; this would make two poems earlier than AD 79: *si prensus fueris* (*CIL* 4 7038) and **35** 2 (although the reading of both inscription and poem is uncertain); and *pedicare volo* (*CIL* 4 2210) and **38** 3.

INFLUENCES AND MODELS

Although the Greek epigram provided the origins and basis, the author of the *Priapea* developed the genre to a much higher degree of skill and diversity. Two only are clearly imitations of the Greek, **24** being little more than a translation of *28*, while **5** bears a close resemblance to *33*. The idea of the two introductory poems may have come from Strato (*AP* 12 1, 2), assuming the *Priapea* to be the later work. Both **1** and Strato 2 have the *non . . . non . . . nec . . . sed . . .* sequence, and both reject the 'raised eyebrow' or 'grave face'. In **2** and Strato 1, both poets declare that their subject is not suitable for the Muses.

The author draws effortlessly from his knowledge of literature and mythology. He is familiar with Homer, Elephantis, Callimachus, Eratosthenes and Philaenis, and the whole corpus abounds in mythological allusions. Nevertheless, his chief skill lies in his ability to borrow ideas, motifs, and even odd phrases and words, and from these to build incomparably witty and well-formed epigrams. There is much imitation of Catullus: **35** ends *pedicaberis irrumaberisque* . . ., recalling the *pedicabo vos et irrumabo* of 16; in **52** 12 *cum tantum sciat esse mentularum* obviously echoes 5 13, *cum tantum sciat esse basiorum*; there are many other examples. There is little from Horace, although the name Lalage in 4 3 recalls *Odes* 1 22 10–23, and *inutile lignum* (**77** 3) is also found in Satires 1 8 1. The relationship with Ovid is close, with about 50 half-lines common to both, and **20**, which compares the weapons of the gods, strongly resembles *Amores* 3 2 27ff.

Links with Martial are even more numerous, and whichever was the later has clearly been greatly influenced by the earlier. Compare Martial 3 68 with **8**: both introduce the Roman matron in the first line; in both she is asked not to look, but keep away, because of the indecency of the book's content; in both she disregards this warning: her interest has been aroused and she reads on. In each the rustic god's member is both the subject of the warning and the cause of the attraction. Buchheit suggests that the Priapean author got his inspiration from line 9 of the Martial.[34] Nor can there be much doubt of a link between Martial 6 71 along with 14 203, and **19**. In the latter, Telethusa is so seductive a dancer that she would be able to move Phaedra's stepson, i.e. Hippolytus, who, in ancient mythology, personified male resistance to female seduction. Other strong similarities include Martial 6 70 5: *ostendit digitum, sed impudicum* and **56**: *et impudicum ostendis digitum*; Martial 9 41 2: *servit amica manus*, and **33** 6 *fiat amica manus*. Martial 10 17 and **57** both set out to describe an old hag; they are the same length and in the same metre. In Martial the woman is so old that "Priam called her nurse", while in **57** she is so old that "she could have been Priam's nurse".

ARRANGEMENT

It has been shown that conscious arrangement is not lacking in the apparently haphazard sequences of poems by Catullus, Martial and others. So it is with the *Priapea*. Take metre: in the first 14 poems there is an alternation between the elegiac couplet and the hendecasyllable, while a reversed alternation follows from 15 to 20. This regularity is not maintained, but although almost half the epigrams are hendecasyllabic, only twice do three of these follow each other, and never more than three; and of the 34 in elegiac couplets, there is one sequence of four, two of three, but 20 of them occur singly. Each of the eight poems in choliambs is well spaced except for a pair near the end.

In most (60) of the poems, Priapus is the speaker, or else takes part in dialogue, or is quoted; in 15 others he is addressed. The 60 are so well distributed that there are at least one and not more than two such poems in each of the eight decades except 21–30, in which there are three. As to length, nineteen of the epigrams are of ten lines or more, and there are nine in the first half (1–40), ten in the second (41–80); no decade has none, but only one (61–70) has as many as four. Ten of the poems are single couplets, but in one instance only do two of them come together. In content too, poems with a similar motif are well spaced throughout, an exception being the concentration of verse rich in mythological allusion in the latter part of the book. Several pairs of epigrams have an unusual word in common, and it is improbable that they are all accidental: **17–18** (*laxior* and *laxa*), **26–27** (*prurientes* and *pruriginis*), **45–46** (*Maurae* and *Mauro*), **46–47** (*erucarum* and *erucis*), **57–58** (*fututor* and *fututorem*), **62–63** (*canes* and *caniculam*), **67–68** (*Penelope*), **71–72** (*pomaria* and *pomarii*).

FORM AND STRUCTURE

Symmetry and unity, economy and clarity are the hallmarks of the composition of these epigrams. The poet's favourite is a quartet consisting of two couplets, the first an introductory statement or question, in which interest or curiosity is aroused, the second a wittily-pointed conclusion or answer. Sometimes the first couplet is the *do* part ("I give thee Priapus . . .") and the second the *ut des* part ("that thou mayest give me . . .") of a *do ut des* dedicatory epigram, e.g. **42**. Twenty-two of the 80 poems are four-liners, and of these only four have a different structure.

Of the ten single-couplet epigrams, eight consist of introductory and concluding statements corresponding to the two lines, e.g. **71**. There are only two three-liners, and it may be no coincidence that they are placed at equal distances from the beginning and the end. In each the arrangement is 2 + 1, an introductory couplet with a single-line conclusion. In **17** they are question and answer; Sir Richard Burton's version of **64** is:

> One than a goose's marrow softer far
> Comes hither stealing for its penalty's sake.
> Steal as he please him: I will see him not.

There are six five-liners, and in all but one the arrangement is 3+2 or 2+3.

The longer poems fall into three groups of roughly equal size. First, there are 13 poems which may be said to be 'framed' or held together between distinct introductions and conclusions. The intervening lines are in elaboration, confirmation or explanation of the opening statement, and may consist of a set of examples coloured with similes or hyperbole (priamels and *cumulationes*), building up with overwhelming argument to the irresistible ending; or they may be skilfully used to create uncertainty and tension, so that the reader is kept guessing. Normally the opening and ending statements are couplets as in **1** (2+4+2) and **3** (2+6+2), but are sometimes longer, as in **2** (3+5+3). Poem **9** is an example of this type. It is introduced by a couplet, each line of which is a question. Then come ten lines of argument, each instancing a god, followed by the concluding couplet which, supported by the evidence adduced, answers the introductory questions.

In the next group there is no introductory statement. The argument, elaboration or accumulation begins with the first line. But there is still a distinct and pointed conclusion to round off the epigram. There are 14 of these; **16** is a good example: the poet plunges immediately into the *cumulatio* with *Qualibus* . . . and follows it up with *qualibus . . . qualis . . . quale . . .*: "Just such fine apples as . . . as . . . as . . .", and brings in the conclusion with *talia*: "such . . . (were given to Priapus)".

Finally, there is a group of 15 poems which lack a formal introductory or concluding part, although the last line or two may sharpen the point of the epigram. They are continuous statements, and may describe an incident, a person or a situation, or take the form of a lament or curse. One of the shorter instances is **23** (trans. Burton):

Whoso of violets here shall pluck, or rose,
Or furtive greens, or apples never bought,
May he in want of woman or of boy,
By the same tension you in me behold,
Go burst, I ever pray; and may his yard
Against his navel throb and rap in vain.

CONTENT

The 80 *Priapea* differ from the epigrams of Catullus and Martial
in that they all have the same subject, and it is the poet's supreme
achievement that they are all, nevertheless, different. Many
distinct motifs are introduced, some running as 'cycles' through-
out the series, and within each motif there are several variations;
there is further distinctive development of some of these
variations. And the variations of one motif intermingle with those
of another to form another breed of mixed-motif epigrams. Even
when, as is often the case, there is inspiration from another poet,
the treatment is novel. In short, there is genuine creative talent.

In the first two epigrams the poet tells both his readers and
Priapus that what follows is not serious but wanton and frivolous.
And indeed, parody, facetiousness, mockery and jest dominate
throughout, and there is the ever-present spice of wit, not to
mention the salaciousness of most of the poems. In only one or
two cases is the link with Priapus obscure or contrived: he is not
really relevant in **19**, and has no place in **61**, unless we assume
that the poems hung upon the tree are *priapea*.

As the distinguishing feature of Priapus is his salient member,
its prominent characteristics are variously emphasized — its
nakedness (**1, 9**); its rustic wooden manufacture (**6, 10, 25, 56,
63**); its size (**1, 6, 8, 18, 30, 36**); its rigidity (**6, 10, 20, 63, 70,
79**); its ruddy colour (**1, 72**); its wetness (**48**). Where there are
several references to a characteristic, they are not found in any
two consecutive poems.

Obscenity is inevitably present, more so than in Catullus and
as much as in Martial. Only 10 may be classified as wholly
innocent, 31 as dubious, 27 as obscene, and 12 as very obscene.
By the standards of the time and place in which they were
written, this obscenity would have been less obtrusive and
offensive, particularly as statues of Priapus, adorned by such
verses, were commonplace. Also, it had its positive, beneficent

aspect: the privy parts stood for fertility and their exhibition was thought to avert evil. The poet does not dissociate himself from the immorality of his work as do Catullus (16 3), Ovid (*trist.* 2 354) and (Martial 1 4 8), who claim that they themselves are pure, even if their verse is not. Straight away, in **1** and **2**, he warns that his writing is not for the chaste or prudish; for, although no one is more appalled by indecent language than he is, if he is dealing with a shameless god, what else can he do (**29**)? Nor is the god himself evasive in this matter: he bluntly rejects circumlocution (**3**). He too is plain spoken (**38**), and in **68**, on the pretext that he is a boorish fellow who knows no better, goes out of his way to use foul language. The main obscenity in the *Priapea* is the god's frequent threat of sodomistic behaviour, of *pedicatio*, which is mentioned or implied in 18 of the epigrams. The lustful god usually finds himself isolated in an orchard where any visitors are likely to be male thieves after the fruit. He is therefore compelled to resort most often to this outlet. His boasts and threats about what he can or will do in this way are not to be taken too seriously, however; it is aggression by foul language, and more bark than bite. Nor must his obsession with *pedicatio* be exaggerated: 14 of the poems refer to *fututio* with women.

The poet himself speaks in both the first and last two epigrams. This last pair are, however, in amusing contrast, for while in **79** *poeta noster* boasts that his member is as big as Priapus', in **80** he is obliged to ask the god's help because it won't stand up, and the work ends with the optimistic couplet:

> Still, while there's life there's hope, they say:
> Priapus, bless my tool, I pray.

The *Carmina Priapea* can be divided according to content into three groupings of about equal size. The first (27 poems) includes those where Priapus is seen as a god. He receives or expects worship; he is compared with other divinities, and he exercises divine powers. These poems could be termed 'religious' but for the fact that they are mostly parodies. Only two of them could be called obscene, although ten refer to his gross erect member, and two more to his testicles; but nine of them are wholly innocent — and there are only ten such in the whole book. Seventeen poems are concerned with dedications or offerings to Priapus; these include fruit (**16, 21, 42**), cake and grain (**70**), garlands (**40, 50**), a pig (**65**), a dancer's gear (**27**), obscene pictures (**4**), willow

penises (**34**), the picture of a penis (**37**); but the commonest
dedication referred to is that of verses (**2, 41, 47, 49, 60, 61**). In
53 he is reminded that he is only a minor god, and cannot expect
much by way of a harvest offering. Those making the offerings are
mostly poets, dancers and whores (**4, 27, 34, 40**), but there is also a
farmer (**42**), a lover (**50**), and a man whose sick member has
been cured (**37**). Five poems compare Priapus and the other gods.
Poems **9, 20, 36** and **39** are arrogant vauntings that he is at least
their equal, if not their superior, while **75** relates that he, like
other major gods, has his own special place. Finally, there are the
poems in which it is made clear that Priapus is not a prudish god,
requiring a solemn and purified approach (**1, 14, 29, 49**), but one
who presides over or assists in erotic activities (**27, 37, 50, 80**).

In the second group, also of 27 poems, we are not concerned
with the deity of Priapus the god, but with the behaviour of the
rudely-carved statues erected in the countryside by farmers and
peasants to scare away birds and thieves, in fact, with individual
Priapuses. Many of these epigrams are obscene because these
talking statues threaten rape against marauders in the hope that
violent language will scare them off. But in **38** the watchman is
prepared to bargain — to allow the thief to take the fruit if he will
submit to sodomy. In **51** he is forced to conclude, from the
popularity of his garden with thieves, that they actually want the
punishment; this is the case too with the catamite in **64**. In **23**
and **58** he is content to curse rather than threaten. In **55** the
thieves steal his sickle: in **56** a thief is contemptuously rude to
him, and all that he can say is that he will send for his master.

In the third group, of 26 poems, we see a sexually-depraved
and degenerate Priapus who has become a cynical fornicator,
pederast or irrumator. Here is portrayed or caricatured the
Roman male at his lowest level of ruthless self-indulgence and
lust. In **19** he is a byword for sexual excitability. In **33** he
bemoans the fact that there are no longer nymphs around to
gratify the lusts of Priapuses, so that they are forced to
masturbate. In **74** he boasts of the three orifices which, according
to age and sex, his member seeks and frequents. Most of the
poems in this group are about his relationship with women. He
assumes that they burn with desire within, even when they
appear outwardly chaste (**8, 10, 39, 43, 66, 68, 73**). They
exhaust him with their insatiable demands (**26, 63**); or they are
so repulsive that even he finds them hard to stomach (**12, 32, 46,
57**); in **78** he curses a man who leaves a girl too sore for his own

use, but in **18** he finds comfort in the size of his member, as for him no woman can be too big. In **6** he threatens a woman with rape. When he is not occupied with women, he is obsessed with *pedicatio* — threatening it (**76**), begging for it (**3, 5, 38**), and making up word or letter games about it (**7, 54, 67**). Like the typical sexually aggressive male of the Roman world, he is contemptuous of passive male partners such as the *cinaedi* he mocks in **45** and **64**. Yet he himself is mocked in the penultimate poem (**79**).

ARTISTIC QUALITY

This is seen in the varied treatment of a single subject, avoiding repetition and tedium; in the faultlessness of the metre; in the interlocking of metre and meaning, and their reinforcement on occasion with sound effects, including alliteration and penta-meter half-line balance and rhyme; in the building of interest-holding, suspense-creating and context-embracing 'arches' from the first line to the last; in the achievement of clarity, pithiness and wit, combined with absolute word economy; in the subtle use of parody and irony; and in the importance attached to contrast and antithesis. The supreme contrast is that between the perfection of the art and the depravity of the matter, a contrast which serves to enhance the former and emphasize the latter. With this go the ironic contrast between redoubtable Priapus, source of life, god of creation, on the one hand, and the contemptible priapus, the crude wooden stock personifying the ultimate in turpitude and vice. Throughout runs mockery of peasant superstition, if not of pagan religious observance as such. What is lacking is any trace of finer feeling or human emotion. The excellence is wholly professional and technical.

That in these poems the epigram reaches a degree of perfection is the verdict of many whose judgement has not been clouded by revulsion against their obscenity. Some of the most distinguished of the early renaissance editors and commentators, while recording their disapproval of the content, could not withhold their admiration for the form. The mere fact that, although they could not believe that the chaste Virgil wrote them all, they were yet ready to concede authorship to poets such as Catullus, Tibullus, Ovid and Martial, shows how highly they valued them.[35] But Floridus, while admitting that many of them were worthy of Virgil, Ovid and the like, thought others contained "much that is clumsily and tastelessly written". A few modern scholars share this view, e.g. Richlin (1983): "the poems in the Priapea are uneven in quality".[36] Maggi in 1923 went further, dismissing any pretentions to quality: "artistically", he wrote, "they are a poor enough thing ... the unfortunate poets of the *Priapea* grope blindly here and there in search of ideas they often do not possess, of an expression they cannot find, and of an image they often do not clearly perceive" (trans.).[37] Most modern critics have, however, come closer to agreeing with Buchheit, that "there is no one poem the composition of which could be called defective". Kenney (1963) saw their author as "a highly professional artist"; Fischer (1969) speaks of "the formal perfection and logical clarity of the composition", and Kytzler (1969) of the "artistic metre, the masterly structure, the fine forms of speech and the high-styled diction of the poems". Rankin (1971) refers to "the smoothness and skill of composition in most of the Priapea".[38]

THE METRE

The metrical perfection of the *corpus Priapeorum* has often been praised. Avancius, writing in 1493, told a correspondent that he had carefully read the work through and weighed the quantity of all the syllables, and, except where the manuscript was corrupt, could not find a single one out of place.[39] In 1921 Radford wrote that it "displays the full perfection of metrical art",[40] and Buchheit's analysis in 1962 confirmed this view. Rules are observed with a meticulousness unmatched by most leading poets of the day and surpassed by none.

The three metres in which the Priapea are written are the hendecasyllabic, elegiac and choliambic, distributed thus:

hendecasyllabic — 2, 4, 6, 8, 10, 12, 14, 15, 17, 19, 23, 25, 26, 28, 29, 32, 34, 35, 37, 39, 41, 44, 45, 46, 48, 50, 52, 56, 57, 59, 61, 64, 66, 69, 70, 75, 76, 77
elegiac — 1, 3, 5, 7, 9, 11, 13, 16, 18, 20, 21, 22, 24, 27, 30, 33, 38, 40, 42, 43, 49, 53, 54, 55, 60, 62, 65, 67, 68, 71, 72, 73, 74, 80
choliambic — 31, 36, 47, 51, 58, 63, 78, 79

The poems total 569 lines: this number includes the line which completes **75**, and the disputed couplet which concludes **80**. The first two lines of **72** have no recognizable metre. Of the remaining 567, 296 lines (38 poems) are in hendecasyllables; 190 (in 34 poems) form elegiac couplets; and 81 lines (in 8 poems) are choliambs or scazons.

Thus 52 per cent of the work is in hendecasyllables. The lines are phalaecian, i.e. they are made up of a spondee, a dactyl and three trochees, with the caesura falling most often after the dactyl. In sharp contrast to Catullus, the spondee in the first foot is universal. Almost as strict is the observance of the 'no two monosyllables at the end of the line' rule: there are five exceptions (**14** 4, **23** 4, **26** 7, **29** 1, **77** 4). There is irregularity in the placing of the caesura of only 3 per cent compared with 9 or 10 per cent in Martial.[41] Such regularity is most difficult to reconcile with a collection drawn from many authors or taken from the walls of shrines, or from the pediments of statues.

Ninety-five elegiac distichs make up another 34 per cent of the work. Most of the poems in this metre are four-liners (14) or single couplets (9), but they include the longest poem by far — **68** (38 lines). The elegiac distich consists of a dactylic hexameter line followed by a 'pentameter', which is really a hexameter with the third and sixth feet halved. Spondees can replace the dactyls except in the fifth foot of the hexameter, and the fourth and fifth feet of the 'pentameter'. We have compared the 95 elegiac distichs of the *Priapea* with a similar number in Catullus (65–68A), Ovid (*am.* 1–5), and Martial (6 2–47). Taking the first four feet of the hexameter, Catullus is heaviest in weight of spondees (63 per cent), followed by Martial (52 per cent), the *Priapea* (51 per cent), and Ovid — only 42 per cent. Catullus has 10 SSSS lines, the *Priapea* 3, Martial 2, and Ovid only 1. Ovid, by contrast has 11 DDDD lines, the *Priapea* 6, while Martial and Catullus each have two. The commonest arrangements of the first four feet are: Catullus DSSS (27) and DSSD (11), Ovid DDSD (15) and DSDS (12), Martial DSSD (19), DSSS and SDSS (10 each), *Priapea* DSSS (18), DDSS (14) and DSSD (12). Martial leads in spondaic first feet, with 36, followed by Catullus (31), the *Priapea* (23) and Ovid (18). Thus, although the *Priapea* are close to Martial in weight of spondees, they are closer to Ovid in spondaic openings.

As for the first two feet of the pentameter, comparison with Platnauer's analysis of Tibullus, Propertius and Ovid[42] shows the *Priapea* closer to the former two (percentages):

	Tibullus	Propertius	Ovid	Priapea
DD	24.0	24.1	30.9	24.2
DS	58.6	43.0	52.4	43.2
SD	5.2	16.5	8.3	10.5
SS	12.2	16.4	8.4	22.1

The *Priapea* appear much heavier than both Ovid and Tibullus in spondaic openings but similar to Propertius. However, these figures relate to the whole works of the three named poets, but only to the 95 couplets of the *Priapea*. There is strict observance of the rule that the last word of the pentameter should consist of two syllables. This is entirely disregarded by Catullus; Propertius, in his first 95 distichs, has 21 breaches of the rule, Tibullus only 7, while Martial has 10, but Ovid none. The *Priapea* have six, but all are special cases: two are mythological names ending single-distich epigrams (Alcinoo **60** 2; Erigone **62** 2); in two the offending word is *supercilium* (and *supercilii*: **1** 2 and **49** 4) which all poets, even Ovid (e.g. *her* 17 16), used as a pentameter ending; and two are needed for balance — the balanced pentameter half-line is a special feature of the *Priapea*: *quod peto, si dederis, quod petis, accipies* (**38** 4), and **68** 8 where *merdaleast* is needed to balance *merdaleon* at the beginning of the couplet. There are, of course, many cases where the two-syllable ending includes an elided *est*, but this is very common also in Ovid. Apart from this, a single-syllable word never forms the pentameter ending, although "even Ovid is more free in this respect, not to mention Martial".[43]

The hexameter caesura is normally penthemimeral (in the middle of the third foot), though occasionally we meet the "more lively and graceful tripartite hexameter".[44] Concidence of word-ending with end of the fifth-foot dactyl, at 44 per cent, is much the same as Ovid (46 per cent) and Martial (47 per cent), but less than Catullus (56 per cent). Coincidence of the end of the couplet with a strong pause (enjambment) does not occur in 12 out of the *Priapea*'s 95. This is a higher proportion than with the other poets,[45] but most instances result from the frequent priamel-type listing, e.g. **20**.

Scazons or choliambs make up only 14 per cent of the *Priapea*, but the eight poems in this metre have an average length of ten lines, one (**51**), with 28 lines, being the second longest in the book. The metre is iambic, except that the final foot is a trochee. There is some variation, especially in the first foot, but here again, the *Priapea* are more regular than some other poets, avoiding opening anapaests, dactyls and tribrachs.[46]

LANGUAGE

The same love of variation which enabled the poet to write 80 different epigrams on the same subject, is seen in his language. Thus, the central feature of the book, Priapus' member, although usually called *mentula* (15 times), is also termed a *columna* (**10** 8), a *contus* or pole (**11** 3), a *fascinum* (**28** 3, **79** 1), *fustis* or club (**63** 9), *hasta* **43** 1, 4), *impudentiae signum* (**63** 13), *inguen* (**1** 6), *ista, quae me terribilem facit* (**56** 3–4), *nervus* (**63** 14, **80** 10), *nota virilis* (**66** 1), *obscaena pars* (**7** 1), *pars* (**37** 8), *pars madida* (**48** 1), *pars maior* (**30** 1), *penis* (**18** 1, **40** 3), *psoleos* = Gr. for *penis* (**68** 5), *sceptrum* (**25** 1, 3), *seminale membrum* (**26** 2), *stator*(?) (**52** 3), *tela* (**55** 4), *vena* (**33** 2) — 21 variants! And although his favourite threat of *pedicare* uses that verb on seven occasions, he varies it on six others with *caedere* (**26** 10), *excavare* (**51** 4), *fodere* (**52** 8), *percidere* (**13** 1, **15** 6), *perforare* (**76** 3) and *scindere* (**54** 2, **77** 9).

The poet is fond of referring to mythological persons in a roundabout way instead of simply naming them (antonomasia), e.g. *soror Phoebi* (**1** 3) for Diana, *qui raptus ab alite sacra* for Ganymede (**3** 5), *Hectoris parente* for Hecuba (**12** 1), etc. Schönberger notes the frequency of ablatives of comparison, e.g. *membrosior aequo* (**1** 5), *tormento citharaque tensiorem* (**6** 5), *ipsa pudicior Vesta* (**31** 2). He lists 22 examples: "no small number for a little book".[47]

"Its poets seem to have been fascinated with abstruse or rare words".[48] O'Connor lists 65 of these, distributed throughout the work and occurring in 41 of the 80 poems. Several of them are post-Augustan and point to such a date for the poems that include them. Others are botanical or medical terms. Thirteen are used for the first time in the extant Latin literature, or used for the first time with a particular meaning.

The author's rigorous adherence to metrical rectitude causes him occasionally to stretch a point in syntax. Thus he uses the ablative for the accusative in *totis noctibus* (**26** 3), *longa nocte* (**47** 5), *autumnis . . . duobus* in **61** 3, and *tota nocte* (**70** 8); also there are one or two instances of subjunctive or future for the present indicative of verbs, and other aberrations, all on account of the metre.[49]

READERSHIP — AND ROMAN SEXUAL ATTITUDES

As it is not certain that it was ever published, the *Priapea* may have had no ancient readership, but from the content we may learn much about the readership for which it was intended, and of the kind of person who would have chosen to read it, given the chance. Like Latin literature generally, it was certainly written by a man and for a male audience, although as **8** suggests, even 'chaste' matrons might well be tempted to read it too.

Its readers would have shared the distinctive sexual attitudes and assumptions of the Roman male which it displays. One such assumption was that women and boys were both generally considered to be legitimate outlets for male sexual desire. Horace writes of "lusting for a thousand girls, a thousand boys" (*sat.* 2 3 325). The gulf between our own traditional mores in this respect and that of the ancients stems largely from the fact that Christian morality followed the Jewish, and Roman the Greek philosophy: "the Greeks regarded the phallus and paiderasty as sacred and the seed as the carrier of arete, while the Jews saw homosexuality as an abomination, the phallus as hideous and seed as unclean".[50] Tatian, in his *Oratio ad Graecos* (28), wrote that pederasty was held a crime among the barbarians, but honoured by the Romans. Most liaisons between Roman men and boys were with slaves, for unions with free-born youths were illegal, but this was on social rather than moral grounds. And when Ovid (*a. a.* 2 683–4) expresses his preference for girls, it is entirely because of greater enjoyment, and not a moral judgement:

I don't like intercourse where both don't share the joys:
  That's why I'm not so keen on love of boys.

Others argued otherwise, as Menelaus in Achilles Tatius: "Boys have a more straightforward nature . . . and their beauty is a more piquant sauce to pleasure" (35). Yet some demurred, as for instance the high-minded Quintilian: he reproached Afranius for polluting his plots "with the abominable loves of boys" (*inst.* 10 1 100). But this doubtless was what Afranius' public wanted and what the readers of the *Priapea* would have expected.

The fact that the more intellectually-inclined Romans of the slave-owning classes read and wrote poetry about the sexual use and abuse of boys did not mean that they were homosexuals. Of the love of grown man for grown man there is very little in Latin literature, and nothing at all in Latin verse, and the passive partner in such relationships was regarded with ridicule or contempt. *Pedicatio* with an adult was associated not with affection but with aggression. Threats of anal and oral rape, such as Catullus' *pedicabo ego vos et irrumabo* and the many in the *Priapea*, are not literal expressions of real intent but terms of verbal abuse and attack. Oral intercourse was considered even more degrading for the recipient partner. Thus, when the reader of the *Priapea* read that the threatened punishment for a single theft was *pedicatio*, but of a second, *irrumatio*, he would have understood the distinction.

Besides the contempt shown to the 'pedicated' and 'irrumated' adult, there was extreme revulsion against elderly females who still lusted after men, and especially the superannuated whore. And whereas the erect male member was regarded with approval as a symbol of manliness, dominance and power, the impotent senile penis, along with female genitalia, and all polluted mouths, were looked upon with distaste. The average reader would have appreciated the disgusting description of the aged female's sexual anatomy in **12** and **46**; he may have come across such in Horace *Epode* 8 and in *55, Quid hoc novi est* . . .. Such language not only expresses hostility but humour as well. For the Roman reader would find these exaggerated invectives funny — jokes at the expense of people he would think should be the butts of a witty poet. For, as in Attic comedy, obscenity is "used to insult some one . . . to add power to comedy, jokes, ridicule or satire".[51]

Who, though, would want to read about such an unpleasant character as the Priapus of the *Priapea*? For he is nasty: aggressive, arrogant, crude, cruel, cynical, egocentric, exhibitionist, filthy-minded, foul-mouthed, lewd, sadistic, sarcastic and selfish, yet self-pitying. But he is witty — and this itself, together with the elegant and technically-perfect Latin in which he is described, would have attracted a large circle of readers who would delight in such entertaining excellence. He embodies, in exaggerated form of course, the worst characteristics of the Roman male of the time: "the ambivalence and irresponsibility of the Roman ruling class in general is revealed in these poems".[52] The decisive factor is that it was a slave-owning society. Most of the slaves came from the north, and were physically attractive to the Italians. Pope Gregory's *Non Angli sed Angeli* comes to mind[53] — and Ausonius' *Bissula*. In the face of such availability and such temptation, sexual indulgence must often have been in the thoughts of the idle classes from whom readers would be drawn. Horace's lines (*sat.* 1 2 114–9) are revealing:

> When parched thy throat, dost thou insist on wine?
> Or starving, all but choicest game and fish decline?
> And when thy member swells, and for thy lust
> A serving girl stands there, in whom to thrust —
> Or a boy slave, would'st rather burst? Not me!
> I like to have it quick and trouble-free.

THE LIBELLUS

In **1** the author speaks of a *sacellum* or shrine of Priapus in which his large member is naked to be seen, and in **2** says that the poems have been written upon the walls of the god's temple. Three other Priapea (**41**, **47**, **49**) refer to this custom. Several early editors took this literally to mean that such wall-writings and inscriptions had actually been copied out, as later did Wernicke (1847), Buecheler (1862), Baehrens (1879) and Vollmer (1923). It seems obvious, however, that the author is speaking figuratively, having composed the epigrams himself in his study for the purpose of compiling a book devoted wholly to Priapus, and it is likely that this libellus carried on its cover a bold picture of the god. The book stands for the shrine, its pages are the walls to which the poems were appended, and the picture represents the god's statue.

MANUSCRIPTS

Possibly some 75 manuscripts contain the *Priapea*, and 40 of these were used by Clairmont to establish his very comprehensive critical apparatus.[54] All but one are very late (15th cent.); the exception is the Laurentianus Plut. 33.31 (*A*), transcribed by Boccaccio (1313–75). The absence of earlier copies probably results from a readiness to destroy and a reluctance to copy because of the nature of the subject matter. Laurentianus Plut. 33.31 (*A*) is in a class by itself, not only on account of its seniority, but also because of its superiority — despite many defects — as a text, and its independent derivation from an ancient source. The original title, probably *VIRGILIJ PRIAPEIA*, has been erased, and *DIVERSORVM AVCTORVM PRIAPEIA* substituted. Likewise, at the end, *EXPLICIT PRIAPEIA* has replaced *PRIAPEIA MARONIS VIRGILIJ EXPLICIT.*[55] The poems follow each other without interval, distinguished only by larger majuscules, although in some instances this has not been done. An analysis of Clairmont's apparatus[56] shows a close relationship with three other manuscripts: Laurentianus Plut. 91 sup. 19, Vat. Lat. 1586, and Parisinus 8205. A close examination of Clairmont's work, and of photographic copies of about half the codices he himself used, leads us to the conclusion that few of them add much of worth to the *codices optimi* of previous editors: these are, besides *A*, the Guelferbytanus 338 Helmst. (*H*), Laurentianus Plut. 39.34 (*L*), Vossianus Latinus 0.81 (*V*), and the Wratislaviensis Rehdigeranus 60 (*W*). They must remain the staple for any edition of the *Priapea*.

The Guelferbytanus 338 Helmst. (*H*) has the title *Publij Virgilij Maronis Mantuani poetae priapeia incipit*, and the subscription *Publij Virgilij Maronis poetae inter omnes Latinos excellentis: Priapeia explicit per me Ioannem carpensem die 15 Novembris 1460. Bene Vale qui Legeris.* At first, individual poems are separated and have brief titles, such as *Carmen Elegiacum* (**3**), *loquitur Priapus* (**6**), but after **20** these intervals cease. Analysis shows a close affinity between *H* and the earlier Bodleianus 30059, the Catinensis (*C*) and Vat. Lat. 2876 (*y*). Laurentianus 39.34 (*L*), like all *Priapea* mss., abounds in defects, but remains valuable. It has no title; the individual poems are separated, and each has a brief title, e.g. *VIRGILIVS, PRIAPVS, IVVENIS, DISTICON*. At the end are two short Greek phrases. It appears to lack close affinity with other mss.; the nearest to it are, as with *H*, Bodleianus 30059, the Catinensis, Perusinus 740, Vat. Reginensis Latinus 1803, and Vindobonensis 3108.

Vossianus Latinus 0.81 (*V*) has had its title erased; there are no titles to the poems, which are not separated. Despite the authority rightly accorded to it, it is badly written and confused. It comes to an end with line 4 of **70**. The remainder of the work is found interpolated between **52** 7 and **52** 8. Some lines (**48** 3 to **50** 5 and **51** 13–20) are scribbled in a later hand. Analysis shows a strong affinity to Parisinus Lat. 8232 (*Q*). It has similar relationships to other manuscripts as do *H* and *L*, suggesting that it belongs to the same 'family'.

Codex Wratislaviensis Rehdigeranus 60 has the title *EXCERPTA EX PRIAPEIA*; the poems are interspaced, with brief titles such as *AD PRIAPVM, PRIAPVS, AD LALAGEM, AD MATRONAS*. Besides the *carmina Priapea*, it has the pseudo-Tibullan *Rusticus (Vilicus) aerari (44)* and *Quid hoc novi est (45)*, after which comes the subscription *FINIS*. It has quite distinct affinities with certain other mss., being closely related to Brit. Mus. Addit. 11355, Vaticanus 1608 (*v*), Vat. Chigianus HV 164, Corsinianus 43 F21 (*c*), and Harleianus 2578.

Besides the 'families' of mss. which are linked with *A*, *HLV* and *W*, there is possibly another, for analysis shows strong similarities between Vat. Chigianus HV 169, Guelferbytanus 371, Vat. Ottobonianus Lat. 2029, and Ambrosianus D267 Inf. (*B*). But by far the largest grouping is that associated with *HLV*, although affinities within this group are not as strong as those within the smaller groups around *A* and *W*.[57]

EDITIONS

There have been at least 70 printed editions of the *Carmina Priapea*, but they have usually been published together with other material. Because the manuscripts are corrupt and full of errors, the task of editors has not been easy.

They were first printed in the *editio princeps* of Virgil (Rome 1469), by de'Bussi, which is clearly close to the Corsinianus ms. It has a few omissions and numerous errors and misprints, some of which were corrected in a second edition (1471).[58] Another Roman edition (1473), that of Udalricus Gallus and Simon de Luca, was the model for numerous editions of Virgil which appeared in various Italian cities over the next 40 years, e.g. Venice 1472, 1475, 1480, 1483, etc.; Vicenza 1476, 1479; Milan 1480, 1481, 1482; Brescia 1484; Florence 1487, and also for the first French and German editions (e.g. Paris 1478, 1489; Nuremberg 1492). Many of the surviving copies have had the *Priapea* torn out, while in some they have not been bound in, although listed in the Contents; this is so with the Bodleian Library's copies of the Milan editions of 1481 and 1482. Vollmer says he could not use the 1517 Aldine edition because the *Priapea* had been removed from it.[59]

Quite exceptional is the Modena edition of 1475. This beautifully-printed book is greatly superior to the other Italians; it has many of the now-accepted readings previously ascribed to

Avancius or Aldus. It does not seem to identify with any
particular manuscript, and whether it is based on one unknown
to us, or whether it is a remarkably well-edited collation we
cannot say. It was followed as a model, among the Italians, only
by the Parma edition of 1492, which, in one or two instances,
itself anticipates later accepted improvements. The first Aldine
(Venice 1517) breaks new ground, but remains essentially one of
the Italians; but the 1534 edition, revised by Asulanus, embodies
many improvements and marks a distinct advance.

Joseph Scaliger was the first to include a commentary
(Leyden 1573). He was regarded as the foremost scholar of the
age, and his edition influenced subsequent work until the late
nineteenth century. His commentary is learned and illuminating,
but, although some of his conjectures have been retained, most
were too far-fetched to survive. In 1595 Lindenbrog republished
Scaliger's Virgilian *Appendix* and *Priapea*, adding a useful com-
mentary of his own. In 1606 a rival edition to Scaliger's appeared
in Frankfurt under the name of Scioppius (Caspar Schoppe) who,
however, denied paternity, claiming that the book had been put
out by Melchior Goldast to discredit him. It is the first edition to
number the poems. It attracted abuse because its commentary
was condemned as more obscene than the poems themselves.
Nobody believed his denials, and the work continues to be
ascribed to him. Most of the new generation of leading scholars
were Protestant Germans and Lowlanders. Scioppius had aban-
doned Protestantism for the Roman faith at a time when the
religious struggle was at its most critical and fanatical stage, and
he was not forgiven. His edition was said to have been originally
published in Ingolstadt in 1595 when he was only 18; it may be
that it was a youthful folly which he later regretted and denied,
but which his enemies, having discovered, used as a stick to beat
him with. He was scurrilously attacked by Scaliger, Barthius and
others as a lecherous monster, and Fleming wrote abusive
sonnets about him.[60] Yet, as Scioppius pointed out, the great
Scaliger himself had not only produced his own edition of the
Priapea, but had gone out of his way to translate one of the most
obscene poems ever written (*45*) into Greek.

The *Priapea*, almost always supplementary to Petronius'
Satyricon, appeared throughout the seventeenth and early eight-
eenth centuries: Padua 1614, 1664; Frankfurt 1629; Utrecht 1654;
Amsterdam 1669, 1676; Magdeburg 1709; Leipzig 1731. Most of
these were merely reprints of Scioppius or Scaliger, but the

editions of Gabbema (1654), Hadrianides (1669) and Boschius (1676) were edited from both. The *Priapea* were included in Volume 2 of Pieter Burman's *Anthologia Latina* (Amsterdam 1773), accompanied by a massive commentary based on the study of several manuscripts, and with numerous quotations from previous editors and commentators. The sheer bulk of material adduced makes its use cumbersome. A few years later came Anton's edition (Leipzig 1781), a slimmer work with one or two interesting conjectures. Also useful, and embodying some necessary improvements, was the second volume of Meyer's *Anthologia Latina* (Leipzig 1835).

The second half of the nineteenth century saw real progress in the continued purification and amelioration of the text, the result of the labours of Buecheler (Berlin 1862, 1892, 1895, 1904), L. Mueller (Leipzig 1874, 1892) and Baehrens (Leipzig 1879). Buecheler was an outstanding Latinist, Mueller was authoritative on metre, while Baehrens drew, for the first time, upon the oldest and best of the mss. (A). Despite the many unlikely conjectures all three attempted, they provided the basic material for building as good a text as we are ever likely to get. For more recent editors, little has remained other than to try to resolve the outstanding conundrums by widening the manuscript base and arguing for and against various readings and conjectures. Whether they have done much to enhance the situation remains open to doubt. Heraeus (Berlin 1912)[61] made a few changes to the Buecheler edition; Pascal (Turin 1918)[62] was a conservative editor, sceptical of conjecture, but Castiglioni, who revised his edition (1931), offered some intriguing suggestions. Vollmer (Leipzig 1923),[63] generally regarded as the best of the twentieth-century editors, often fails to make the most convincing choice from the possibilities available. The editions of Maggi (Naples 1923) and Cazzaniga (Turin 1959) were severely criticized by Fraenkel and Buchheit respectively.[64] Yet another Italian edition was that of Serra (Pisa 1976); nine mss. are adduced, but there is no apparatus. The most recent edition, the doctoral dissertation of Clairmont (Chicago 1983), although accompanied by an unprecedently comprehensive apparatus, drawing upon 40 mss., has, with but one or two exceptions, a traditional text.

During the past century there have been several editions with an accompanying translation into a modern language, usually in verse. The three into English listed below were all privately printed. Such translations known to us are:

into English: 'Neaniskos' (prose) (Athens 1888)
                'Neaniskos' [prose], 'Outidanos' [verse]
                (Cosmopolis 1890)
                Buck, M. S. (Philadelphia 1937)
into French: t'Serstevens, A. (Paris 1929)
into German: Fischer, C. & Kytzler, B. (Salzburg 1969)
                Kytzler, B. & Fischer, C. (Zurich & Munich 1978)
into Italian: Bach, G. (Rome 1945, 1950)
                Vespini, A. (Naples 1976)
                Vivaldi, C. (Milan 1976)
into Spanish: Cartelle, E.M. [translation only] (Madrid 1981)

STUDIES AND COMMENTARIES

Besides those who have produced full editions of the text, many other scholars have contributed to the discussion of various points or special aspects. But there are also four or five comprehensive studies. The earliest and briefest was the work of Avancius of Verona (1495),[65] who succinctly pointed out, epigram by epigram, errors in the text of the early Italian editions. A more substantial work was the *Priapeia* of Wernicke (1853).[66] This is a comprehensive review of the contributions of previous scholars, with special attention to the quality and metre of the poems and their authorship. Very different in quality and importance was the work of Franz Buecheler (1863);[67] examining each poem in turn, he has original and illuminating comments on almost all the difficult questions; many of his emendations have been accepted, while others have proved too daring or contrived. Almost exactly a hundred years later (1962), came Buchheit's brilliant study,[68] full of revealing insights. His main themes are authorship, relationship with the Greek and Latin epigram, perfection of the metre, artistic quality of composition, and date — arguing for after Martial. Finally, the doctoral thesis of O'Connor (1984), which, after surveying the historical, religious and literary backgrounds, proceeds to an analysis, sometimes fascinating, sometimes provocative, never dull — of each poem.

DIVISION, SEQUENCE AND NUMBERING

In the manuscripts and early editions, sometimes complete poems, sometimes isolated lines, were often omitted. Poems now assumed to be separate were joined together, while others, now regarded as one, were divided; but the practice was not uniform. Pairs usually joined were **14** and **15**, **25** and **26**, **43** and **44**, **58** and **59**, **73** and **74**, **76** and **77**, while **30**, **68**, **72** and **80** were often divided into two. The early editions, following the codex *W*, transposed **43** and **44**. Obviously there could be no standard numbering while there was no agreement as to whether a poem was to be counted as one or two. The first poem, entitled *Ad Lectorem*, at first went unnumbered, with the second poem starting as **1**. Aldus, Burman and Meyer each brought the division and joining of the poems closer to the modern practice, but Mueller (1874) still divided **72** and combined **76** and **77**; Buecheler (1862) joined **72** and divided **76** from **77**, but divided **80**. Baehrens (1879) was the first to number through from **1** to **80** in the modern way. The present arrangement is not, however, necessarily the correct one.

Although almost all manuscripts end the *Priapea* with line 10 of **80**, the W group add *44* and *45*, and are followed in this by the early Italian editors (though not by the Modena). Aldus in 1517 added a Martial epigram (*55*) and the three *priapea* from the *Catalepton* (*39, 40, 41*); in this he was followed by Scaliger and his successors. Burman dropped the Martial. Buecheler and Mueller retained the rest as **82–86** and **81–85** respectively. Baehrens and Pascal (1918) omitted them, but they reappear as **82–86** in Vollmer (1923), and as **81–85** in Maggi (1923), who has the Tiburtine hymn (*60*) as **86**.

THE TEXT

In establishing the text we have had regard to the manuscript tradition, the arguments of editors and commentators, the exigencies of grammar and metre, and the need to make sense. The Latin superscriptions are nearly all taken from manuscripts, for the most part from Guelferbytanus 10.9. Aug.4.

The apparatus is comprehensive enough to enable scholars to judge for themselves the weight of manuscript authority and editorial opinion. It does not take account of variations in the use of capital or small letters in proper names or to begin lines, nor, normally, of obvious spelling errors or nonsense. Because of the lateness and corruption of the mss., more attention than usual is given to the choices and comments of editors and commentators.

THE TRANSLATION

We are aware of only two previous translations into English verse. The first was by Sir Richard Burton, using the pseudonym 'Outidanos'. His rendering is often clumsy, stilted and unnatural. He uses the second person singular (thou, thee, etc.) where appropriate. His translation is quite literal; only once or twice does he rhyme. The second was by M.S. Buck, an American. He rhymes, and translates the second person singular of the original as 'you' and 'your'.

In the present translation no attempt has been made to match metre or line length. Traditional English metres are used and nearly all the verses are rhymed. Rhyme can add to the piquancy of the verse and thus bring it closer to the original. Nothing seems more inappropriate for a rendering of highly formal and disciplined classical poetry than the formless, seemingly chaotic word arrangement of much modern verse. Where a material liberty has been taken with the text, this is noted in the commentary. The use of both 'thou' and 'you' (but not within the same poem) when addressing a single person may be criticized as inconsistent.

The translation of erotic or obscene language often employs blunt and forceful Anglo-Saxon words characterized by the English dictionary, if they are included at all, as "not in decent use". Difficulty arises from the absence of acceptable English words for the private parts and sexual activities that has resulted from taboos, now partially lifted, upon their literary use. The choice lies between Latin words more appropriate to medicine and the law, and bad language. But the author of the *Priapea* makes it clear that his language is not for chaste ears, and his Priapus, who is the speaker in most of the epigrams, is portrayed as lewd and coarse. Burton used either anglicized Latin terms such as 'mentule' and 'irrumate', or pseudo-archaisms like 'prickle' and 'coynte', but these only add to the rather bizarre nature of his work. Buck imitates him in the use of such Latinisms as 'mentule' and 'pedicate', and he too renders *cunnus* by 'coynte'. To avoid the blunt bad language is, however, to pervert the intention of the poet, who makes it plain that circumlocution and euphemism are not for him.

The English superscriptions are not translations of those above the latin text, but provided by the editor.

PRONUNCIATION

The name Priapus — Priapos or Priepos in Greek — had a 'long' second syllable. For this reason the OED gives the stress on this syllable; it also gives a long 'i' in the first syllable. As the name is normally used only by those with some classical education, this pronunciation survives, but were the word to have a wider currency in spoken English, it is unlikely that the long 'i' and the stressed 'a' would last long together; either the 'i' would shorten or the stress would move back to the first syllable, giving Prĭápus or Prĭápus, or both would happen, giving Prĭăpus. In the translation we have used Priápus, mindful of the god's threat, according to A.G. Kaestner:[69]

E longo Priapum qui me fecere Priapo
Efficiam, media sint quoque parte breves.

Those who, instead of Priăpus, me Prĭăpus make,
Their middles too to shorten, I shall measures take.

REFERENCES

1. Suetonius *de poetis: virg. 17*; for Donatus and Servius, see Vollmer, F. *Sitzb.Bayer.Akad.Wiss.* (1907) 339.
2. Keil, H. *Grammatici Latini* (Leipzig, 1857), 512.
3. Radford, R.S. *Trans.Am.Phil.Ass.* 52 (1921), 174.
4. Bloch, H. *Strassburger Festschrift* (Strassburg, 1901), 271.
5. In Bembus, P. *Ad Herculem Strotum* (Venice, 1530), b1a–b.
6. In Gruterus, J. *Lampas* 1 (Frankfurt, 1602), 1045.
7. Baptista Pius, G. *Annotationes posteriores* (Bologna, 1511), cap. 41; Gyraldus, L.G. *Historiae poetarum dialogi* (Basel, 1545), 4 452.
8. Barthius, C. *Adversarii* (Frankfurt, 1624), 44 6.
9. *Catulli, Tibulli, Propertii Carmina* (Leipzig, 1874), xliii–xliv.
10. *Carmina ludicra Romanorum* (Turin, 1918), xiv.
11. *Rh.Mus.* 18 (1863), 382.
12. *Poetae Latini minores* (Leipzig, 1879), 54.
13. *Poetae Latini minores* 2.2 (Leipzig, 1923), 36.
14. Rand, E.K. *Harv.Stud.* 30 (1919), 129–30.
15. *Trans.Am.Phil.Ass.* 52 (1921), 177.
16. Thomason, R.F. *The Priapea and Ovid* (Nashville, Tenn., 1931); Steele, R.B. *A review of 'The Priapea and Ovid'* (Nashville, Tenn., 1932).
17. *Miscellaneorum* (Florence, 1489), lix.
18. *Jugendverse* (Leipzig, 1910), 2.
19. Vollmer *Sitzb.Bayer.Akad.Wiss.* (1907), 350–1; Rand *Harv.Stud.* 30 (1919), 110.

20. Radford *Trans.Am.Phil.Ass.* 52 (1921), 172.

21. *Latomus* 22 (1963), 31–55.

22. Ménage, E. *Anti-Baillet* 1 (The Hague, 1690), 366.

23. *Zetemata* 28 (1962).

24. O'Connor, E.M. *Dominant themes in Greco-Roman priapic poetry* (diss. Univ. Calif. Santa Barbara, 1984), 97.

25. Fischer, C. and Kytzler, B. *Priapea* (Salzburg, 1969); Cartelle, E.M. *Priapos* (Madrid, 1981), 23–4; Goodyear, F.R.D. *Camb.Hist. Class.Lit.* 2 (Cambridge, 1982), 631–2.

26. Kenney, E.J. *CR 77* (1963), 72.

27. O'Connor *Priapic poetry*, 123.

28. *Rh.Mus.* 18 (1863), 383.

29. *PLM* 2.2., 37.

30. Galletier, E.P. *Vergilii Maronis* (Paris, 1920), 21; O'Connor, *Priapic poetry*, 45.

31. *Adversarii*, 27, 8.

32. *Zetemata* 28, 108–23.

33. Citroni, M. *M. Valerii Martialis epigrammaton liber primus* (Florence, 1975), 131; Cali, C. *Studi su i Priapea* (Catania, 1894), 5–6.

34. *Zetemata* 28, 112–13.

35. As for instance, Aldus *Diversorum veterum poetarum in Priapum lusus* (Venice, 1517), 1; Victorius, P. *Variarum lectionum* (Florence, 1553), 11, 17, 167; Scioppius, C. *Priapea* (Frankfurt, 1606), 4; Barthius *Adversarii*, 27, 8.

36. Floridus, F. in Gruterus *Lampas* 1 (Frankfurt, 1602), 1045; Richlin, A. *The Garden of Priapus* (New Haven, 1983), 42.

37. *I Priapea* (Naples, 1923), xxiv.

38. Buchheit *Zetemata* 28, 40; Kenney, *CR 77*, 74; Fischer *Priapea* (1969), 141; Kytzler *ibid.*, 129; Rankin, H.D. *Petronius* (The Hague, 1971), 60.

39. In Gruterus *Lampas* 1, 1045.

40. *Trans.Am.Phil.Ass.* 52 (1921), 162.

41. Buchheit, *Zetemata* 28, 22.

42. Platnauer, M. *Latin elegiac verse* (Cambridge, 1951), 38.

43. Buchheit, *Zetemata* 28, 22.

44. Radford *Trans.Am.Phil.Ass.* 52 (1921), 84.

45. Platnauer *Latin elegiac verse*, 27.

46. Sommer, P. *De Vergilii Catalepton* (Halle, 1910), 93–5.

47. *Glotta* 28 (1940), 90.

48. O'Connor *Priapic poetry*, App. B.

49. Schoenberger, J.K. *Glotta* 28, 93–5.

50. Vanggaard, T. *Phallos* (London, 1972), 136.

51. Henderson, J. *The maculate muse* (New Haven, 1975), 7.

52. Rankin, H.D. *Class.Med.* 27 (1966), 235.

53. Bede *Historia Ecclesiastica* 2 1.

54. Clairmont, R.E. *Carmina Priapea* (diss. Loyola Univ. Chicago, 1983), 109–11.

55. Sabbadini, R. *Le scoperte dei codici latini e greci* (Florence, 1905), 32–3, 41.

56. A complete analysis could not be made because Clairmont does

not list the mss. giving the readings he has selected, but only those with the readings he has rejected.

57. But see also Buchheit, V. *Gnomon* 35 (1963), 36 and Clairmont, *Carmina Priapea*, 85–107.

58. Giomini, R. *Appendix Vergiliana*, 2nd. ed. (Florence, 1962), lvii.

59. *Poetae Latini minores* 2,2 (Leipzig, 1923), 42.

60. Tarraeus Hebius [Barthius, C] *Cave canem . . . de vita Gasperis Scioppii apostatae* (Hanover, 1612); Lappenberg, J.M. *Paul Flemings Lateinische Gedichte* (Stuttgart, 1863), 575, 595.

61. *Petronii Satirae et liber Priapeorum* (Berlin, 1912).

62. Pascal, C. *Carmina ludicra Romanorum* (Turin, 1918).

63. Vollmer, F. *Poetae Latini minores* 2,2 (Leipzig, 1923).

64. Fraenkel, E. *Deutsche Literarurzeitung* 45 (1924), 353–5; Buchheit, V. *Gnomon* 35 (1963), 34–8.

65. *In Val. Catullum et in Priapeia emendationes* (Venice, 1495).

66. *Priapeia sive diversorum poetarum veterum in Priapum lusus* (Thorn, 1853).

67. 'Vindiciae libri Priapeorum', *Rh.Mus.* 18 (1863), 381–415.

68. 'Studien zum Corpus Priapeorum', *Zetemata* 28 (1962), 1–147.

69. Qu. in Wernicke *Priapeia* (Thorn, 1853), 33.

Note to the Reader

Traditionally known as the *Priapea*, these 80 poems are now often referred to also as the *Carmina Priapea* (*CP*) or the *corpus Priapeorum*. References to individual poems by number are made in bold type, thus: **7**; numbers in italics, thus: *18*, refer to the priapic poems listed in the tables on pp. 3 and 11.

Sometimes, in the translation or the commentary, the reader will find, not 'Priapus', but 'priapus'. Priapus was the phallic god of generation and of fertility; a priapus is his simulacrum: one of a multitude of statues placed in gardens, orchards and fields in the belief or hope that it would not only increase yields, but also deter marauding birds and thieves. The poems that follow cannot be fully appreciated unless it is borne in mind that thieves abounded in the Italian countryside, and the plundering of produce by vagrants and others was the chief bane of the horticulturalist of those times.

The Priapea: text and translation

CODICES

A	= Laurentianus Pluteus 33.31	*a*	= Alanus
B	= Ambrosianus D267 Inf.	*b*	= Vat. Barberinus Lat. 135
C	= Catinensis S. Nicolai 30	*c*	= Corsinianus 43 F.21
G	= Gotingensis Philol.116	*g*	= Guelferbytanus 10.9 Aug. 4°
H	= Guelferbytanus 338 Helmst.	*h*	= Guelferbytanus 336 Helmst.
L	= Laurentianus Plut.39.34	*p*	= Parisinus Latinus 8236
N	= Laurentianus Plut. 33.22	*u*	= Vat. Urbinas Lat. 350
O	= Vat. Ottobonianus 1465	*v*	= Vat. Latinus 1608
P	= Parisinus Latinus 8206	*w*	= Vindobonensis 3108
Q	= Parisinus Latinus 8232	*x*	= Vat. Latinus 3269
R	= Parisinus Latinus 8205	*y*	= Vat. Latinus 2876
S	= Vossianus Latinus F.78	*z*	= Vat. Latinus 1628
U	= Vat. Urbinas Lat. 745		
V	= Vossianus Latinus 0.81	Hi omnes codices saeculi XV	
W	= Wratislaviensis Rehd.60	videntur praeter *A* (saec.XIV)	

EDITIONES

ed.pr.	= Romana 1469	*Lind.*	= Lindenbrogii 1595
ed.Rom.	= Romana 1473	*Sciop.*	= Scioppii (1595) 1606
ed.Mutin.	= Mutinensis 1475	*Burm.*	= Burmanni 1773
ed.Venet.	= Venetia 1475	*Anton.*	= Antoni 1781
ed.Vincent.	= Vincentis 1476	*Meyer*	= Meyeri 1835
ed.Brix.	= Brixiensis 1484	*Buech.*	= Buecheleri 1862, 1863,
ed.Florent.	= Florentina 1487		1892
ed.Parm.	= Parmensis 1492	*Muell.*	= Luc.Muelleri 1874
Ital.	= editiones Italicae	*Baehr.*	= Baehrensii 1879
Ald.1517	= Aldina 1517	*Her.*	= Buecheleri-Heraei
ed.Argent.	= Argentina 1520		1912
Ald.1534	= Aldina 1534	*Pasc.*	= Pascali 1918
	(Asulani)	*Voll.*	= Vollmeri 1923
Ald.	= Aldinae 1517 &	*Maggi*	= Maggii 1923
	1534	*Cazz.*	= Cazzanigae 1959
Scal.	= Scaligeri 1573	*Clair.*	= Clairmontii 1983

The Priapea

I

Poeta de opere suo ad legentes

Carminis incompti lusus lecture procaces,
    conveniens Latio pone supercilium.
non soror hoc habitat Phoebi, non Vesta sacello,
    nec quae de patrio vertice nata dea est.
sed ruber hortorum custos, membrosior aequo,   5
    qui tectum nullis vestibus inguen habet.
aut igitur tunicam parti praetende tegendae,
    aut quibus hanc oculis aspicis, ista lege.

Inscriptio *G*   3 hoc] hic *codd. deteriores plerique*
4 nec AHL: non *QV* ˙   7 tegendae] pudendae *Scal.*   8 hanc
HV: haec (hec) *ALh*   aspicis] perspicis *Meyer*

1–2. Cf. Mart. 1 4 1s: *Contigeris nostros Caesar si forte libellos,/terrarum dominum pone supercilium*; Auson. 9 2 1s: *Carminis incompti tenuem lecture libellum,/pone supercilium.*

2. *Latio.* Tatio castigant Holstenius et Scriverius, teste et adprobante N. Heinsius ad Ovid I Art. Am. 650 quod etiam defendit Gevartius Lib. II Elector cap. 6 ut *Tatium* ponat pro duro et rigidi supercilii homine Martialis Lib. XI Ep. 105[104]. *Non ego sum Carius, non Numa, non Tatius* — BURMANNUS.
Et hoc primum Epigramma unum est ex illis Decem, quae universus Character mihi persuasit a Martiali profecta venisse — BARTHIUS.

1

A warning to the reader

> These verses here are full of rudery,
> So lay aside your Roman prudery:
> Dian' and Vesta dwell not in this fane,
> Nor goddess who from head of father came,[1]
> But ruddy orchard guard with tool that's blessed
> With immense size, and hidden by no vest.
> So cover up his shameful member — or,
> Gazing on it, with those same eyes read more.

[1] the goddess Athene, who sprang from her father Zeus's head,
after he had swallowed her mother, Metis.

At once the author displays the epigram-building skill that he will demonstrate throughout his work. Two central couplets warn of the nature of the verses that are to come; the first negatively — they are *not* about chaste goddesses like Diana, Vesta or Athene; the second positively — they *are* about that garden protector whose naked member knows no equal. These two balancing couplets are framed by an introduction, warning that here is no reading for prudes, and a conclusion, in which each line offers a choice: either cover up the erect member, or go ahead and read. The book — or roll — may have had a picture of Priapus upon the cover. If so, the poem invites any one who should look upon the roll, either to cover it up if it gives offence, or to open it and read.

Strato has a somewhat similar preface to his poems on the love of boys (*AP* 12 2): both ask the reader not to bring too severe a moral attitude to such reading. Martial also uses the phrase *pone supercilium*, "lay aside severity", when asking the Emperor Domitian to be indulgent to his verses (1 4 1–2). Much later, Ausonius (4th cent. AD) prefaced his poems to Bissula with a close imitation of **1**, and again advises, *pone supercilium*.

II

Excusatio poetae ad Priapum

Ludens haec ego teste te, Priape,
horto carmina digna, non libello,
scripsi non nimium laboriose.
nec Musas tamen, ut solent poetae,
ad non virgineum iocum vocavi.   5
nam sensus mihi corque defuisset,
castas, Pierium chorum sorores
auso dicere mentulam Priapi.
ergo quicquid id est, quod otiosus
templi parietibus tui notavi,   10
in partem accipias bonam, rogamus.

Inscriptio *g*   5 ad *HW et codd. plerique*: at *ALV*   virgineum
ALmv: ingenium *CV et codd. plerique*, inguen *H*   locum *HL*:
chorum (corum) *A et codd. plerique*, iocum *Wv ed. pr.*   vocavi]
invocavi *u*   7 Pierium (pyerium) *ALGu Buech. et edd. recen-
tiores*: Pieridum (pyeridum) *CHVWv edd. veteres*

3. Cf. Mart. 11 6 3: *versu ludere non laborioso*; 11 106 3: *nimium
laboriosus*.

5. *virgineum. ingenuum* codex Broukhusii . . . non spernanda videtur
haec lectio. nam *locus non ingenuus* idem notat, quod Ovidio dicitur
Lib. I. A.A. v.100 . . . Ingenuum enim omne liberale et honestum
est — BURMANNUS.

7. Martial (7 69 8) has *Pierio*, but Ovid (*tr.* 5 3 10) writes *Pieridum*.
Catullus tells what would happen if Priapus's member *did* go to
the Muses (105): *Mentula conatur Pipleum scandere montem: / Musae
furcillis praecipitem eiiciunt.*

haec . . . carmina . . . scripsi (1–3) . . . *quod otiosus templi parietibus tui
notavi* . . . Der Dichter von c.1 und c.2 beansprucht somit, der
Autor sämtlicher Gedichte zu sein — BUCHHEIT.

2

The author dedicates his verses to Priapus

You've seen, Priapus, these fruits of my wit:
More for a garden than a book they're fit,
And without too much trouble I've them writ.
Although 'tis poets' custom, I have not
Summoned the Muses to this unchaste spot.
For the heart and the will I haven't got
To bring such chaste sisters — the Pierian lot[1] —
So close to the member of Priapus hot.
And so, whatever in my idle scrawl
You find I've written on your temple wall,
Please be so good as to accept it all.

[1]one manuscript reading refers to the Muses as the Pierian or Thessalian chorus; an alternative reading makes them Pierides, i.e. daughters of Pieros, their Macedonian father.

Again, with mock modesty, the poet apologizes for his verse; it is rustic rather than literary, and written *non nimium laboriose* — without taking pains, and consisting of mere idle scribblings.

The central part of the poem, five lines in which the author explains why he has not called upon the Muses as poets usually do, is — once again — framed between an introduction and conclusion, each of three lines. Together these make up the dedication: "I have not produced elegant verses for you, Priapus — but please accept them". The conceit that was introduced in **1** is continued in **2**: the book is imagined as a shrine of Priapus, and the pages inside are conceived to be the temple walls hung with dedicatory verses.

This poem has some similarity with Strato's first prefatory verses (*AP* 12 1): it is imitated in Ausonius's first poem to Bissula.

III

Priapus se excusat quod obscena loquitur

Obscure poteram tibi dicere: "da mihi, quod tu
    des licet assidue, nil tamen inde perit.
da mihi, quod cupies frustra dare forsitan olim,
    cum tenet obsessas invida barba genas,
quodque Iovi dederat, qui raptus ab alite sacra,   5
    miscet amatori pocula grata suo,
quod virgo prima cupido dat nocte marito,
    dum timet alterius vulnus inepta loci."
simplicius multo est "da pedicare" Latine
    dicere. quid faciam? crassa Minerva mea est.   10

---

4 cum (quom) *AVW edd.*: dum *CHLNPv Clair.*   tenet] teget
Ald. 1534 Scal. Burm. Meyer. Muell.   6 grata *CHLW edd.* : sacra
AV   8 alterius *CHNWv codd.*   *plerique*: illius *ALV*   9
Latine *edd. Mut. & Parm.*: latino (latoino *H*) *codd. fere omnes*

2. Cf. Ov. *a.a.* 3 90: *Mille licet sumant, deperit inde nihil.*

6. Cuius sensum ita quoque expressit Plautus Casina (V.ii.41)
Illo haud verbum facit, et sepit veste id, qui estu,
Ubi illum saltum video obseptum, rogo. ut altero sinat ire —
BURMANNUS.

7. Sen. *contr.* 1 2 22: *novimus, inquit istam maritorum abstinentiam qui
etiamsi primam virginibus timidis remisere noctem, vicinis tamen locis
ludunt . . . Ovidianum illud "inepta loci".* Cf. Mart 11 78 5s: *pedicare
semel cupido dabit illa marito, / dum metuit teli vulnera prima novi*; Ov.
fast. 4 153: *cum primum cupido Venus est deducta marito.*

10. Macrobius Lib.I Saturn. cap. 24. *Sed nos, quos crassa Minerva
dedecet, non patiamus abstrusa esse adyta sacri poematis.* Horatius Lib.II
Sat. 2.3.   *Rusticus, abnormis, sapiens, crassaque Minerva —*
BURMANNUS.

3

Priapus declares his intention of speaking plainly

In riddles I might speak to thee,
And say: "Give and again give me
That which to yield would mean no loss;
For which, when whiskers spoil the gloss
Of thy smooth cheeks, in vain thou'lt sigh;
That which the boy, who, snatch'd from high
Mount Ida's top to mix Jove's wine,[1]
Gives to his lover lord divine;
That which the newly-wedded bride,
While striving hard one place to hide,
Will this then to her mate betray".
'Tis simpler in plain speech to say:
"Give entry, lad, to thy behind".
What else to do? I've but a dullard's mind.

[1]Ganymede, a shepherd boy. His beauty excited the lust of Zeus, who carried him off from the hills near Troy and made him his cup-bearer. It was nectar, rather than wine, that Ganymede served his master.

So succinct is this poem that four of its five couplets have necessitated three lines each in translation. Note how the central lines skilfully elaborate the introduction with three examples of evasive circumlocution — of speaking *obscure*. This heightens the suspense until the sharp conclusion shocks with its crudity. It is the god's first appearance, and he sounds his battlecry: *Da pedicare*, "let me bugger you". This epigram has been ascribed to Ovid because of an allusion in Seneca to *inepta loci* (line 8 of the original) as Ovidian (see pp. 34–6).

Deprecatio Lalagae dicantis Priapo

Obscaenas rigido deo tabellas
ductas ex Elephantidos libellis
dat donum Lalage rogatque temptes,
si pictas opus edat ad figuras.

Inscriptio *g*   2 ductas *Castiglioni*: ducens *H et codd. plerique,
edd. vett. Baehr. Cazz.*, dicans *LNPV v ed.Parm. Burm. Meyer Muell.
Buech. Voll. Clair.*, dicens *A ed. Mut.*   3 temptes *AHVv ed.
Mut. edd. recentt.*: tentes *LC et codd. plerique, edd. vett.*   4
pictas] pietas *A*

Ex huius ergo libris ductas picturas Lalage Priapi sacello
suspendit, rogans ut se stuprare velit et tentare, an omnes istos
pictos coeundi modos fideliter imitari poscit. Hic sensus est
carminis, aliud qui dicunt, campas loquuntur — SCIOPPIUS.

2. The reading *dicans*, termed "certain" by Buecheler, and
adopted by most editors since, is unacceptable. Not only would it
be the only iambic beginning to the hendecasyllabic line in the
whole work, but with *dat* in v.3, would be blatantly tautological.
Ducens has good manuscript authority, but is a difficult reading.

Elephantidos. Cf. Mart. 12 43 4: *nec molles Elephantidos libelli*; Suet.
caes. 3 43: *cubicula plurifariam disposita tabellis et sigillis lascivissi-
marum picturarum et figurarum librisque Elephantidis instruxit, ne cui in
opera edenda exemplar impetratae schemae deesset.*

3. Lalage. Cf. Hor. *od.* 1 22 10, 23; 2 5 16.

Priapus is invited to try some positions pictured in a book

Lalage gives to the hard-membered god
Pictures obscene from Elephantis' books,
And in return requests that he should try
With her to bring the deeds they show to life.

This is the first of several dedicatory poems in which a gift is
offered to the god with a request that he do something in return.
The wanton girl, Lalage, offers Priapus the illustrations of coital
positions by Elephantis, and challenges him to practise them
himself — presumably with her. Although Elephantis' works
have not survived, the emperor Tiberius, according to Suetonius,
made use of them on the Isle of Capri:

In various places he decorated rooms with pictures and
figurines of the most lascivious paintings and sculptures,
which were taken from the books of Elephantis, so that those
taking part in his orgies would find models for the positions
they were to adopt.

And Martial (12 43) refers to the work in these lines:

Too much, Sabellus, in your verses I have read
Of many lecherous ways of making love in bed.
Of such lascivious tricks, Diodym's whores know nought.
For them in Elephantis' books in vain I've sought.
You give new ways of doing it, one can't deny,
That e'en the most abandoned rake would love to try.

Horace also refers to a girl called Lalage. It was evidently a name
commonly used to denote a woman of easy virtue.

V

Lex Priapi dicta puero

Quam puero legem fertur dixisse Priapus,
 versibus his infra scripta duobus erit:
quod meus hortus habet, sumas impune licebit,
 si dederis nobis, quod tuus hortus habet.

Inscriptio *g*   2 his *LVa Voll*.: hic *codd. fere omnes, edd. vett.,*
Muell. Buech. Cazz. Cairn., haec (hec) *A Baehr. Pasc.*   4 Si
mihi tu dederis *H*   *hoc carmen om. Wc ed. pr.*

3–4. A similar distich is found in an anonymous epigram
published by Pithoeus (16th cent.):

Quod meus hortus habet, gratanti suscipe mente:
sic fruaris laetus, quod tuus hortus habet. (Meyer 1074 15s)

Here, however, neither *hortus* is meant obscenely, as it is in the
fourth verse of **5**. But both meanings — garden and privy part —
are similarly found in successive lines in an epigram quoted by
Menagius (17th cent.) in his work on Diogenes Laertius (see p.
28):

Horto Hesperidum, Sabelle, cultis
vestrae cultior hortus est puellae:
mirari, o bene, desinas, Sabelle,
hortorum Deus ipse nam Priapus
cunctius hunc fodit et rigat diebus.

1 Horto] Hortis *Burm.*   2 vestrae] *aliter* nostrae

Diogenes himself (2 116) used the Greek equivalent of *hortus*,
κῆπος, for *cunnus*.

5

How Priapus bargained with a boy in the orchard

> The rule which Priapus laid down for the boy,
>> In two lines set below you may see: '
> "What my garden holds thou may'st freely enjoy
>> If what thine contains thou givest me".

Priapus now appears in his commonest role, that of horticultural watchman. Usually he deters would-be robbers of fruit and vegetables with his menacing member, but here he is prepared to betray his trust for the perverse sexual gratification he is constantly seeking.

It was not uncommon for the ploughing or digging up of land to be used metaphorically to express penetration by the male member, and the Greek and Latin words for garden or orchard are sometimes used in this way (*see opposite*).

There are two similar epigrams in the Greek Anthology (*AP*16 240, 241), but how much more polished and pointed is **5**, with the two sides of the god's proposition neatly corresponding to the two lines of the second couplet. *AP* 16 240 is a dialogue between a vagrant (*V*) and Priapus (*P*):

V. Your figs are ripe, I see. May I pick some?
P. No, not one.
V. You are not very friendly.
P. It's no good your talking; you're wasting your time.
V. Now, please, please!
P. Give me something then that I would like.
V. Whatever can you want of me?
P. "Give and take" is a good rule, you know.
V. You are a god, and yet you want payment?
P. No, it's something else I'd like.
V. What's that?
P. If you are to get my figs, let me have that fig you've got behind.[1]

[1]'Fig' was commonly used, both in Greek and Latin, in an obscene sense.

VI

Comminatio Priapi ad puellam

Quod sum ligneus, ut vides, Priapus
et falx lignea ligneusque penis,
prendam te tamen et tenebo prensam
totamque hanc sine fraude, quantacunque est,
tormento citharaque tensiorem   5
ad costam tibi septimam recondam.

Inscriptio *g*   1 Quod] Qui *L¹ Baehr. Pasc.*, Quom
Muell.   sum *ACHLQg ed. Mut.*   Heins. *Anton. Meyer edd.*
recentiores: sim *VWav et codd. plerique, edd. veteres Muell.*   3
prendam] praehendam (pre-) *plerique codd. deteriores*   tenebo]
tenendo *A*   prensam *CHQW edd. vet. Muell. Pasc.*: pressam *AV*,
praehensam (pre-) *codd. plerique*, prensum *L Buech. edd. recentt.*,
prehensum *alii*   5 tensiorem *ALV*: tentiorem *HWv et codd.*
plerique

4. Supply *mentula*; cf. Mart. 9 47 6.

VII

Excusatio Priapi balbutiensis

Cum loquor, una mihi peccatur littera: nam te
pe-dico semper blaesaque lingua mihi est.

Inscriptio *z*   1 loquor] loquar *A*   te] T (t) *GHLN Voll.*,
prae (pre) *codd. pauci*   2 mihi *AHLV edd. recentiores*: mea *W et*
plerique codd., edd. veteres

6

Priapus warns of what his tense member, though made of wood, can do

> Although Priapus made of wood you see,
> With sickl'and penis both of wood to be,
> I'll take thee yet, my girl, and hold thee fast,
> And sure will hide it all, although 'tis vast
> And tense as string of catapult or lute,
> Inside thee deep, the distance of a foot.[1]

[1] Literally, up to thy seventh rib.

Priapus speaks, and for the first time his sickle (*falx*) is mentioned. The manuscript evidence points to a female target for these menacing lines (the readings *prensam*, *prehensam*, etc.). Modern editors, following Buecheler, prefer the masculine *prensum* because Priapus is assumed to be threatening thieves who are usually male. But here there is no reference to stealing; and in both **10** and **73** he reproves girls for their attitude to him because he is made of wood.

7

Priapus blames a speech defect for his indecent words

> I have a lisping tongue, and when I speak, one letter goes
>   astray.
> For though it's Tea I try for, Pee is what I always say.

This couplet is a letter game, but it cannot be translated into English and still retain its original meaning. Priapus says *nam Te Pe dico* — "for 't' it's 'p' I say", but *te pedico* means "I bugger you". He thus, while making an apparently innocent statement, contrives an obscenity.

VIII

Priapus ad matronas castas

Matronae procul hinc abite castae:
turpe est vos legere impudica verba.
non assis faciunt euntque recta:
nimirum sapiunt videntque magnam
matronae quoque mentulam libenter.   5

Inscriptio *g*

Ein deutliches Beispiel von der glänzenden Begabung unseres
Dichters — BUCHHEIT. Martial 3 68 has a similar theme. In
both poems the matron(s) is/are asked to keep away, in both the
request is ignored, and in both a *mentula* is the attraction. In v.8 of
the Martial epigram it is described as: *quam recepit sexto mense
superba Venus*. This line has long been a mystery, for "ein Fest der
Venus und des Priapus welches . . . im Juni begehen lässt, wird
sonst nirgend erwähnt" — MARQUARDT. It has also been the
subject of such ill-informed comment as: "au mois d'août les
dames romaines fidèles au culte d'Isis apportaient solennellement
un phallus au temple de Vénus Erycine" — ISAAC. According to
Schilling's convincing explanation, this line refers to the rite of
the Arrephoria, held in Athens in June and described
by Pausanias (*Attica* 1 27 3), in which 'unmentionables'
(ἄρρητοι) were carried to Aphrodite; some of these objects were
cakes made in the shape of a phallus (Rabe, *Schol. in Lucian.* 276
13).

3. *assis*. Cf. Catul. 42 13: *non assis facis*.

8

Priapus tries to warn off respectable women

> I tell the chaste matrons to keep away.
> "What you'll read here is unseemly", I say.
> They care not a fig, but they come right on,
> And knowingly, willingly, gaze upon
> My monstrous big member without dismay.

Roman matrons, formidable in their reputation for rectitude, have come upon the book, with its cover-picture of the big-membered god, and are told not to look further. The warning is ignored. And so they must, Priapus concludes, be very experienced to gaze upon him with such pleasure.

Here, as in **4**, Priapus is passive rather than active. It is not he who displays the sexual activity or interest; instead it is he who attracts or arouses it. **10** and **66** also depict sexually-interested approaches to the god by the supposedly chaste or bashful, and the conclusions of **8**, **10** and **66** are all introduced by *nimirum*: "too great by far" is the attraction of his huge member.

Compare this poem with Martial 3 68:

> Matron, my book so far has written been for thee.
> "For whom the rest?", thou askest. Why, for me!
> Now we at baths and changing rooms arrive. Beware,
> Lest thou catch sight of men who're stripped and bare!
> Terpsichore, from wine unsteady, wanton plays,
> Puts shame aside, and knows not what she says;
> No niceties for her: she names in words rough-hewn
> The phallus to proud Venus borne in June,
> That which the farmer's man sets up to guard his land;
> Which, lest she see, the maid puts up her hand.
> Ha, ha! My book — thou wast about to let it fall!
> But now thou'lt eagerly devour it all.

IX

Priapus excusat se quod mentulam detectam habet

Cur obscena mihi pars sit sine veste, requiris?
    quaere, tegat nullus cur sua tela deus.
fulmen habens mundi dominus tenet illud aperte;
    nec datur aequoreo fuscina tecta deo.
nec Mavors illum, per quem valet, occulit ensem;   5
    nec latet in tepido Palladis hasta sinu.
num pudet auratas Phoebum portare sagittas?
    clamne solet pharetram ferre Diana suam?
num tegit Alcides nodosae robora clavae?
    sub tunica virgam num deus ales habet?   10
quis Bacchum gracili vestem praetendere thyrso.
    quis te celata cum face vidit, Amor?
nec mihi sit crimen, quod mentula semper aperta est:
    hoc mihi si telum desit, inermis ero.

Inscriptio *P*   1 requiris] requirens *A Voll.*, requiras *y*   2
quaere (quere) *A Muell. Buech. edd. recentiores*: quaero *codd. fere omnes*,
edd. veteres Pasc.   tela *ACL Ald. 1517 edd.*: signa *codd. reliqui*,
Ital.   3 habens *A Voll. Cazz.*: habet *codd. reliqui, edd.*   6
in tepido]   intrepidae *Castiglioni*   7 num] nec *A*   auratas]
hamatas *HC*   8 clamne *HVW et cett.*: clam nec *AP*, clamve
codd. plerique, edd. veteres   9 tegit] tenet *A*   10 tunica:
tunicam *LQV*   num] non *Pha*   13 quod] quis *HPR*

2. *quaere* et ipse conjeci et Lucianus Muellerus de re metrica p.51 –
BUECHELER.

6. *in tepido.* Castiglioni's *intrepidae* (Palladis) is tempting.
Puto esse Ovidii — SCALIGER.

9

Why, Priapus asks, should he be the only god to hide his weapon

Unclothed are my privates, and you ask me why.
"Does any god else," — I ask in reply —
"Disguise his own weapon?" The lord of the sky
His thunderbolt plainly to all will reveal:
Does Neptune, the sea god, his trident conceal?
That warrior Mars has a sword is quite clear,
And Pallas attempts not to hide her long spear
Within her warm cloak. Does Phoebus feel shame
Displaying his arrows, with sunlight aflame?
Diana her quiver does not cover up,
Nor Alcides put clothes on his knobbly club;
His magical wand has winged Mercury dressed?
And has Bacchus decked up his staff in a vest?
Whoever saw beautiful Cupid in clothes?
No crime can it be if my prick I expose:
Without it I'd have no defence 'gainst my foes.

This poem is one of several in which Priapus compares himself to
the other gods; the others are **20**, **36**, **39** and **75**. He even dares to
equate his member to Jupiter's thunderbolt. This epigram is
another masterpiece of witty content and formal perfection. In
construction it is again 'framed': ten lines of proof or substantia-
tion are enclosed by the opening question and the concluding
answer; and, in the original, one god or goddess, with his or her
weapon, is neatly fitted into each of the ten lines. The translation
does not accord exactly with this arrangement: the opening
couplet here takes two and a half lines, and the whole rendering is
two lines longer.

X

Priapus ad puellam se quod ligneus esset irridentem

Insulsissima quid puella rides?
non me Praxiteles Scopasve fecit,
non sum Phidiaca manu politus;
sed lignum rude vilicus dolavit
et dixit mihi: "tu Priapus esto".   5
spectas me tamen et subinde rides?
nimirum tibi salsa res videtur
adstans inguinibus columna nostris.

Inscriptio *Harleianus 2578*   3 non *ALVWv ed. Mutin. Voll. Cazz.
Clair.*: nec *H et plerique deteriores, edd.   veteres Muell. Buech.
Pasc.*   7 salsa *Ald. 1517 ed. Argent. 1520 edd.*: falsa *codd. fere omnes
Clair.*

2–5. Cf. Col. 10 29ss:

*Neu tibi Daedaliae quaerantur munera dextrae,
nec Polyclitea nec Phradmonis, aut Ageladae
arte laboretur: sed truncum forte dolatum
arboris antique numen venerare Priapi
terribilis membri, medio qui semper in horto
inguinibus puero, praedoni falce minetur.*

2. Cf. Mart. 4 39 3ss:

*solus Praxitelus manum Scopaeque
solus Phidiaci toreuma caeli,*

8. For *columna* as *mentula* cf. Mart. 6 49 3: *de ligno mihi quolibet columna est*; and 11 51 1s: *Tanta est quae Titio columna pendet / quantam Lampsaciae colunt puellae.*

10

Priapus reproaches a girl who laughs at him

What are you laughing at, you silly wench?
I was not made on Praxiteles' bench;
Nor Scopas nor Phidias smoothed me with sand.
I was carved out of wood by a rustic's hand.
"Be Priapus!" he said, as he finished his work.
Yet you look at me and you giggle and smirk.
Only too well do you see't as a joke
That such a thick pole from my loins should poke.

Phidias (5th cent. BC), Praxiteles and Scopas (both 4th cent. BC)
were Athenian sculptors of great renown.

Distinct from Priapus, potent god of reproduction, was the
'priapus', the roughly-hewn scare-thief set up by his peasant
'master' who had had him 'made'. Compare Horace *Satire* 1 8:

A fig-tree once I was, which useless wood
The carpenter in doubt was if he should
To a priapus turn — or to a chair.
He chose the god, and so my job's to scare
Away the thieves . . .

Columella (1st cent. AD) has similar lines to **10**, although his
sculptors are different:

Not by Daedalus' hand this statue that you look upon,
Nor yet by Polyclitus' art 'twas worked, nor by Phradmon
Nor Ageladas carved. It is the trunk of some old tree,
That has been roughly shaped to show Priapus' deity,
Which, standing ever in the orchard's midst may, by the
     sight
Of member terrible — the boys, of sickle — thieves afright.

XI

Priapus in furem callidum

Ne prendare cave. prenso nec fuste nocebo,
   saeva nec incurva vulnera falce dabo:
traiectus conto sic extendere pedali,
   ut culum rugam non habuisse putes.

Inscriptio *y*   1 prendare *Buech. edd. recentiores*: prensare *A et
codd. fere omnes, Ital.*, prensere *codd. pauci Ald. 1517 Scal. Burman.
Meyer*, pressare *W*   prenso *PWay Ald. 1517 edd.*: prensus *AHL et
cett., Ital.*, prehenso *Avanc.*   4 rugam *AHL et plerique, ed.
Mutin. Buech. Voll. Cazz.*: rugas *VWav edd. veteres Muell. Pasc.*

1. *prendare* scripsi: *prensare* libri plerique, quod qui mutarunt in
prensere, Latine nesciebant, quia nemo unquam *furem* aut *male-
ficium prensare* dixit sed *prendare* aut *deprendere* — BUECHELER.

3. Cf. Mart. 7 14 10: *mentula . . . sesquipedalis.*

11

Priapus says which of his three weapons he will use

> Watch out I don't catch thee! I'll not use my stick,
> Nor will my curved sickle thee savagely nick.
> But when I thrust up thee my great thick pole,[1]
> Stretched without wrinkle will be thine arsehole.

[1] literally 'foot-long pole', or possibly — with typical priapic exaggeration — 'foot-wide pole'.

Priapus was often said to carry a sickle; on this occasion he is also armed with a cudgel, club or stick (*fustis*). These were, of course, subsidiary to his main weapon, his huge member, which here he calls a *contus* or pole.

XII

Priapus de anicula coitum petente

Quaedam serior Hectoris parente,
Cumaeae soror, ut puto, Sibyllae,
aequalis tibi, quam domum revertens
Theseus repperit in rogo iacentem,
infirmo solet huc gradu venire   5
rugosasque manus ad astra tollens,
ne desit sibi mentulam, rogare.
hesterna quoque luce dum precatur,
dentum de tribus exscreavit unum.
"tolle" inquam "procul ac iube latere   10
scissa sub tunica stolaque rufa,
ut semper solet, et timere lucem,
qui tanto patet indecens hiatu,
barbato macer eminente naso,
ut credas Epicuron oscitari."   15

Inscriptio *Harleianus 2578*   1 serior *a¹u¹ Avanc. ed. Argent. Scal. Sciop. Burm.*: senior *WCcv et cett., Ital.*, segnior *Ald. 1534*, iunior *AHLPV et cett., edd. Mut. & Parm. Ald. 1517 Buech. Voll. Clair.*, haud iunior *Heins. Meyer Pasc. Maggi*, putrior *Buech.*, turpior *Jahn*   3 aequalis] et qualis *H*, aequali *Cazz.*   7 desit] desim *Avanc. Voll. Cazz.*   sibi] tibi *A*   mentulam *L et codd. plerique, edd.*: mentula *AHVWv Avanc.*   8 luce *libri*: nocte *Buech. Baehr.*   9 ex(s)creavit *LP edd.*: hic screavit *HV et codd. plerique*, ecscreavit *Muell.*   11 rufa *edd. vett. Buech. Clair.*: ruffa *HLPQRVWv*, russa *A Baehr. Muell. Voll. Cazz.*   15 Epicuron *Ald. 1517, edd.*: epicuros *P*, epicurii *A*, epicureo *L*, epicureos *HVW et codd. plerique, Ital.*   oscitari *A ed.Mut. Ald. 1517, edd.*: obscitari *L*, citari *HW et cett., Ital.*

1. *serior*. Buchheit defends *iunior*, claiming that it here means "ein bisschen jünger als Hecabe".

8. *luce*. miror ne scripsit *hesterna quoque nocte*: nam noctu ad Priapum lascivientes illae vetulae accedunt — BUECHELER. Hier ist nirgends von der Nacht der Rede … es heisst hier einfach neutral 'gestern' — BUCHHEIT.

15. Cf. Cic. *n.d.* 1 26 72: *ista . . . quae Epicurus oscitans alucinatus est.*

12

Priapus rebuffs an old hag who asks a favour

A hag as old as Hecuba,[1] who could have been
The Cumaean Sibyl's[2] sister, or that old crone seen
By Theseus homeward-bent, laid out on funeral mound,[3]
Comes here; and that a fuck for her by me be found,
With wrinkled hands raised up, implores the skies,
And spits out one of only three teeth as she cries.
"Be off!", I say, "and 'neath your ragged garment hide
That which by light of day should never be escried;
That which, with hairy lump protruding by its side,
Like Epicurus yawning, shameless gapes and wide."

[1]Hector's parent in the original. Hecuba was wife of Priam, king of
Troy, and mother of Hector.   [2]The Sibyl of Cumae, a town
in Campania, was a priestess of Apollo who asked the god for
eternal youth, which he would give only in return for her virginity.
This   she   refused   and   became   hideously   old   and
shrunken.   [3]Hecale, who hospitably received Theseus, on his
way to slay the bull of Marathon; on his return he found her dead.

Such mockery of the superannuated courtesan who, despite her
decayed charms, still seeks copulation, was a stock-in-trade of the
classical poets, both Greek and Roman. Horace's eighth Epode
paints an even more disgusting picture. Epicurus seems to have
been famous for his yawns — Cicero refers to 'yawning Epicurus'.

XIII

Monitio Priapi facta puero et puellae

Percidere puer, moneo: futuere puella:
barbatum furem tertia poena manet.

Inscriptio *g*   1 Percidere *Salmasius edd.*: Praecidere (Preci-
dere) *libri, edd. veteres*, Paedicere *Scal.*, Perscindere *Muell.*

Cf. *AP* 49; Procopius *Anecdota* 9 18.

1. Intellege *Percidere, futuere* temporis futuri — PASCAL. *Percidere*
= *pedicare*, cf. Mart. 12 35 2: *dicere percisum te mihi saepe soles.*

2. *tertia poena manet.* Scilicet oris stuprum — LINDENBRUCH.

Priapus threatens three kinds of punishment

> Take heed: a boy behind, a girl in front I'll take;
> For bearded ones who steal remains a third ordeal.

This is the first of the poems to refer to *irrumatio*. It is also the first of three single-couplet epigrams which succinctly state the 'three-fold punishment' meted out to thieves by Priapus, according to their sex and maturity, the others being **24** and **74**. Such concentrated obscenity has no parallel in priapic verse, although it is found elsewhere in the Greek epigram as the 'harlot's three-fold service to the customer', e.g. in *AP* 5 49 by Gallus, loosely rendered as:

> With utmost speed our Lydia serves three men:
> That's one behind, and one down there, and then
> Here's one on top. "I take all kinds,"[1] she'll say:
> "E'en though I've got two now, don't go away".

[1] In the original these are listed as "the lover of boys, the lover of women, and the lover of moisture".

Licentia introeundi ad Priapum

Huc huc, quisquis es, in dei salacis
deverti grave ne puta sacellum.
et si nocte fuit puella tecum,
hac re quod metuas adire, non est.
istud caelitibus datur severis: 5
nos vappae sumus et pusilla culti
ruris numina, nos pudore pulso
stamus sub Iove coleis apertis.
ergo quilibet huc licebit intret
nigra fornicis oblitus favilla.   10

Insciptio *g*   2 deverti *lapis edd.*: diverti *A et codd. fere omnes, edd.*
veteres   4 non est *libri*: noli *lapis*   5 istud *ALNVa Baehr.*
Pasc. Voll. Clair.: istuc *HW et codd. plerique, Buech. Muell.*   9
quilibet *lapis AHCa Avanc. Meyer Buech. Voll. Clair.*: cuilibet (quoi
libet) *LW et codd. plerique Ital. Burm. Muell. Baehr.*   10 nigra
lapis HLVWvw et codd. fere omnes: nigri *A et pauci codd., ed. Venet. 1475
Voll. Cazz.*   favilla *libri*: fabilla *lapis.*

Cf. *CIL* 11 3862 = *CLE* 1305

7–8. Cf. 29 3s: *sed cum tu posito deus pudore / ostendas mihi coleos patentes.*

10. Cf. Mart. 12 61 8: *nigri fornicis ebrium poetam.*   nigra. favilla
autem *nigra* saepius vocatur, et in hendecasyllabis poetae
adiectivum substantivumque ita componere amant ut principium
et finem versus occupent — BUECHELER.

No need, says Priapus, to be on your best behaviour with me

Come along, come along! Don't go off!
This is the shrine of a lecherous god.
Even if you had a girl last night
You can still come in, it's quite all right!
Approach top gods, of course, without sin:
We rustic chaps don't give a pin!
We cast aside all shame, and dare
Stand here and flaunt our bollocks bare.
So enter do, and have no fear:
Straight from a brothel you can come here.

In 1878 this epigram was found inscribed on marble in Capua, where it probably adorned a temple of the god. It has the framed construction so beloved of the priapic poet: the first couplet introduces the subject — unchasteness is no bar to approaching Priapus, while the last, strongly opened by *ergo*, 'therefore', confirms this. These two couplets enclose six lines of amplification and explanation.

This is one of several poems in which Priapus speaks deprecatingly about himself as a boorish fellow of little worth. Other examples are **3**, where he confesses to having a "dull intellect", **63**, where he calls himself a "wooden pumpkin-keeper", and **68**, which begins:

No scholar I, but country bred, so pardon me
If I be crude: trees is my trade, not books, you see.

Comminatio Priapi ad eos, qui turbabunt agellum sibi commissum

Commisso mihi non satis modestas
quicunque attulerit manus agello,
is me sentiet esse non spadonem.
dicat forsitan haec sibi ipse: "nemo
hic inter frutices loco remoto   5
percisum sciet esse me", sed errat:
magnis testibus ista res agetur.

Inscriptio *g*   sentiet *codd. fere omnes, edd.*: sentiat *A*   4–5]
5–4 *ponunt LV et codd. plerique, edd. vett.*   4 haec (hec) *ACVWvy*
Ital. edd. praeter Voll. Cazz.: hoc *HLa ed. Mut. Voll. Cazz.*   sibi
LVW codd. plerique, *edd.*: tibi HC*y*, tibine *A Voll. Cazz.*
Clair.   ipse] iste *Muell.* ipse: "nemo] quisquam *A Voll.*
Cazz.   5 hic *av et codd. minores, edd.*: huc *AHLV et codd.*
plerique, edd. Mutin & Parm.   6 percisum *pauci codd. minores,*
edd.: praecisum (pre-) *AHLW codd. fere omnes, edd. vett.*, perscissum
Muell. Pasc.   sciet *CHVWvy edd.*: sciat *ANa Voll. Cazz.*

6. Cf. Mart. 2 72 3: *os tibi percisum*

7. Cf. Mart. 2 72 8: *quid quod habet testes, Postume, Caecilius?*
Phaed. 3 11 5: testes quis desunt mihi.   Plaut. *curc.* 30, 32: *semper*
curato ne sis intestabilis / Quod amas ama[to] testibus praesentibus;
mil. 1420s: salvis testibus /ut te hodie hinc amittamus; & 1426: *si posthac*
prehendero ego te hic, carebis testibus.

Priapus warns that there will be witnesses

To look after this orchard — that's my job;
And if any thief comes here to rob,
He'll soon find out that I'm virile and strong.
And if he kids himself that no one sees,
In this remote orchard, among the trees,
That he's been rogered, then he'll be wrong.
My balls will witnesses be of his shame —
In Latin the word for both is the same.

One can only guess at the precise wording of lines 4 and 5. The manuscripts disagree, even about the order of the lines, but the free rendering above gives the sense of what clearly was intended. Since the shame of the chastisement was as potent a deterrent as the physical pain, the thief is told that he need not think that it won't be seen in such an isolated place: there will be *testes* present — for *testes* means both testicles and witnesses — hence the explanatory eighth line added to the translation.

XVI

Comparatio pulchritudinis pomorum oblatorum Priapo

Qualibus Hippomenes rapuit Schnoeneida pomis,
   qualibus Hesperidum nobilis hortus erat,
qualia credibile est spatiantem rure paterno
   Nausicaam pleno saepe tulisse sinu,
quale fuit malum, quod littera pinxit Aconti,   5
   qua lecta est cupido pacta puella viro:
taliacumque pius dominus florentis agelli
   imposuit mensae, nude Priape, tuae.

Inscriptio *g*   2 Hesperidum *Ald. 1517*: hippomanes (yppoma-nes *et al.*) *libri*   4 Nausicaam *C Avanc. edd.*: Nausicam (Nasicam) *codd. fere omnes, Ital.*   6 lecta est cupido *LPVWv et codd. plerique Voll. Cazz. Clair.*: cupido lecta *A Baehr.*, lecta, cupido *H edd. veteres, Muell. Buech.*,   est *ad finem AH et alii, edd. vett. Muell. Buech. Baehr.*   7 taliacumque (talia cumque) *HLVay Ald. 1517 Scal. Burm. Pasc. Clair.*: qualiacumque *A Voll. Cazz.*, talia cuncta *Baehr.*, talia quinque *Wcv Ald. 1534 Meyer Lessing Muell.* pius *A et codd. pauci Baehr. Her. Voll. Cazz. Clair.*: puer *HVW et codd fere omnes Meyer Muell. Buech. 1892 Pasc., fortasse* petis *Buech.*, pauper *Buech. 1863*   dominus] domini *Muell.*

7. *Taliacumque pius* — CLAIRMONT.
Qualiacumque pius — codex A, HERAEUS, VOLLMER, CAZZA-NIGA.
Taliacumque puer — codex H, editiones veteres, BUECHELER (1892), PASCAL.
Talia quinque puer — codices Wcv, editio Aldina 1534, LESSING, MEYER, MUELLER.
Talia nunc pauper — BUECHELER (1863).
Talia cuncta pius — BAEHRENS.

puer dominus agelli ab omni probabilitate; neque enim erilem filium quisquam Latine puerum dominum dixerit — BUECHELER (1863).

A gift of fine apples for Priapus

Apples as fine as those with which Hippomenes[1]
   Won Atalanta; such as Hesperides'[2]
Renownëd garden gives; such as the Pheacian maid,[3]
   Who often through her father's orchard strayed,
Her lap did fill; such as the fruit the damsel found
   Which bore the words that her t'Acontius[4] bound:
Priapus nude, of fertile land the pious lord
   Has placed such fruit upon thine altar board.

[1]Hippomenes successfully wooed Atalanta with three golden apples; she had previously rejected and killed all her suitors. [2]The Hesperides were nymphs who watched over the garden of the gods, in which grew apples of gold. [3]The Pheacian maid, i.e. Nausicaa, was the daughter of Alcinous, king of the Pheacians, whose orchards were renowned. [4]Acontius, enamoured of Cydippe, wrote a promise to marry him on a quince. This he threw to the girl, who picked it up and read out the promise, thus plighting her troth.

A glance at the opposite page will show the variety of possibilities offered by the manuscripts and by ingenious editors for line 7. By adopting one or other of these, the final couplet could read:

Such fruit the boy has placed upon thine altar board,
   Priapus nude — of fruitful land he's lord.

or

The boy's placed five such apples on thine altar board,
   Priapus nude — of fruitful land he's lord.

XVII

Reprehensio Priapi in circitores

> Quid mecum tibi, circitor moleste?
> ad me quid prohibes venire furem?
> accedat, sine: laxior redibit.

Inscriptio *g*

There are no problems with the text of this epigram, nor with that which follows. It is generally true that the shorter the poem, the less likely it is to have become confused in transcription.

XVIII

Commoditas penis Priapi

> Commoditas haec est in nostro maxima pene,
>   laxa quod esse mihi femina nulla potest.

Inscriptio *g*

96

17

Priapus is deprived of his prey

> You nasty watchman, why not let
> The thief approach? I don't object.
> When he gets home he'll find, I bet,
> My laxative has ta'en effect.

Or, more literally, and keeping to the three lines of the original,
Sir Richard Burton's version:

> What hast thou, meddling watch, with me to do?
> Why baulk the robber who to me would come?
> Let him draw nigh: the laxer shall he go.

Some farmers evidently did not rely upon Priapus alone to keep
the thieves away, but employed a watchman. The god protests
the interest he has in catching them, and stresses the efficacy of
his punishment.

18

Priapus sees an advantage in size

> The size of my member has this great use:
>   For me no woman can be too loose.

Or,

> Aye in this prick of our the bonniest boon to be found is,
>   Loose for my daily use no woman can be. (Burton)

(although there is no mention of 'daily' in the original), or even,

> My mighty penis is a comfort to me
> Since, so, no dame could ever be too roomy. [!] (Buck)

XIX

De Telethusa optime crissante nates

Hic quando Telethusa circulatrix,
quae clunem tunica tegente nulla
extans altius altiusque motat,
crissabit tibi fluctuante lumbo:
haec sic non modo te, Priape, possit,   5
privignum quoque sed movere Phaedrae.

Inscriptio *w*   1 Hic] Si *Q Baehr.* Hic quando] Ecquando *Scal. Muell.* 3 extans *Holland*: extis *libri Buech. 1892 Pasc. Cazz. Clair.,* aestis *p,* aestu *Baehr.,* exos *Voll.,* exossem *Vorberg,* sistris *Buech. 1863 Muell.*   altius *Wx Voll. Clair.*: saltius *V'y,* satius *AHLV et codd. plerique,* aptius *pv edd. vett. Buech. Muell.,* acrius *Ellis,* latius *b Baehr. Pasc.,* sacrius *v,* scitius *Cazz.*   altiusque *av Buech. Baehr. Voll. Clair.*: altiusve *AHLV et cett. Cazz.,* aptiusque *SW,* acriusque *Muell.,* motat *A Ald. 1517 edd. vet. Baehr. Voll. Cazz. Clair.*: movit *Wv et cett.,* ed. *Rom. 1473 Buech. Pasc.,* movet *HL et cett., Ital.*   5 haec sic *u edd. recentt.*: haec si *AL, om.* haec *HV et codd. fere omnes,* sic ut *HPW et codd fere omnes,* edd vett. *Muell.*   possit *bx Muell. Baehr. Pasc.*: posset *codd. fere omnes, edd. vett. Buech. Voll. Cazz. Clair.*

3. *extis* v.3 ist unverständlich . . . Denkt man an die ekstatischen Bewegung der Mänaden, so wird man auf einen Ausdruch wie *extans* geführt . . . vgl. Ov. her. xiii 103 *altior extat* — HOLLAND. For various versions of v. 3 see Appendix A.

4. Es stört aber jedes Verständnis, wenn man nach Vers 4 ein Fragezeichen setzt und damit zu erkennen gibt (fast alle Herausgeber), dass *quando* also Fragepronomen interpretiert wird. Denn die erwartete Antwort auf die angebliche Frage bleibt aus; in dem *haec sic* ist sie jedenfals nicht enthalten. Fasse wir jedoch *quando* kondizional, so gewinnen wir einen ausgezeihneten Sinn: "Sollte die Telethusa einmal vor dir (Priap) tanzen . . . , so dürfte sie nicht nur dich, sondern auch den Stiefsohn der Phaedra in Wallung bringen" — BUCHHEIT.

19

The erotic effect of Telethusa's dancing .

If here the dancer Telethusa lewd,
She who contrives to move her buttocks nude
Above her breasts, up, down, and to and fro,
Should now her pulsing thighs before thee show,
She would, Priapus, fire not only thee,
But Phaedra's stepson's[1] stern frigidity.

[1]Hippolytus. Phaedra conceived a passion for him, but, furious
because he repulsed her, told her husband, Theseus, he had tried
to rape her. This led to his death and to Phaedra's suicide.

The poet prefers an indirect indication — Phaedra's stepson — to
the outright naming of his mythological characters, thereby
bringing the whole myth into the picture and so subtly enriching
the epigram. Hippolytus was renowned for his chastity, and
ability to arouse him was supreme proof of female charm. Ovid
says of another woman who moved her body lasciviously, that if
Hippolytus had been there, he would have become Priapus
(*Amores* 2 4 29ff). And Martial thus describes the girl from Cadiz,
a town noted for its dancers:

So artfully she moves her thighs, so wantonly gyrates,
That seeing her — why, even Hippolytus masturbates!
    (14 203)

Of another Telethusa — or perhaps the same? — Martial again
(6 71):

In time to Andalusian music she can prance;
    She's learnt to move Cadizian-way in dance.
E'en palsied Pelias, and Hecuba's old spouse,
    She, Telethusa, could them both arouse.
She has her former lord and master on the rack:
    He sold her slave; as mistress bought her back.

The manuscripts are corrupt, and there are nearly as many
readings and conjectures as there are copyists and editors.

XX

Priapus, de comparatione sui ad alios deos

Fulmina sub Iove sunt, Neptuni fuscina telum;
  ense potens Mars est; hasta, Minerva, tua est;
sutilibus Liber committit proelia thyrsis;
  fertur Apollinea missa sagitta manu;
Herculis armata est invicti dextera clava: 5
  at me terribilem mentula tenta facit.

Inscriptio *P*   1 telum] *add.* est *p Burm. Cast. Cazz.*   3
sutilibus (suttilibus) *Apx ed. Mutin. Avanc. edd.*: subtilibus *HLPVW
et codd. plerique ed. Vincent. Sciopp.*   5 invicti *ALN Avanc. Ald.
1534 Burm. Meyer Voll. Cazz. Clair.*: invicta *AHv codd. fere omnes, Ital.
Ald. 1517 ed. Argent. 1520 Buech. Muell. Baehr.*

Cf. Ov. *am.* 3 3 27ss: *Mavors . . . ense, Palladis . . . hasta, Apollonis
arcus, Iovis . . . fulmen.*

3. *sutiles thyrsos* intellege hedera, pampino, vittis adsutis ornatos
— BUECHELER.

5. *invicti dextera clava* non *invicta* — AVANCIUS.   edebant
invicti, et invictus Hercules profecto saepissime cognominatur. at
in libris est *invicta*, et non sine gravitate tentae Priapi mentulae
opponitur Herculis clava invicta — BUECHELER.

20

Priapus, like other gods, has his weapon

Jupiter rules over thunderbolts; and
Neptune is seen with a trident in hand;
Mars has a sword; Minerva a lance;
Bacchus[1] in battle with thyrsus[2] doth prance;
Phoebus[3] has arrows; there's Hercules' stick:[4]
But I am alarming because of my prick.

[1]*Bacchus.* The original has *Liber,* the old Italian name for the wine god.   [2]*thyrsus.* A staff entwined with ivy and vine tendrils. [3]*Phoebus.* The original has *Apollinea* — belonging to Apollo. His full Roman name was Phoebus Apollo.   [4]*Hercules' stick.* Although the weapon he used when performing his feats of valour was often the arrow, Hercules was associated with the *clava* — staff or cudgel, as in the saying *clavam Hercule extorquere* (to seize Hercules' staff, i.e. to attempt the impossible), and as in the name of the plant *Clava Herculis.* It would be quite in character for the rustic god to call the staff a stick.

This epigram is closely similar to **9**. Except for the omission of Diana, it lists the same gods, with the first four in the same order.

XXI

Quidam ad Priapum

Copia me perdit: tu suffragare rogatus,
  indicio nec me prode, Priape, tuo,
quaeque tibi posui tamquam vernacula poma,
  de sacra nulli dixeris esse via.

Inscriptio *g*   1 perdit *libri*: periit *Scal.*, deperiit (*om.* me)
Muell., servet *Baehr.*   rogatus] rogantum *Barth.*, rogatis
Heins   2 me *LVW av edd. veteres Buech. Muell. Pasc. Clair.*: nos
AHP et codd. plerique, ed. Parm. Voll. Cazz. Buchheit   3 quaeque
AHW et cett. ed. Mutin. Ald. edd. recentt.: haec (hae, hec) quaecum-
que (que-) (*om.* tanquam) *LV et cett. edd. veteres Pasc.*

1. hinc equidem ex mera coniectura recepi: *Copia me periit* —
SCALIGER.   Priapo queritur aliquis tot rogatores se
pomorum suorum caussa pati, ut nec Deo ipso ponere ea audeat
nisi sub ostentatione silenti. Scribendum igitur puto . . . *tu*
suffragare rogantum — BARTHIUS.   sensu caret illud *copia*
me perdit . . . Itaque de propria coniectura scripsi *copia deperiit*, h.e.
funditus periit — MUELLER.   loquitur enim fur qui cum
magnum numerum pomorum se sacra via abstulisset, partem
eorum dedicavit Priapo, ut onere aliquantum relevaretur, et hunc
deum . . . conciliaret — BUECHELER.   ista copia videli-
cet furum fuit, quibus salax dominus eam legem dixerat quam
puero fertur dixisset Priapus 5 3sq. — HOUSMAN.   Wer
beide Deutungen aufmerksam vergleicht, wird die in ihrer
Einfachheit bestechende Auslegung Buechelers der . . . von
Housman vorziehen — BUCHHEIT.

2. *nos.* scil. furem cum pomis — CAZZANIGA (prave).

3–4. Cf. Ov. *a.a.* 2 265s: *Rure suburbano poteris tibi dicere missa, / illa*
vel in sacra licet empta via.

21

Someone (a thief?) asks Priapus not to betray him

Too much has ruined me. If questioned, do not me betray:
　　Thou wouldst, Priapus, if thou wert to say,
The apples on thine altar, which as home-grown I did lay,
　　In fact were brought here from the Sacred Way.[1]

[1] a street in central Rome which ran eastwards from the temple of Vesta. Fruiterers traded there.

Several uncertainties make this epigram difficult to understand. It is by no means clear who is speaking — the landowner, a thief, a whore, or, as the title to the poem in one manuscript has it, a priest. What do the initial words, "Wealth (or plenty) is ruining me", mean? And, while some manuscripts read "do not betray me", others give "do not betray us", implying that Priapus is in some way an accomplice. Finally, the text does not say whether the apples from the Sacred Way have been bought or stolen. Ovid, in strikingly similar lines, does make this clear: he is advising a lover to present his lady with a basket of fruit (*Art of Love* 2 265f.):

They came from your suburban garden, you may say.
　　Although you bought them on the Sacred Way.

Another rendering, making more assumptions and taking the reading *nos* (us) instead of *me* in line 2, but more intelligible, runs:

I took too much, and 'twould both you and me betray,
　　Priapus, if when asked, thou wert to say,
The fruit upon thy board as home-grown I did lay,
　　Was stolen by me from the Sacred Way.

There have been many attempts at interpretation, none of them entirely satisfactory; for discussion of these see *Appendix B* (pp. 201–2).

XXII

Priapus loquitur de poena furum

Femina si furtum faciet mihi virve puerve,
haec cunnum, caput hic praebeat, ille nates.

Inscriptio *Q*   1 faciet] faciat *Cau*   virve puerve *Muell. edd. recentiores*: virque puerque *libri edd. veteres*

1. Cf. Ov. *pont.* 4 9 96: *femina de nobis virve puerve queri.*

XXIII

Priapus male optat furibus

Quicumque hic violam rosamve carpet
furtivumve olus aut inempta poma,
defectus pueroque feminaque
hac tentigine, quam videtis in me,
rumpatur, precor, usque mentulaque   5
nequiquam sibi pulset umbelicum.

Inscriptio *P*   1 violam rosamve] rosam violamve *g*   3 defectus pueroque feminaque *codd.optimi* (-ve -ve *L*) *ed. Mutin. Ald. Scal. edd.*: defecti puerique feminaeque *pauci codd. deteriores, Ital.*   4 quam *HWv* et *codd.plerique*: qua *AV*, quem *L*   6 nequiquam *Muell. edd. recentt.*: nequidquam (nequicquam) *libri edd. vett.*, nec quisquam *C*, ne sibi quicquam *N*

3–4. Cf. 33 5: *sed ne tentigine rumpar.*

Plate 1a. Red-figure *kylix*:
young man carving a herm of Priapus. Late 6th cent. BC.

Reproduced by courtesy of National Museum,
Copenhagen, Dept. of Near Eastern and Classical
Antiquities.

Plate 1b. Attic cup.
Woman worshipping a herm of Priapus.

Reproduced by courtesy of Antikenmuseum Staatliche
Museen Preussischer Kulturbesitz Berlin.

Plate 2. Attic *krater* (bell bowl).
Pan chasing a shepherd; statue of Priapus.

Plate 3. Boeotian *skyphos*:
the hero Cephalus sacrifices to Priapus. 5th cent. BC.

Reproduced by courtesy of Archaeological Institute,
University of Tübingen.

Plate 4a. Carnelian gemstone: Priapus and two Cupids, one playing the double flute, the other sacrificing at an altar. 2nd/3rd cent. AD.

Reproduced by courtesy of Kestner Museum, Hannover.

Plate 4b. Carnelian gemstone: a satyr sacrifices to Priapus. 1st cent. AD.

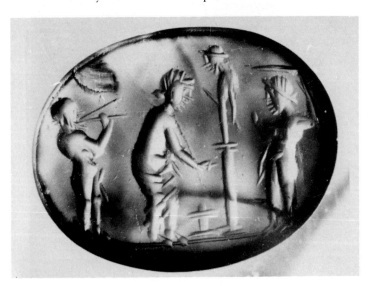

Reproduced by courtesy of Kestner Museum, Hannover

Everyone has something for Priapus

> Whoever the robber may be, each has something to offer
> me:
> The woman her cunt, the man his gob; if a boy, his arse will
> do the job.

This poem is the second of a 'three-fold punishment' trio, the others being **13** and **74**; but whereas **13** deals with three different kinds of sexual activity, **22** takes the three orifices — an example of the poet's ability to vary a single theme. Its obscenity apart, it is beautifully contrived, and so concise that the translation — by no means verbose — uses twice as many words as the original.

23

Priapus lays a curse upon garden thieves

> If any man should here a flower pluck,
> Or steal a cabbage, or an apple sweet,
> May he be tortured with desire to fuck,
> Yet find no boy or girl to cool his heat;
> So may his swollen prick be out of luck:
> Vainly against his navel let it beat.

This is the first of five maledictory poems in which misfortune is invoked upon those who fall foul of the garden god. It introduces a new variation to the theme of the priapic member: the curse is literally, "may he suffer from *hac tentigine quam videtis in me* — that tension which you see in me", a point lost in the translation. Also, in line 1, where the translation has "flower", the original reads *violam rosamve*, "a violet or a rose".

XXIV

Priapus custos furibus indicit poenam

Hic me custodem fecundi villicus horti
mandati curam iussit habere loci.
fur habeas poenam licet indignere "feram" que
"propter olus" dicas "hoc ego?" propter olus.

Inscriptio z   3 habeas] caveas *Muell.*   4 hoc] haec (hec)
C, hanc *plerique codd. deteriores*

3. *habeas.* Scripsi *caveas* . . . Nam in hoc carmine non magis quam
in reliquis Priapus inducitur poenam exercens sed minitans,
idque ipsum asseritur epigr. Leonidae, ex quo expressum esse
latinum plerique annotarunt — MUELLER.

Cf. *AP* 16 236. Doch kann von einer sklavischen Übertragung
keine Rede sein, wie die Anpassung der persönlichen Note im
Leonidas-epigramm an die generelle Aussageform der *carmina
Priapea*, sonstige Änderungen und die geschliffenere Form
beweisen — BUCHHEIT.

Even the smallest theft will bring retribution

> To me here the steward has given the care
> Of this fruitful garden, so, thief, beware!
> "You mean for a cabbage you'd do that to me?"
> For only a sprout I'll do it to thee.

We may safely assume that the threatened punishment is that aggression, using his terrible member, about which he is usually more explicit. Richlin (1983) describes this epigram as "very awkward". It is the only one of the 80 *Priapea* to be a fairly close translation of an earlier Greek epigram, the original being a poem by Leonidas (3rd cent. BC):

> I'm Priapus set up on the wall of the yard
>   By Dinomenes, his greens to guard.
> Sir thief, see how taut I am. "For greens, just a few,
>   All this?" Yes, for just one or two.

XXV

Priapus quamvis sit ligneus fures puniet

Hoc sceptrum, quod ab arbore est recisum,
nulla iam poterit virere fronde;
sceptrum, quod pathicae petunt puellae,
quod quidam cupiunt tenere reges,
cui dant oscula nobiles cinaedi,   5
intra viscera furis ibit usque
ad pubem capulumque coleorum.

Inscriptio *z*   1 ab *AHV et cett., edd.*: in *Wv et codd. plerique, Ital.,* ex *L,* ubi *Baehr. Pasc.*   est recisum *libri edd.*: ut recisum est (recisumst) *edd. veteres Muell. Buech.*   2 iam *HLV et codd. fere omnes, edd.*: etiam *ANR,* et iam *Voll. Clair.*   5 nobiles] nubiles *Heins.*

1. Cf. Virg. *aen.* 12 206ss:

Ut sceptrum hoc (dextra sceptrum nam forte gerebat)
nunquam fronde levi fundet virgulta, nec umbras,
cum semel in silvis imo de stirpe recisum.

4. hoc versu non dubitavit quin certos suae aetatis homines poeta designare voluerit . . . : aut enim quidam principes civitatis, quos impotentiae causa reges iam Cicero vocitabat, infamis nequitiae accusantur, velut Caesar Bythinica regina — BUECHELER.

Surely *reges* is, in its most basic meaning here, another mock-heroic allusion; and appropriately, kings long to hold the "scepter", an *ad hoc* metaphor for penis — O'CONNOR.

25

Priapus's 'staff', though made of dead wood, is yet a potent weapon

This is the staff which, lately cut
From tree, will ne'er again bear leaf:
Which yet is sought by girls in rut;
Which even kings love to possess;
And high-born 'gays' kiss and caress;
But which I shall, don't doubt it, push
Right up the arse of any thief
As far as my own balls and bush.

Here once more is the tripartite construction of introductory couplet, central elaboration, and conclusion. The first couplet introduces Priapus' 'staff' as being of dead wood. Yet, say the middle three lines, what it stands for is an object of desire for each of the three sexes. But the conclusion is that this wooden instrument, so coveted by man, will bring brutal retribution to a thief caught in the act. The first and last couplets (the last takes three lines in the translation) would together form a complete epigram, though without the richness of the intervening development which builds up suspense in expectation of the conclusion.

By its sudden transition from religious adoration of the god to the obscenity of the orchard watchman, the poem brings into sharp contrast the distinction between Priapus, the widely worshipped phallic god of sexual activity, and the dissolute garden 'priapus' looking for carnal gratification at the expense of a trespasser.

The phrase "staff which will never again bear leaf" parodies its epic use in Homer's *Iliad* 2 234ff, where Achilles swears by a gold-studded staff which shall never again grow green with leaves; both Virgil in his *Aeneid* (12 206ff.) and Valerius Flaccus (1st cent. AD) in the *Argonautica* (3 707ff.) had imitated it. So it was ripe for parody.

XXVI

Priapus rogat Romanos ne pereat prae nimia libidine

Porro — nam quis erit modus? — Quirites,
aut praecidite seminale membrum,
quod totis mihi noctibus fatigant
vicinae sine fine prurientes
vernis passeribus salaciores,   5
aut rumpar nec habebitis Priapum.
ipsi cernitis, exfututus ut sim
confectusque macerque pallidusque,
qui quondam ruber et valens solebam
fures caedere quamlibet valentes.   10
defecit latus et periculosam
cum tussi miser expuo salivam.

Inscriptio *z*   3 totis mihi] mihi totis *W*   6 rumpar]
rumpat *A*   7 exfututus (effututus) *Avanc. edd. vett. Buech.
(1892) Voll. Clair.*: ecfututus *Buech. (1863) Muell. Baehr. Pasc. Cazz.*,
ut fututus *A*, ut fututurus, futuiturus, futurus *et aliter, alii*   9
valens] rigens *Buech.*, vigens *Muell.*, calens *Baehr.*   10 cae-
dere] scindere *Muell.*   11 defecit *A Ald. edd.*: deficit *HLPWhv
et cett.*   defecit latus] latus deficit *v et cett., Ital.*   periculosam]
periculosum *L*

Cf. Macr. *sat.* 2 7 4: *porro Quirites libertatem perdimus*; Apul. *met.* 8 29
4: *Porro Quirites proclamari gestivi.*   *porro Quirites* formola
esclamativa di chi chiedeva aluto o protezione — MAGGI.

9. *valens* codd. omnes, quod repudiarunt editores et in diversa
abierunt (*calens, vigens, rigens*), propter illud *valentes*, quod sequitur
repetitum. Sed ut alia mittam, hoc est non scribam sed poetam
corrigere — PASCAL.

26

Priapus complains that women are wearing him out

> O citizens, Romans, I pray you please,
> There must be a limit — I'm brought to my knees;
> For passionate women from hereabout
> Importune me nightly and tire me out;
> And always they're lustful as sparrows in spring.
> So, either you'll have to cut off my thing,
> Or Priapus' life will soon ebb away.
> See how with fucking I'm pallid and grey!
> I used to be hale and lusty and strong,
> And able to deal with the thieves that did wrong;
> But now I am in a most dangerous state,
> And shudder and cough and expectorate.

Priapus is in a very sorry state indeed. Although often portrayed — especially by himself — as possessing inexhaustible potency, he is now worn out by the insatiable demands of the local women. Consequently he is no longer able to punish thieves in the manner about which he has so often boasted.

Some liberty has been taken with the arrangement of the lines. Literally the first lines read: "Help, Quirites (i.e. Romans), where will the limit be? Either cut off my seminal member, which the prurient women of the neighbourhood, more lustful than sparrows in spring, endlessly exhaust, or I shall be done for . . .".

The translation, by using the words "brought to my knees" to express the severe debility described in the original, echoes a Greek epigram by Apollonides (1st cent. BC), in which Priapus explains that he has been brought to his knees because the statue of a beautiful girl stands next to his (see p. 8).

XXVII

Auctor ad Priapum de donis Quintiae meretricis

Deliciae populi, magno notissima circo
   Quintia, vibratas docta movere nates,
cymbala cum crotalis, pruriginis arma, Priapo
   ponit et adducta tympana pulsa manu:
pro quibus, ut semper placeat spectantibus, orat,   5
   tentaque ad exemplum sit sua turba dei. ·

Inscriptio *P*   2 Quintia] Quinctia *Scal. Burm.*   3
Priapo] Priape *PQp*   4 adducta *Wv ed. Vincent. edd.*: abducta
codd. fere omnes., *Ital.*, obducta QV

1. Cf. Plaut. *most.* 15: *urbanus scurra deliciae pop(u)li.*

XXVIII

Priapus minatur furi cuidam

Tu, qui non bene cogitas et aegre
carpendo tibi temperas ab horto,
pedicabere fascino pedali.
quod si tam gravis et molesta poena
non profecerit, altiora tangam.

Inscriptio *P*   1 et] sed *pw*, non *R*

27

A dancing girl offers Priapus the tools of her trade

> Quintia, the circus star, she whom the crowd enjoys,
>   Who so seductively can shake her bum,
> Has dedicated to Priapus all her toys:
>   Her cymbals, rattles, bones and beaten drum,
> That she may always please the watching men and boys,
>   So that their cocks taut as the god's become.

This is the type of dedicatory epigram often known as *do ut des* —
"I am giving something that you may give something in return".
Quintia, the darling of the circus crowd, offers her gear to
Priapus, with the hope that, in return, he will ensure that she so
excites her fans that they become as tense as the god himself.

28

Priapus again threatens an orchard thief

> If, evil-minded wretch, you have to steal,
> Then my huge penis up your arse you'll feel;
> And if that doesn't make you leave your loot,
> Then at a higher place I'll aim to shoot.

Here, as in **13**, **22**, **35**, **44** and **74**, Priapus threatens not only
pedicatio, but also *irrumatio*, a practice considered more humiliat-
ing by the Romans.

Cur licet poetae obscene loqui

Obscenis, peream, Priape, si non
uti me pudet, improbisque verbis.
sed cum tu posito deus pudore
ostendis mihi coleos patentes,
cum cunno mihi mentula est vocanda.   5

2 improbisque verbis *W ed. Rom. 1473, edd.*: improbis (improbris)
AHLV et codd. fere omnes verbis *Wv ed. Rom.1473, edd.*: probris *Baehr.*
Pasc. Cazz.: probisque (probrisque) *AHLV et codd. fere omnes*
4 ostendis *HVPW Muell. Clair.*: ostendas *AL et cett., edd.*

1. *si non*. One of only five instances in the *Priapea* in which a
hendecasyllabic line ends with two monosyllables.

Quidam petens a Priapo iter ad fontem

"Falce minax et parte tui maiore, Priape,
    ad fontem, quaeso, dic mihi, qua sit iter."
Vade per has vites, quarum si carpseris uvam,
    cur aliter sumas, hospes, habebis aquam.

Inscriptio *g*   1 minax] minans *AWc*   3 uvam *HLV et.*
cett., edd. Mutin. et recentt.: unam *A*, uvas *vx, edd. vett. Buech.*
Muell.   4 cur (quor) *AHLV et cett. Ald. edd. recentt.*: quas *W et*
codd. plerique, edd. vett. aquam *AL et cett. Ald. edd. recentt.*: aquas *HV*
et cett., edd. vett. Muell.

4. Cf. Ov. *tr.* 2 50: *habebis cur aliter sumas.*

The god sets a bad example

Priapus, let me die if I am not appalled
To use indecent words that may 'obscene' be called.
But, if you, shameless god, your testicles display,
Then 'prick' along with 'cunt' I well may say.

This poem, like **14**, illustrates the contrast between the purity of language and behaviour with which one should normally approach a god, and the indecency which is acceptable and appropriate to Priapus. The translation, although condensing the five lines of the original into four, remains quite literal.

30

A wayfarer asks where he can get a drink of water

'You are terrific with your sickle and that enormous thing!
Priapus, I beseech you, tell me how to find the spring."
Go through these vineyards: if from them a single grape you
    take,
Why look elsewhere? There's water here, my friend, your
    thirst shall slake.

Another instance of a threat of *irrumatio*. There may also be an allusion here to Priapus as a signpost god. The sixteenth-century editor, Joseph Scaliger, wrote in a note on this epigram: "Priapus and Hermes . . . were placed at crossroads or where three or four roads met, who, stick in hand, pointed the way to the spring." (trans.) Here too, as often in priapic literature, Priapus is holding a sickle.

XXXI

Ad mulieres Priapus

Donec proterva nil mei manu carpes,
licebit ipsa sis pudicior Vesta.
sin, haec mei te ventris arma laxabunt,
exire ut ipsa de tuo queas culo.

Inscriptio *w*   1 mei *W et cett. Ital. Ald. Meyer edd. recentiores*: mihi *ed. Argent. Scal. Burm. Muell.*, mea *A et codd. plerique*, tua *Lg*   mei manu] manu mei *hw*   4 ipsa *libri, veteres edd. Muell. Pasc. Clair.*: ipse *Scal. Baehr. Buech. Voll. Cazz.*   culo *libri, edd.*: cunno *Sciopp. Muell.*   ordo de tua ut ipsa *w*, queas de tuo culo *V*

1. Cf. 58 3: *quaeque hic proterva carpserit manu poma.*

4. vitium agnovit Scioppius qui *culo* in *cunno* iussit mutari . . . viro autem si minari Priapum statuimus, lenius in quarto versu mutabimus *ipsa* in *ipse* — BUECHELER.   sed, frustra obpugnante Buechelero, res est de pedicanda femina — PASCAL.

116

31

Priapus warns a visitor

> If you don't steal from me with wanton hand,
> You may as chaste as goddess Vesta stand:
> My member else had carved a hole so vast
> That through your own backside you could have passed.

Because of the comparison with Vesta, a goddess renowned for her chastity, and the use of the feminine form *ipsa* in line 4, Priapus appears to be addressing a woman, and since he, according to **13** and **22**, punished them in the more natural way, Scioppius (early 17th cent.) substituted *cunno* (cunt) for *culo* (arse) in the fourth line, giving:

> That through your cunt you could yourself have passed.

For the same reason Buecheler (1863), while retaining *culo*, changed the *ipsa* ('you yourself' *F.*) into *ipse* ('you yourself' *M.*). But the manuscripts are unanimous for both *ipsa* and *culo*.

XXXII

Priapus narrat qualem vetulam nocte futuat

Uvis aridior puella passis,
buxo pallidior novaque cera,
collatas sibi quae suisque membris
formicas facit altiles videri,
cuius viscera non aperta Tuscus   5
per pellem poterit videre aruspex,
quae suco caret ut putrisque pumex,
nemo viderit hanc ut expuentem,
quam pro sanguine pulverem scobemque
in venis medici putant habere,   10
ad me nocte solet venire et affert
pallorem maciemque larualem.
ductor ferreus insularis aeque et
lanternae videor fricare cornu.

Inscriptio *P*   3 collatas *H ed.Parm. edd.*: collatasque (conl-)
LVWvw et codd. plerique, Ital., collataque *A et cett.* quae *A¹ HL ed.
Parm. edd., om. APVW et cett., Ital.*   7 *om. A* ut putrisque *hp edd.
Argent. & Ald. 1534 Burm. Clair.*: ut putris (putrix) usque *Wv*, ut
perusta *Melissus*, ut porosa (*vel* perosa) *Heins.*, usque putris
(putrix) *HV Voll.*, usque et usque *c edd. pr. & Mutin.*, usque quaque
Buech., utque putris *Ital. Ald. 1517*, atque putris *Meyer*, atque petra
Scal. Gabb., atque putra *Voss.*, est putusque *Muell.*, estque pura
Baehr., os putrisque *Her.*   13 insularis aeque *libri, edd. vett.
Buchheit* (*add.* et): insulariusque *Burm. edd. recentt.*, insulariusve
Voll., insulariaeque *O'Connor*

2. Cf. Ov. *pont.* 1 10 28: *membraeque sunt cera pallidiora nova.*

5–6. Cf. Cic. *cat.* 3 19: *cum haruspices ex tota Etruria convenissent.*

7. Cf. Plaut. *per.* 1 2 42: *nam tu aquam a pumice non postulas.*

32

Priapus is visited by a hag who lacks moisture in every part

More than the raisin is this girl dried out,
More pallid than fresh wax or boxwood she,
The thinness of whose legs is but disguised
By swarms of ants that crawl all over them.
The priest[1] her in'ards need not open up,
For he can spy them through her see-through skin.
Old pumice stone has as much juice as she.
No one has ever seen her spit; and as
For blood, the doctors swear her veins are stuffed
With powder or dry dust. Such is the maid,
A pallid, parched, and spectre-like old hag,
Who comes to me at night: in whom I rasp
As th'iron bar that holds the lantern high
Above the street, grates harshly in its ring.

[1] *Tuscus . . . aruspex* in the original. The *(h)aruspices* were diviners who made predictions and interpretations from an inspection of internal organs. They were thought to have originated in Tuscany.

This is one of several instances of exaggerated invective against old women in Latin literature. Within the *Priapea* we have already met one in **12**, and there is another to come: **57**. Here the poet uses twelve lines of hyperbole to emphasize the dessication of a woman who comes to him by night, building up to the vivid climax in which he likens his unlubricated efforts to an iron lampholder grating and scraping against the ring of the lantern.

This interpretation of the last two lines is but one of several, for they have given great difficulty to commentators: words are used with rare or obscure meanings, leading some to believe them to be corrupt and to make emendations. For more on this, see *Appendix C* (pp. 202–3).

XXXIII

Priapus conqueritur quod careat mulieribus

Naidas antiqui Dryadasque habuere priapi,
  et quo tenta dei vena subiret erat.
nunc adeo nihil est, adeo mea plena libido est,
  ut nymphas omnis interiisse putem.
turpe quidem factu, sed ne tentigine rumpar.   5
  falce mihi posita fiet amica manus.

Inscriptio *P*   2 quo] quoi *Muell.*   subiret] subaret
Muell.   3 mea *AHLV et codd. plerique, edd.*: mihi *Wv et*
cett.   est] *om. W et codd. plerique, edd. veteres*   5 factu *codd. fere*
omnes Avanc. edd. recentiores: fatu *codd. pauci deteriores Scal. Heins.*
Anton., dictu *L*   ne *AV edd.*: si *HLP codd. plerique*   6 mihi
Buech. edd. recentiores: manu *libri, edd. vett. Pasc.*, tamen *Burm.*

5–6. Cf. Mart. 11 73 3–4: *cum frustra iacui longa prurigine tentus,*
          succurrit pro te saepe sinistra mihi.

6. Cf. Mart. 9 41 2: *servit amica manus.*   poeta non potuit
quin scriberet: *falce mihi posita* — BUECHELER.
manu posita. sic codices omnes, frustra a Buechelero temptatum
propter nomen manus bis iteratum; qui cum scriberet *mihi posita,*
verborum lusum qui iteratione illa efficiebatur omnino sustulit.
Intellege: "cum nulla nympha mihi amica sit, mentula in manu
posita, fit amica manus" — PASCAL.

33

All nymphs have gone, so Priapus is driven to masturbate

> Woodland and river maids were plentiful at first,
>   And priapuses their tense members could relieve.
> But now nymphs are there none, and so with lust I'm
>   cursed:
>   That all such girls have vanished I must now believe.
> I'll lay my sickle down, for if I'm not to burst,
>   My hand as girl I'll use, some pleasure to achieve.

The maids described in the first line as *Naidas* and *Dryadas* were water and woodland nymphs, and there are several references by Ovid and others to Priapus as a nymph-chaser. This epigram recalls Martial, who writes of a lover who, tired of waiting for his girl, uses his hand (11 73); elsewhere he employs almost the same expression as in Priapea **33**: "your hand as girl you'll use" (9 41).

We write 'priapuses' with a small 'p', because, being in the plural, it can scarcely refer to the god Priapus, but to the numerous talking wooden figures which populated the countryside and are the subject of most of these poems.

XXXIV

Votum puellae offerentis tot tabulas quot sustinuerat mentulas

Cum sacrum fieret deo salaci,
conducta est pretio puella parvo
communis satis omnibus futura:
quae quot nocte viros peregit una,
tot verpas tibi dedicat salignas.   5

Inscriptio *z*

XXXV

Priapus ad furem

Pedicabere, fur, semel; sed idem
si prensus fueris bis, irrumabo.
quod si tertia furta molieris,
ut poenam patiare et hanc et illam,
pedicaberis irrumaberisque.   5

Inscriptio *g*   2 prensus (praensus) *Wv edd. Rom. veteresque Voll.*
Cazz. Clair.: deprensus (depraensus) *ed. Parm. Meyer Muell. Buech.*
Pasc., prehensus *Lp*, deprehensus *p¹a ed. Mutin.*, precisus *AHV et*
codd. plerique, praedatus *Baehr.*, praesens *Sciopp.*   fueris *Wv edd.*
vett. Voll. Cazz. Clair.: eris *AHLV et codd. plerique Meyer Muell. Buech.*
Pasc.   4 patiare] patiaris *L codd. plerique*   et] *codd.fere omnes*
praeter AGLNc

2. Cf. *CIL* 4 7038 = *CLE* 1934; *si prensus fueris [pueris] poenam*
patiare necesse est.

5. Cf. Catull. 16 14: *pedicabo ego vos et irrumabo.*

122

34

A whore gives Priapus a thank-offering

When worshipped was the lusty god of glee,
A girl was introduced of virtue light,
Who would by everybody rogered be.
As many men as had her in one night,
So many willow pricks she'd offer thee.

Women of easy virtue dedicate offerings to their god in **4**, **27** and **40**, as well as in this poem, of which Payne-Knight wrote:

On an antique gem in the collection of Mr Townley, is one of these fair victims, who appears just returned from a sacrifice of this kind, and devoutly returning her thanks by offering upon an altar some of these images; from the number of which, one may observe that she has not been neglected.

35

Priapus announces a scale of penalties for stealing

In your back way I'll go if once you thieve;
If twice, me in your mouth you will receive;
And if a third such theft you should attempt,
Both penalties you'll have to undergo;
In arse and mouth my potent force you'll know.

This is further evidence that the Romans regarded *irrumatio as* more disgusting than *pedicatio*, since the latter is the punishment for one theft, the former for two. And references to the 'foul mouths' of those who may have been 'irrumated' abound: "the strongest Latin invective is that against the *os impurum*, the unclean mouth" (Richlin).

XXXVI

Priapus de excellentiis deorum et sui

Notas habemus quisque corporis formas:
Phoebus comosus, Hercules lacertosus,
trahit figuram virginis tener Bacchus,
Minerva flava, lumine est Venus paeto,
frontem vides cornutos Arcadas Faunos,   5
habet decentes nuntius deum plantas,
tutela Lemni dispares movet gressus,
intonsa semper Aesculapio barba est,
nemo est feroci pectoriosior Marte;
quod si quis inter hos locus mihi restat,   10
deus Priapo mentulatior non est.

Inscriptio *P*   1 quisque corporis *Ald. edd.*: corporis quisque *codd. fere omnes*, corporis formas quisque *codd. pauci*   quisquis *Avanc.*   3 trahit *AHLV ed. Mutin. Ald. Meyer et edd. recentt.*: trahitque *Wv et pauci, edd. veteres*   *ordo* figuram virginis tener Bacchus *ALV ed. Mutin. Meyer et edd. recentt.*: virginis tener B. formam *Wv et pauci, Ital.*, B. virginis tener formam *Scal. et edd. vett.*   tener] celer *H et cett.*, sacer *L*   4 flava *de Rooy Voll. Clair.*: flavo *libri, edd. vett.*, ravo *Haupt. Muell. Buech.*, glauco *Anton.*   est *PQ om. codd. fere omnes, Ital.*   5 *ordo* frontem vides cornutos Arcadas Faunos *Buchheit*: fronte (frontem) crinitos (*vel sim.*) Arcadas vides Faunos *vulgo* frontem *B*   *Ald. 1534 Scal. Burm. Meyer Muell. Baehr. Cazz. Clair.*: fronte *AHLVW Ital. Buech. Pasc. Voll.*, at fronte *ed. Argent. Lind.*, fronde *Heins.*   cornutos *ed. Mutin. Buchheit*: cornuta *Lind.*, comatos *Avanc. Ald. 1534 Burm. Meyer Clair.*, bicornes *Buech.*, cruentos *Scal.*, caprinos *Muell. Baehr.*, ceruchos *Cazz.*   10 hos *h et codd. pauci Meyer Baehr. Muell. Pasc.*: haec *AHLV et codd. fere omnes, vet. edd. Buech. Voll. Cazz. Clair.*

5. *cornutos*, as in the Modena edition of 1475, is not only appropriate to the Fauns, but unlike the other conjectures, could easily have been misread as *crinitos*. But, like *crinitos*, it is not satisfactory in the choliambic metre as the second word in the line, wherefore Buchheit would change the order to that given above.

36

Priapus, like the other gods, has his distinguishing feature

We each are known by some outstanding mark:
Phoebus — his locks; and Hercules, his brawn;
Tender Bacchus has such a girlish face;
Minerva — yellow hair; and Venus squints;
Arcadian Fauns have horns upon their heads;
The gods' own envoy[1] has such splendid feet;
Lemnos' protector[2] limps upon his way;
Aesculapius' beard goes quite untrimmed;
And who is more big-chested than fierce Mars?
So if a place for me be found among this host,
'Tis 'cause no other god a larger prick can boast.

[1]Mercury.   [2]Vulcan.

This is the third of four poems in which Priapus compares himself
with other gods, emphasizing his penis as his main attribute. But
whereas the deities listed in **9** and **20** are almost identical, this
poem also brings in Venus, Vulcan, the Fauns and Aesculapius;
the other six are common to all three.

The manuscript readings for lines 4 and 5 are difficult. In line 4
Minerva is described as *flavo lumine* or 'yellow-eyed' — a novel
attribute, yet the favoured substitution of *ravo*, 'grey-eyed',
scarcely gives an 'outstanding' feature. De Rooy placed a comma
between *flava* (for *flavo*) and *lumine*, giving "Minerva is yellow
(haired), Venus is squint-eyed".

In line 5, the manuscript reading *crinitos* would give the Fauns
a hairy face, whereas they were usually thought of as bald. Their
distinguishing mark was their horns, and for this reason
Lindenbruch (1595) substituted *cornuta*, 'horned', Buecheler
(1863) *bicornes*, 'two-horned', and Mueller (1874) *caprinos*, 'goat-
like'.

XXXVII

Responsio cuiusdam requisiti, cur in tabella sit pictum praepucium

Cur pictum memori sit in tabella
membrum quaeritis, unde procreamur?
cum penis mihi forte laesus esset
chirurgique manum miser timerem,
dis me legitimis nimisque magnis,   5
ut Phoebo puta filioque Phoebi,
curandam dare mentulam verebar.
huic dixi: "fer opem, Priape, parti,
cuius tu pater, ipse pars videris.
qua salva sine sectione facta   10
ponetur tibi picta, quam levaris,
compar consimilisque concolorque".
promisit fore mentulamque movit
pro nutu deus et rogata fecit.

Inscriptio *g*   3 mihi forte *Av edd.*: forte mihi *HLVW*   4
chirurgique (cirugique) *A Ald. vet. edd. Baehr. Voll. Cazz. Clair.*:
chirurgamque *CPQpy Muell. Buech. Pasc.*   5 dis (diis) me
legitimis *CHLPW et cett., edd.*: me dis legitimis *a Cazz.*, me duci
medicis *AL et cett.*, dum divis medicis *Baehr.*   7 curandam *AL
et. cett. Baehr. Pasc.*: curatum HVWv et codd. plerique, *edd. vet.
Buech. Muell. Voll. Cazz. Clair.*   9 pars *cod. Griselli, Gronovius
edd.recent.*: par *libri, vet. edd.*, Lar *Muell.*   12 compar *Scal.
Burm. Meyer Muell. Voll. Clair.*: parve et *A*, parva et *HLV et codd.
plerique*, parva *Wv Ital.*, parque *Ald. Sciopp.*, par vel *Baehr. Pasc.*,
verpa *Cazz.*

7. Cf. Mart. 11 74 1: *curandum penem commisit Baccara Raetus.*

14. Cf. *Iliad* 1 528.

37

A man, whose member Priapus has cured, offers him a picture of it

Why, you ask, does this painted tablet show
That member male to which our life we owe?

My poor penis had suffered injury,
And I was scared of surgeon's remedy.
The proper gods are much too great to care —
Such as Phoebus or Phoebus' son and heir[1] —
To bring them my sick tool I was afraid.
"Priapus", cried I, "Please come to my aid.
Kindly bring health back to my private part
Without recourse to surgeon's knifely art.
A picture of it then I'll give to you,
Exactly like in size and shape and hue."

Priapus promised me to grant the boon:
His penis gave a nod: he cured me soon.

[1] Aesculapius, who was renowned for his skill in medicine; his father, Apollo, or Phoebus, was god of medicine.

Of this masterpiece Buchheit writes, "the epigram can offer nothing like it". He singles out for praise the way in which Priapus moves his penis to indicate assent, recalling the nod of Zeus in Homer's *Iliad*. Thetis had climbed Mt Olympus to persuade Zeus to give her son, Achilles, vengeance for the wrong Agamemnon had done him. Zeus agreed with his famous 'nod', that shook the mountain to its foundations.

This poem skilfully parodies prayers to the gods for healing as well as the dedicatory poem. Note the neat structure, whereby the story is framed between an introductory interrogatory couplet and the final couplet which brings the *dénouement*.

XXXVIII

Priapus ad quendam volentem poma decerpere

Simpliciter tibi me, quodcunque est, dicere oportet,
   natura est quoniam semper aperta mihi:
pedicare volo, tu vis decerpere poma:
   quod peto, si dederis, quod petis, accipies.

Inscriptio *g*   1 tibi me] me tibi *h*   4 petis] cupis *hp*

3. Cf. *CIL* 4 2210 (= *CLE* 1785): *pedicare volo.*

XXXIX

Priapus ad puellas

Forma Mercurius potest placere,
forma conspiciendus est Apollo,
formosus quoque pingitur Lyaeus,
formossissimus omnium est Cupido.
me pulchra fateor carere forma,   5
verum mentula luculenta nostra est:
hanc mavult sibi quam deos priores,
si qua est non fatui puella cunni.

Inscriptio *g*   4 omnium est cupido *ed.Argent. edd.*: est omnium cupido *Lv Ital.*, omnium Cupido est *Ald.*, omnium est apollo *APR*, est apollo omnium *HQVWhp et codd. plerique.*

128

38

Priapus does not beat about the bush

> I'll plainly tell you what I have to say
> (My nature to be open is and blunt).
> You'd like some apples; I want your back way:
> Give me what I seek — you take what you want.

This beautifully-balanced little epigram recalls the 'plain speaking' of **3**, and the 'fair exchange' of **5**. The translation, otherwise closely literal, avoids the obscenity of *pedicare volo*, a phrase incidentally found as an inscription at Pompeii.

39

Priapus says that "handsome is as handsome does"

> Fair Mercury's a pleasing sight;
> Apollo's beauty shineth bright:
> Lyaeus[1] pretty too they call;
> Cupid is fairest of them all.
> In looks I know I can't compete,
> My penis though is quite a treat!
> And any girl whose cunt's no fool,
> To all these gods prefers my tool.

[1] Bacchus.

Priapus again compares himself to other gods. The obscenity of the last couplet reflects the brutal cynicism with which he regards the female sex: he maintains that any girl will prefer him, ugly as he is, to the handsomest of gods, because he has a *mentula luculenta* — a beautiful prick — that is, unless she has a *fatuus cunnus* — a stupid cunt.

XL

Ad quandam puellam cingentem penem Priapi

Nota Suburanas inter Telethusa puellas,
  quae, puto, de quaestu libera facta suo est,
cingit inaurata penem tibi sancte corona:
  hunc pathicae summi numinis instar habent.

Inscriptio *g*   1 Suburanas (suburranas) *ed. Venet. edd.*: sub-
urbanas *libri ed. Mutin.*   Telethusa *Burm. Meyer et edd. recentiores*:
thelethusa *et similia HLVWv* et *plerique, edd. veteres,* Celisinas *A,*
Telesina (thelesina) *G Cazz.* 2 puto *codd. fere omnes, edd.*: puta *H
Muell. Baehr.*   est *om. HV*   4 hunc *LW edd.*: hoc (*scil.*
numen) *A Voll. Cazz.,* hanc. *HV et codd. fere omnes*

1. *Subura.* Cf. Mart. 6 66 1s: *Famae non nimium bonae puellam, / quales
in media sedent Subura;*   11 61 3s: *quem cum fenestra vidit a Suburana
/ obscena nudum Leda;*   11 78 11: *ergo Suburanae tironem trade
magistrae.*   *Telethusa.* Cf. Mart. 6 71 5: *urit et excruciat dominum
Telethusa priorem;* 8 50 23: *si Telethusa venit promissaque gaudia
portat.*   *Telesina.* Cf. Mart. 2 49 1s: *Uxorem nolo Telesinam
ducere: quare? / moecha est. Sed pueris dat Telesina. Volo.*

40

Telethusa thanks Priapus for her freedom

Telethusa, Suburan harlot most renowned,
  Whose profits from the trade have set her free,
Has solemnly your tool with gilded garlands crowned:
  In you the whores their supreme godhead see.

The Suburan quarter of Rome was much frequented by prosti-
tutes, and both Telethusa and Telesina (the alternative name
according to some manuscripts) are names used by Martial to
designate women of easy virtue. A Telethusa has been mentioned
already in these poems as the seductive dancing girl of **19**. Most
prostitutes were slaves or women who had bought their freedom.
Such women were prominent among the devotees of Priapus, as
were the keepers of brothels. An incident in the *History of
Apollonius, King of Tyre* (source for Shakespeare's *Pericles*), where
the maid Tharsia is kidnapped and sold into prostitution, is
evidence of this:

the girl was brought to the brothel-keeper, who took her
into the reception room. There he had a statue of Priapus,
covered with gold and jewels, and he told her: "you must
worship my potent god".

XLI

Priapus admonet poetas ingressuros hortum suum ut aliquid scribant iocosum

Quisquis venerit huc, poeta fiat
et versus mihi dedicet iocosos.
qui non fecerit, inter eruditos
ficossissimus ambulet poetas.

Inscriptio *z*. *Deest hoc carmen in A*

4. *ficosissimus.* plenus ulceribus, quae nascuntur cinaedis et pathicis a nimio attritu — SCIOPPIUS.

Priapus is saying, then, "Let anyone who won't condescend to writing Priapea go ahead and be a Vergil, a Hesiod or an Ennius, i.e. a poet proper; but he shall do so only after having been sodomized by me" — O'CONNOR.

XLII

Villicus dicans Priapo cerea poma

Laetus Aristagoras natis bene vilicus uvis
de cera facili dat tibi poma, deus.
at tu sacrati contentus imagine pomi
fac veros fructus ille, Priape, ferat.

Inscriptio *g*   1 Laetus] doctus *A*   2 facili *Scal. Burm. Muell.*: facta *libri edd. vet. Pasc. Voll. Cazz.*, ficta *Melissus*, pacti *Heins.*, flava *Buech. 1863*, parili *Baehr.*, Cera decocta *Clair.* poma] dona *Haupt.*

2. Cf Ov. *met.* 15 169: *utque novis facilis signatur cera figuris.*

Lego, *de cera facili* . . . sic clare legitur in codice Voss . . . *facta* enim hic metri caussa cum *cera*, non vero cum poma conjungendum . . . Scaligeri tamen emendationi aquiescendam opinor — BURMANNUS.

132

Priapus hopes that poets will bring him funny verses

Whoever cometh here, a poet let him be,
Dedicating verses full of fun to me.
If this he fail to do, with piles let him go,
And with the learned poets wander to and fro.

Priapus wants *versus iocosos* — funny poems, i.e. *priapea* like those
in this book. But should a serious-minded *eruditus poeta* visit him,
he would send him off badly afflicted with piles to consort with
his likes. This could well mean, as O'Connor suggests, that the
piles are to result from Priapus's usual method of punishing
thieves, or it could simply be a curse, not to be taken too literally,
like the old malediction, "a pox upon him".

42

Priapus is offered waxen apples, in hopes that he will bring a fine harvest

The farmer Aristagoras has fine grapes in his yard,
    And happily offers the god some fruit of wax.
Priapus, Lord, if thou these holy gifts dost well regard,
    At harvest reward him with real fruit in his sacks.

This is a simple dedication followed by a prayer, the *do ut des* type:
I am giving you something — waxen offerings — in the hope that
you will give me something — abundant fruit on my trees — in
return. Each line neatly corresponds to a complete step in the
thought-process of the epigram.

XLIII

Priapus ad quendam dicentem, quid velit eius hasta

Velle quid hanc dicas, quamvis sim ligneus, hastam,
  oscula dat medio si qua puella mihi?
augure non opus est: "in me" mihi credite, dixit
  "aptetur veris usibus hasta rudis".

Inscriptio *g*   1 hanc] hac *Heins.*   dicas] dicat *Sciopp.*
Dorvillius   sim] sic *Dorvill. Muell.*   hastam] astem *Dorvill.*
Muell., adstans (astans) *Baehr. Schwarz. 1941*   2 si qua] sicca
Scriverius   3 dixit] dicit *Baehr.*   4 aptetur *Mariotti*: utetur
libri edd., utatur *Baehr.*   veris] verae *Ouwens.*, Veneris *Heins.*
Pasc., nervi *Muell.*   usibus *libri edd. veteres Clair.*, viribus
Ouwens edd. recentiores, ictibus *Broukhusius*, lusibus *p Heins. Pasc.*
rudis] nudis *P*

Vide etiam appendicem, p. 203.

XLIV

Verba Priapi monentis fures

Nolite omnia, quae loquor, putare
per lusum mihi per iocumque dici.
deprensos ego ter quaterque fures
omnes, non dubitetis, irrumabo.

Inscriptio *w*   1 loquor *AV edd.*: dico *HLPW et codd. plerique,*
Ital.   3 deprensos *edd.*: deprehensos *codd. fere omnes*, depren-
dens *A*   ego] om. *H*, quoque *Whpv et codd. plerique*   ter] terque
GNQW et cett.   4 non *codd. fere omnes, edd. Mutin. recentioresque*:
ne *Gw Ald. Scal.*   ne dubitetis] ne dubitet quis *Barth.*

3. *ter quaterque.* Cf. *od.* 5 306 and Virg. *aen.* 1 94.

Priapus explains why a girl kisses him

Why is't, you ask, though wooden is my 'spear',
  A girl gives kisses to my 'middle' here?
It is no riddle, this. For so, in truth, said she:
  "It can be put to splendid use in me".

This is one of several poems in which Priapus maintains that,
although he is made of wood, he is still effective, whether in
punishing thieves or in satisfying women. It recalls the custom,
condemned by early Church fathers, whereby women seated
themselves on Priapus' member — or that of his Roman
predecessor, Mutinus Tutinus, "in whose shameful lap young
brides seat themselves so that the god may be seen to have been
the first to cull their virginity" (Lactantius).

For more on this epigram, see *Appendix D*, p. 203.

44

Priapus warns thieves to take him seriously

Please do not think that everything I say
Is spoke by me in game or jest or play.
All thieves caught three or four times in the act
Shall take me in their mouths — and that's a fact.

This epigram recalls **35** where the more serious punishment of
irrumatio is also the penalty for repeated theft. The poem, as so
often in these 'four-liners', falls into two equal parts, the first
couplet carrying a caution, the second a threat.

XLV

Priapus deridet quendam sibi capillos ustulantem

Cum quendam rigidus deus videret
ferventi caput ustulare ferro,
ut Maurae similis foret puellae,
"heus" inquit "tibi dicimus, cinaede,
uras te licet usque torqueasque,   5
num tandem prior es puella, quaeso,
quam sunt, mentula quos habet, capilli?"

Inscriptio *z*   1 quendam] quandam *Avanc.*   4 cinaede *v*
ed. Rom. edd.: cineda *Avanc.*, cinedo *AHLVW et codd. fere omnes, edd.*
pr. et Mutin.   5 torqueasque *Ald. edd.*: torquearis *libri*,
Ital.   6 num] non *L et codd. plerique*   es *AHL et ceteri, edd.*
Rom. et Mutin. Baehr. Voll. Cazz.: est *P et pauci codd. deteriores Ald. edd.*
veteres Muell. Pasc.   7 quam *HPVW et codd. fere omnes, edd.*: qua
AL, quoi *Baehr.*, quod *Shack. Bailey*   sunt *codd. fere omnes,*
edd. veteres Muell. Pasc.. Clair.: sint *A Baehr. Voll. Cazz.*

7. In manu scripto infimae notae libro legebatur. *Qua sunt* non
quam sunt. An prior, inquit, es puella, id est melior, ea parte, qua
pili sunt? Stultus qui ex illius partis depilatione videri vellet
puella — SCALIGER.

num te potiorem puella fieri credis, si ipsos capillos qui mentulam
comitantur ferro ustulare et calimistro componere laborares? —
GOETHE.

id est non tu citius eris puella facta quam renati erant pili
virilitatis testes (cf Martialis VIII 52) et non tu plus valebis
puella quam mentulae pili — BUECHELER.

tu non magis poteris fieri puella quam pili, quos mentula habet,
fieri capilli — VOLLMER.

cur potiorem habes puellam Mauram crinibus expertem quam
crinitam mentulam — PASCAL.

For *quam* read *quod* (*sunt*): "num melior es puella quod capilli sunt
qualis mentula habet?" — SHACKLETON BAILEY.

Priapus shouts to a catamite who is curling his hair

> When the god with rigid rod a youth did spy
>   using hot irons his hair to curl
>   so as to look like a Negro girl:
> "Hey, nancy boy," he shouts, "howe'er you try
>   to heat and twist your hair this way,
>   you'll be no more a girl, I'd say,
> Than are the hairs that all around your penis lie.

The last two lines are awkward in their syntax and obscure in their meaning. Several not very convincing attempts have been made to explain them, and it is possible that they are corrupt in their present form and inexplicable without departing from the ms. version. Literally they appear to say, "surely, pray, you are no better a girl than the hairs which your prick has?". Perhaps because it has none, because they have been plucked out (Scaliger 16th cent.)? Vollmer saw the explanation as lying in the distinction between *capilli*, normally hairs of the head, and *pili*, other hairs: "you can no more become a girl than the hairs which your prick has can become head hair". Cazzaniga (1959) developed this idea beyond what the words actually say: "you can no more become a girl than the hairs (*capilli*) of your head can curl like the hairs (*pili*) of your prick . . . in other words, you are a catamite and not a girl, and I, Priapus, will not fuck you but bugger you" (trans.).

The diversity of interpretations arises largely from the several senses that *prior* (line 6) can have. Thus, taking another tack, Sir Richard Burton's:

> Is then a damsel more of worth, I ask   (i.e. to look like a girl)
> Than are the hairy honours of thy yard?

XLVI

Priapus ad puellam quandam deformem

O non candidior puella Mauro:
sed morbosior omnibus cinaedis,
Pygmaeo brevior gruem timenti,
ursis asperior pilosiorque,
Medis laxior Indicisve bracis: 5
mallem scilicet ut libenter ires;
nam quamvis videar satis paratus,
erucarum opus est decem maniplis,
fossas inguinis ut teram dolemque
cunni vermiculos scaturrientes.   10

Inscriptio *g*   2 sed] O sed *Scal.*   morbosior] mollior *Wv et
pauci*   5 Indicisive *Buech. et edd. recentiores*: Indicisque *Ald. Scal.
Meyer, Clair.*, Indicis *libri*   bracis *Avanc. edd. recentiores*, braccis
Ald. Scal. Meyer, libratis *libri*, bactris *p*   6 mallem *Voss.*: manes
libri Ald. Cazz. Clair., mantes *Alciatus*, mandes *codd. pauci Scal.
Sciopp. Baehr.*, manda *Muell.*, maneas *primus Heins. (Burman-
ni)*   scilicet *Voss. Muell.*: hic licet *libri edd.*, hinc 1. *Voll.*, his 1.
Scal., huic 1. *Baehr.*   libenter] ut libet *Muell. Baehr.*, liberet *Voll.
Clair.*   ires] perire(s) *Buech.*, te inire *Baehr.*, erres *p*, perennis
Muell.

6. *mallem scilicet ut libenter ires* — VOSSIUS.
manes hic licet ut libenter ires — libri
mantes hic licet ut libenter ires — ALCIATUS.
mandes his licet ut libenter ires — SCALIGER, SCIOPPIUS
mandes hic licet, ut lubenter ires — GABBEMA.
manes, hac licet, ut libebit, ire — DORVILLIUS.
mallem scilicet ut libet perire — BUECHELER.
ad mane hic licet ut libet moreris — BUECHELER.
manda scilicet, ut libet, perennis — MUELLER.
mandes huic licet, ut libet, te inire — BAEHRENS
malles huc (licet et libet) redires — ELLIS
manes hinc, licet ut liberet, ires — VOLLMER.
manes hinc licuit libenter ires — HOLLAND.
manes hinc, foret ut libenter ires — SHACKLETON BAILEY.

46

Priapus seeks to repel an ugly woman

> As Negro or as Moor you are about as white,
> And, girl, you're more diseased than any catamite;
> You are yet shorter than the timid pygmy rare,
> And rougher-skinned than bears — and with more hair;
> Than Medes' or Indians' dress you're wider down below.
> I'd much prefer that willingly away you'd go:
> For, though I look as though I'm ready for the deed,
> Ten crates of strongest aphrodisiac I'd need
> 'Fore I could labour in that ditch betwixt your thighs,
> And in your cunt those swarming maggots squash — and
> > flies.

This is another of those epigrams in which the defects of the woman of loose morals who has lost her appeal, are listed and exaggerated into a vituperative diatribe. Line 6 is corrupt and defies meaningful reconstruction in good Latin reconcilable with the manuscript readings. The various conjectures (most of which are listed opposite) turn upon the first word in the mss., *manes*: the souls of the dead or Hades. In favour of keeping it is the supposition that a scribe would be least likely to miswrite the first word of a line. Keeping it, and adapting the rest of the line, Vollmer makes his Priapus tell the hag she may go to hell if she likes, while Shackleton Bailey's says, "you should have gone to the underworld to get yourself a good time". Others for *manes* substitute: *mantes*, "you may stay"; *mandes* "you may ask" — for Scaliger, the god tells her she may ask *his* (for *hic*), "these", meaning those watchmen who, in **52**, stand on guard with him; *mallem*, "I would prefer" — for you to go away (Vossius), to die (Buecheler); *malles*, "you may prefer" — to go away and come back later (while I buy a vast quantity of aphrodisiac rockets to make me equal to the task) (Ellis). Buecheler also recasts the whole line, to mean that she may stay till morning, "for night was the time when old crones were supposed to visit Priapus".

XLVII

Priapus male optat poetis non scribentibus sibi versus

Quicunque vestrum, qui venetis ad cenam,
libare nullos sustinet mihi versus,
illius uxor aut amica rivalem
lasciviendo languidum, precor, reddat,
et ipse longa nocte dormiat solus   5
libidinosis incitatus erucis.

Inscriptio *P*   5 et *codd. fere omnes*: ut *A*, at *Castiglioni*   longa
nocta *L edd.*: nocte longa *codd. fere omnes*   6 libidinosis]
libidinosus *Scal.*

5. Cf. Ov. *pont.* 15 315: *sola iaces viduo tam longa nocte cubili.*

6. *erucae libidinosae.* quae ad libidinem incitant, ut *salaces erucae*
Ovidio *Rem. Am.* 799 — BURMANNUS.

XLVIII

Priapus ad quosdam respicientes eius mentulam

Quod partem madidam mei videtis,
per quam significor Priapus esse,
non ros est, mihi crede, nec pruina,
sed quod sponte sua solet remitti,
cum mens est pathicae memor puellae.

Inscriptio *g*

140

Priapus curses those who fail to bring him verses

If any of you who come here to dine,
Of verse fail to offer me one single line,
May your rival go homeward completely worn out
Because your own girl friend gave him such a bout,
While you spend a long night alone and on fire
With herb-stimulated erotic desire.[1]

[1]Stimulated by the *eruca*, the colewort or rocket. Cp. Columella:
     Of rocket, near Priapus bearing fruit, we sow the seed,
     That it may rouse the sluggish married man to Venus' deed.

Here Priapus is addressing his master's dinner guests; or perhaps
these lines are an inscription for a domestic model of the god,
such as that which, laden with fruit, adorned the table at
Trimalchion's feast in Petronius' *Satyricon*.

48

Priapus explains why there is moisture on his member

That part of me that's wet, as you can see,
By which I'm known a Priapus to be:
It's neither dew nor frost, believe you me,
But what comes to a man spontaneously,
When on a lusty wench he thinks lasciviously.

XLIX

Priapus se excusat quaere carmina inhonesta in templo suo sunt posita

Tu, quicunque vides circa tectoria nostra
    non nimium casti carmina plena ioci,
versibus obscenis offendi desine: non est
    mentula subducti nostra supercilii.

Inscriptio *z*   1 circa] circum *L et pauci codd. deteriores*   tectoria *Scal.*: tentoria *codd. fere omnes, Ital.*, temptoria *AL et pauci*   2 ioci] loci *LPh*

2. *Circa tentoria.* Scribo *tectoria* . . . Nam parietibus templorum Priapi, quicunque intrabant, pro symbola quisque carbone Epigramma enarrabat — SCALIGER.

4. Cf. Gell. 19 7 16: *subductisupercilicarptores.*

Priapus asks that you should not take offence at these poems

> If you should look upon our walls, you there will find
>   Poems not chaste, but of the jocund kind.
> They are obscene. But do not take offence: our prick
>   To raise its eyebrows prudely is not quick.

The poet reminds us that his little book is to be imagined as a shrine, upon the walls of which are posted verses consecrated to Priapus, and he reverts to his earlier warning to the reader (**2**) about their nature. For this reason it has been argued that this is an introductory poem to a collection of *priapea* which has been merged with others to form the *corpus Priapeorum*. We agree with O'Connor (1984) that "*CP* 49, while an 'apology' by Priapus, seems far less like an introduction to a collection than a simple address to a passer-by".

L

Votum iuvenis ad Priapum ut sibi amica faveat

Quaedam, si placet hoc tibi, Priape,
ficosissima me puella ludit
et nec dat mihi, nec negat daturam,
causas invenit usque differendi,
quae si contigerit fruenda nobis,   5
totam cum paribus, Priape, nostris
cingemus tibi mentulam coronis.

Inscriptio *w*   2 ficosissima *HLVW et codd. plerique, edd. veteres Cazz. Clair.*: fucossissima *AC et codd. pauci minores Guyetus Muell. Buech. Baehr. Pasc. Voll.*, tricosissima *Haupt.*, sucosissima *Ellis*, iocosissima *h et pauci*   3 nec] non *vy et codd. minores, edd. veteres*   4 causas *libri Buech. Baehr. Voll. Pasc. Clair.*: causasque *Scal. Burm. Meyer Muell.*   6 cum paribus *Rgp Scal. Meyer Buech. Baehr. Voll. Clair.*: comparibus *ALW et codd. plerique edd. veteres Cazz.*, similibus *HLV et codd. plerique*, sutilibus *Heins. Muell. Pasc*, subtilibus *Cz*   nostris *codd. fere omnes, edd.*: nostrae *HPz et codd. pauci*, noster *C Heins. Muell.*, nodis *Buech., Baehr.*, nostri *Ellis*

2. turpissimis enim ulceribus abundantem puellam num tanti quispiam aestimaverit ut solemni voto eam a Priapo expeteret? — BUECHELER.   Ineptum est *ficosissima* neque satis *fucosissima* . . . Scribendum est *tricosissima* — HAUPTIUS.   Cum puella describatur ad venerem apta . . . non *ficosissima*, nec *fucosissima* debuit esse, sed *sucosissima*, h. e. corpore solido et suci pleno, ut ait Terentius Eun. II 3 27 — ELLIS.

6. puto igitur significatam a poeta esse totam cum scroto mentulam, atque hanc sententiam cum ipsa verborum in versu dispositis adiuvat tum *paribus* vocabulum quo nullum erat aptius ad demonstrandos testes . . . propono *totam cum paribus, Priape, nodis cingemus tibi mentulam coronis* — BUECHELER.

144

50

A young man asks Priapus's help with his girl friend

> A word with you, Priapus, please.
> This wretched girl's an awful tease:
> She won't say yes, she won't say no;
> Such putting-off I undergo!
> But if at last I get my way,
> Upon your prick and balls we'll lay
> Encircling garland tributes gay.

Unlike the *do ut des* epigrams already encountered, the speaker here promises to give only after the god has given. The gift of garlands is not anticipatory but conditional. Here also we see the god in his role as amatory helper, as in some of the early Greek *priapea*.

In line 2 the girl is described as *ficosissima* (badly affected with 'figs', i.e. piles) whence Burton's rendering: "a girl with piles full many piled"; but would the speaker be so keen to make love to such a girl? Hallett (1981) took it to mean that she had piles because she was addicted to anal intercourse, and that this was the gratification the frustrated lover was seeking. We think this unlikely. An alternative manuscript reading is *fucosissima*, from *fucosus*, an uncommon word which means 'coloured' or 'beautified', but in a derogatory sense unsuited to this context. We were tempted to adopt *tricosissima*, as conjectured by Haupt (1874), because *tricosus* means tricky, difficult, wily, which is apt in the context. But we concluded that *ficosissima* is intended to be merely a term of abuse arising from the frustration of a teased lover, and not to be taken literally.

Admiratio Priapi ob furum multitudinem venientium

Quid hoc negoti est quave suspicer causa
venire in hortum plurimos meum fures,
cum quisquis in nos incidit, luat poenas
et usque curvos excavetur ad lumbos?
non ficus hic est praeferenda vicinae   5
uvaeque, quales flava legit Arete,
non mala truncis adseranda Picenis
pirumve, tanto quod periculo captes,
magisque cera luteum nova prunum
sorbumve ventres lubricos moraturum.   10
praesigne rami nec mei ferunt morum
nucemve longam, quam vocant Abellanam;
amygdalumve flore purpurae fulgens.
non brassicarum ferre glorior caules
betasve quantas hortus educat nullus,   15
crescensve semper in suum caput porrum.
nec seminosas ad cucurbitas quemquam
ad ocimumve cucumeresque humi fusos

Inscriptio *w*   1 suspicer *HVWv edd.*; suspicor *AL*   3
incidit *AV Scal. edd.*: incidat *HLW et codd. fere omnes, Ital.*   *ordo*
incidit (incidat *Q*) in nos *V*   4 excavetur *AHLV et codd. fere
omnes, edd.*: excaveris *Wv Ital.*   6 uvaeque] uvaeve *Voll.
Cazz*   legit] legis *HV et codd. pauci Pasc.*   Arete *codd. optimi
ed. Mutin. Scal.*: Crete *W et codd. pauci, Ital.*   7 mala] poma
L   adseranda (ass-) *Ald. edd.*: asservanda (aser-) *ALWvy Ital.*
inserenda *Sciop.*, observanda *QVx et cett.*, observata *H*   8
periculo *L edd.*: pericula *AHV et codd. plerique*   9 magisque]
magisve *u Anton. Voll.*   11 praesigne] praepingue *Ph Avanc.*,
praepinguem *Wv et cett., Ital.*   12 quam vocant *Ald. Meyer
Buech. Clair.*: quae vocatur *AHLV codd. et edd. fere omnes* Avellanum
(Ab-) *Ald. Meyer Clair.*: Alva *A Voll. Cazz.*, alana *x ed.Rom. Pasc.*,
alna *PHgpy*, Albana *Scal. Heins. Muell. Baehr.*   13 purpurae *ed.
Ven. Burm. edd. recentiores*: purpureo *libri edd. veteres*   14
bras(s)icarum *libri Ital. Scal. Anton. Meyer edd. recentiores*: brassicae
Q Ald. Sciopp.   ferre glorior *Burm. edd. recent.*: fero (fere *H*, ferro
y) glorosior *libri*, fero gulosior *ed. Vinc. edd. veteres*, fero glosior *ed.
Rom.*   15 betasve *V ed. Mutin. edd.*: betaeve *codd. fere omnes,
Ital.*   18 cucumeresque *AH* (-osque *V*) *ed. Mutin. Baehr. Voll.
Cazz. Clair.*: cucumeresve *LWv edd. vett. Muell. Pasc.*

Priapus wonders why his garden attracts so many thieves

Why do so many thieves enter my yard,
When, if they're caught, I thrust it up them hard?
The figs here are no better than next door;
The grapes, compared with Arete's[1] are poor.
Nor are my pears and apples the best breed —
And yet they take them without any heed
For risk they run. Nor is my yellow plum,
Nor are my sorbs (no good for a loose bum!)
So special. Mulberries fine they will not gain
From branches here, nor filberts Abellane.[2]
My almond trees don't shine with purple flowers;
I do not glory in my cauliflowers,
Nor claim my garden grows fine beet or leek.
I should be much surprised should any seek
To buy my seedy gourds, cucumbers too,
Lettuces, basil, onions tart: yet who
The rocket herb and garlic nightly steals?
And who the scented mint and rue that heals?
Although I have all these within my fields,
My neighbours' plots are better in their yields.
So why pick on me, you nasty thieves,
When you well know what anyone receives
Who is found out? It seems the treatment rude[3]
Is what attracts them: so I must conclude.

[1]wife of Alcinous, renowned for his gardens. [2]from Abella, a place
in Campania which abounded in nuts — now called Avella.
[3]described in line 2.

(LI)

venire credo, sessilesve lactucas
acresque cepas aliumque furatum,   20
nec ut salaces nocte tollat erucas
mentamque olentem cum salubribus rutis.
quae cuncta quamvis nostro habemus in saepto,
non pauciora proximi ferunt horti;
quibus relictis in mihi laboratum   25
locum venitis, improbissimi fures:
nimirum apertam convolatis ad poenam,
hoc vos et ipsum, quod minamur, invitat.

19 credo *AP ed. Mutin. Ald. edd.*: crede *codd. fere omnes, Ital.* 20
v.20 post v.22 libri et edd. veteres Muell. furatum] fibratum *Scal.
Sciopp. Burm. Meyer Muell.* 22 mentamque] mentamve *codd.
minores Muell. Pasc.* 23 quamvis nostro habemus *Ald. edd.
recent.*: quamvis nostro habeamus *libri,* nostro ut habeamus *ed.
Mutin.,* nostro ut ambiamus *Scal.,* nostro quamquam habemus
Muell. 27 poenam] praedam *Wv Ital.* 28 hoc vos et
Santenius: et vos id *Avanc. Baehr.,* et vos hoc *GHVW codd. fere omnes,
edd. veteres,* et hoc vos *L,* vos hoc et *Muell.,* cum vos hoc *A*

10. Cf. Mart. 13 26 1: *sorba . . . molles nimium tendentia ventres.*

14. verbum enim *ferre* propter sensum abesse nequit, eaque sede
illud reponi, jubet lex metri: et *glorior* insistit omnibus fere
vetustis codicibus mss. in quibus *gloriosior,* unde enata est
absurda lectio *gulosior* — BURMANNUS.

18. Cf. Mart. 3 47 8: *sessilesque lactucas.*

In this, the second longest of the *Priapea*, a priapus confesses that he has failed to achieve the two main purposes for which his master has set him up. For he represents Priapus, who was both god generator, or god of fertility, and god protector — the warder-off of evil. He was expected, therefore, to bring his owner good harvests on the one hand and to deter thieves on the other. But not only are the yields poor, thieves even flock to the garden. Why is this, he asks, since they receive the punishment that robbers get from priapuses when they are caught? He is forced to conclude that this punishment is an attraction rather than a deterrent.

Praise of the garden was a common motif in classical poetry, the oft-imitated original being the famous description of King Alcinous' splendid garden in *The Odyssey* (7 112ff.). In **16** there is a reference to this garden by way of the king's daughter, Nausicaa; here the allusion is through his queen, Arete. Priapus inverts the motif, dispraising the garden he looks after, instead of praising it.

His reference to the neighbour's garden (why don't the thieves go there?) recalls the third *priapeum* of Virgil's *Catalepton* 20f:

> The neighbour's rich,
> His priapus neglectful of his charge:
> This very path will take you to his place.

and the *Greek Anthology* (*AP* 6 302) where Leonidas tells the mice, who raid his larder, that he is but a poor man, but if they go elsewhere they will fare better.

LII

Increpat Priapus inmodestiam furum com admonitione magnae mentulae

Heus tu, non bene qui manum rapacem
mandato mihi contines ab horto:
iam primum stator hic libidinosus
alternis et eundo et exeundo
porta te faciet patentiorem.   5
accedent duo, qui latus tuentur,
pulcre pensilibus peculiati;
qui cum te male foderint iacentem,
ad partes veniet salax asellus
nilo deterius mutuniatus.   10
quare, si sapiet malus, cavebit,
cum tantum sciat esse mentularum.

Inscriptio *z*   2 contines] continens *HSy*   4 alternis
LVWv ed. Mutin. Avanc. edd.: alterni *AHy et codd. plerique*   et
eundo *LP ed.Mutin. Avanc. Ald. edd. recent.*: sed eundo *AHVW et codd.
fere omnes, edd. vet.*, ineundo *Scal. Muell.*   exeundo *AHPR ed.
Mutin. Avanc. edd. recent.*: redeundo *LVhgp et codd. plerique*   5
porta *LVW et cett., edd.*: portam *AHRy*, in portam *Baehr.* te faciet
HVW edd.: te facient *ACRz*, patefiet *L*   8 qui cum *L edd.*:
quicumque *AHV et codd. plerique*, quique *Wv et codd. pauci*, et qui te
Avanc.   9 partes *Salmasius (fortasse vere — Buech.)*: partis *Voll.*,
partum *AHVhgy et codd. plerique*, partem *Meyer Buech. Muell.*,
pratum *Housman Cazz.*, portam *LW et codd. plerique Pasc.*, pastum
Baehr.   10 nilo *Anton. Muell. Buech.*: nihilo *Scal.*, nihil *CHP et
codd. plerique Ald.*, nil est *v Ital.*, et nil *A Baehr. Voll.*, nil iam
L   11 si *libri Ital. Baehr. Pasc. Voll. Cazz. Clair.*: qui *Ald. 1534
Scal. Muell. Buech.*   sapiet *codd. fere omnes ed. Mutin. edd.*: sapis *Wv
et cett. Ital.*   malus *Baehr. Pasc. Voll. Cazz.*: malum *codd. fere
omnes, edd. veteres Muell. Buech. Clair.*, manum *L*   12 *post*
tantum hic *add. Scal. Burm.*   sciat *z ed. Mutin. Baehr.*: sciet *AHlv
Ald. edd.*, scias *W et codd. pauci Ital.*

3. *stator.* quem supra [xiii] *Circitorem* vocavit. *Statores* proprie sunt
carcerum, aut aedium custodes — SCALIGER.

6. *Accedunt duo, qui latus tuentur* nihil aliud quam Latrones eo
designantur: qui prius *Laterones*, quod latus tegerent. Hi et
Statores quoque ipsi sunt — SCALIGER.

Commentarius ad appendicem (vid. p. 204) continuatar.

52

Priapus warns of violent and repeated punishment for orchard thieves

Hey, you, who the temptation can hardly withstand
Upon our rich orchard to lay a deft hand:
This watchman'll go in and out your back door
With gusto until you can't stand any more;
Two more will come afterwards, from either side,
With beautiful penises richly supplied,
And they'll set to work, and dig deeper in;
An ass with huge member on you'll then begin.
It surely makes sense not to play any tricks,
When it means being punished by so many pricks!

Nowhere is the anal-punishment motif developed so energetically as here, but for the modern reader, confused by a corrupt text and numerous conjectures, the interpretation is none too clear. The chief difficulty arises from the meaning of the unusual word *stator* in line 3. It is he who is to inflict the first punishment upon the thief, but there is disagreement as to whether he is the statue of Priapus or a watchman of some kind (like the *circitor* of **17**). In **17** Priapus deplores the employment of a watchman, whereas here he would boast of the fellow's prowess; such contrasting attitudes are, however, to be met with in the *Priapea*. As for the next inflictors of penile punishment, the "two who guard the side", Buecheler (1863) suggested that they were *priapisci* or small images of the god standing on either side of his main statue, but in none of the representations of Priapus extant is such a grouping to be seen. Suess (1910) suggested that they were the god's testicles, but the *tantum . . . mentularum* ('so many pricks') in the last line argues against this. Scaliger (1573) maintained that they were none other than *latrones* or *laterones* — soldiers who guarded the *latus*, the flank or side. This may be, but *latrones* more commonly means robbers, and this would not be apt in this context.

LIII

Quidam deprecans Priapum

Contentus modico Bacchus solet esse racemo,
  cum capiant alti vix cita musta lacus,
magnaque fecundis cum messibus area desit,
  in Cereris crines una corona datur.
tu quoque, dive minor, maiorum exempla secutus,   5
  quamvis pauca damus, consule poma boni.

Inscriptio *g*   2 capiant] capiunt *Muell.*, capiat *H*   alti
Avanc. edd.: altos *libri praeter L Ital.*, altus *L*   cita *AHLV et codd.*
fere omnes Meyer edd.recentiores: sua *pauci codd. deteriores*, nova *x*
Buech.   3 desit] defit *CWv Pasc. Cazz.*

2. Cf. Ov. *trist.* 3 10 72: *nec cumulant altos fervida musta lacus.*

CP 53 employs motifs of ritual prayer: one is the alliteration of
"c", the other is the motif of the small but dutiful offering —
O'CONNOR.

LIV

Forma pingendi Priapum

ED si scribas temonemque insuper addas,
  qui medium vult te scindere, pictus erit.

Inscriptio *g*   1 ED (Ed, Edi) *libri edd. veteres*: CD *Buech.* et
edd. recentiores   scribas] iungas *Avanc.*   2 vult te *AHLV*
codd. optimi, edd. Mutin., Parm. et recentiores: vult T *Ald.*, vult D *Scal.*
Gabb. Hadr. Burm. te vult *PQhgp Muell.*, T vult *ed. Argent.*, D vult
ed. Venet.1480 Sciopp. Meyer, d vult *edd. Rom., Venet. et Vincent.*

vix curam ullam meretur Epigramma putidum et insulsum —
BURMANNUS.

a graffito like those scrawled on the walls at Pompeii —
O'CONNOR.

53

Priapus is told that even top gods get only a token harvest offering

Content with single bunch of grapes is Bacchus divine,
E'en though huge vats can scarcely hold the new wine;
And when yields are so great we cannot store such vast
      stocks
Of grain, just one coronal's spared for Ceres' fair locks.
Thou, Priapus, do as these greater gods do, and though
We give few fruits, thy favours still upon us bestow.

This is one of those *priapea* in which the god is deprecated or
mocked, either by himself or by others. A tight-fisted farmer is
anxious lest his priapus should expect too much after a record
harvest. Unlike the other poems in which Priapus is set alongside
other gods, this is not his usual triumphant boast of superiority;
instead he is firmly put in his place as a lesser god.

54

Priapus conveys his warning through a drawing

Join 'E' and 'D' together, with a bar between the two,
And you will have depicted what will slice your middle
      through.

All modern editors have followed Buecheler (1863) in beginning
this couplet with the letters 'CD', although all the mss. have
'ED', and earlier commentators had little difficulty with the
interpretation. Some manuscripts have *D* instead of *te* in the
second line. Scioppius (1606) appears to argue that this second
'D' represents the part to be penetrated, both because of the
shape of the letter, and because D could be pronounced as *te* or
'thee'. Most manuscripts, however, and all the best ones, read *te*,
not *D*, in the second line.

For more on this epigram, *see Appendix F, p. 204.*

LV

Lamentatio Priapi, cur fures sibi subripuere falcem

Credere quis possit? falcem quoque — turpe fateri —
  de digitis fures subripuere meis.
nec movet amissi tam me iactura pudorque,
  quam praebent iustos altera tela metus:
quae si perdidero, patria mutabor, et olim   5
  ille tuus civis, Lampsace, Gallus ero.

Inscriptio *g*   1 possit *APh Muell. et edd. recentiores*: posset
HLWv et codd. fere omnes, edd. veteres   2 subripuere (surr-)
AHPRVpgh edd. Mutin. et recentiores: subripuisse *LWv et plerique, edd.
veteres*   3 amissi] amissa *L*   tam me *ALW et codd. plerique,
edd.*: me tam *CHPV et cett.*   4 iustos] veros *g*   metus]
motus *Meyer*   5 mutabor *A Heins. Baehr. Voll. Cazz. Clair.*:
mul(c)tabor *codd. omnes praeter A, edd. vet. Muell. Pasc.*

6. *Gallus*. Luditur huius vocabuli ambiguitate, quod et *Galliae
incolum* et *castratum* significat — ANTON.

LVI

Priapus, ad quendam furem ipsum deridentem

Derides quoque, fur, et impudicum
ostendis digitum mihi minanti?
heu heu me miserum, quod ista lignum est,
quae me terribilem facit videri.
mandabo domino tamen salaci,   5
ut pro me velit irrumare fures.

Inscriptio *g*   3 heu heu *AL Avanc. Burm. Meyer Voll. Cazz.
Clair.*: eheu *Ital. Scal. Buech. Muell. Baehr. Pasc*, heheu *Ald.*, heu *codd.
fere omnes*   quod *z Meyer Muell. Baehr. Pasc.*: quid *libri Ital. Scal.
Voll. Cazz. Clair*   ista (*sc.* mentula)] hasta *Salmasius Burm.*

55

Priapus bemoans a loss — but it could be worse .

Just would you believe it — I am in a pickle —
From my very hand they've just stolen the sickle!
But that other tool I'd be even more sorry
And upset to lose — it's a terrible worry.
In fact, I should no longer myself think to call
A Lampsacus man — for I'd be a Gaul.

This epigram treats, in a novel way, the central theme of the
Priapea, which is the god's member. What if he were to lose it, as
he has just lost his sickle? He would no longer be a citizen of
Lampsacus, his home town: he would have become a Gaul, for
the word *Gallus* also means a eunuch. The literary Priapus often
carries a sickle, yet representations of him in the pictorial and
plastic arts rarely — if ever — show him so armed.

56

Priapus has his bluff called

Shamelessly, thief, you laugh and mock.
And with your fingers a snook you cock,
For though it looks fierce, you know it's no good:
Alas, woe is me, it's only of wood.
I'll call my master — he's full of lust;
His prick into any thief's mouth he'll thrust.

In contrast to a Priapus lusty and ready for action, we
occasionally see a despondent, dejected, or even impotent god.
He is, after all, made of wood, and once his bluff has been called,
what use is he? In this instance his master will do his job for him,
though as O'Connor suggests, the attack would probably be
verbal: "Be off, or I'll irrumate you".

LVII

Preces anus ad Priapum

Cornix et caries vetusque bustum,
turba putida facta saeculorum,
quae forsan potuisset esse nutrix
Tithoni Priamique Nestorisque,
illis ni pueris anus fuisset,   5
ne desit sibi, me rogat, fututor.
quid si nunc roget, ut puella fiat?
Si nummos tamen haec habet, puella est.

Inscriptio *w*   2 turba] *add. et Scal. Burm. Meyer*   putida
CHLNPVp edd. recentiores praeter Clair.: putrida *W et codd.plerique, edd.*
veteres Clair., pudica *A et cett.*   4 Priamique] Priamive
Muell.   Nestorisque] Nestorisve *Muell.*   6 desit *CGw Ald.*
Scal. Burm. Meyer Muell. Pasc.: desim *AHLVW Ital. Buech. Baehr.*
Voll. Cazz. Clair.   7 roget] rogat *plerique codd. minores*   *8*
nummos L Ald. Scal. edd. recentiores: minimos *Hv Ital.,* numos *A,* si
minus *V,* nutrios *ed. Parm., om. ed. Mutin.*   haec] hoc *V et pauci.*

8. Barthius, Adv.1.21, c.10 recte coniecit, hunc versum esse
spurium, partim quia Priapo non conveniunt nummi, partim
quia totius epigrammatis acumen inest in versu superiore, in quo
absurda aliqua re per interrogationem proposita, poeta, preces
absurda esse, indicat — SCALIGER.   Hunc versum a
sciolo per interpolationem adiectum esse priori carmini adsentior
plerisque; ut tamen eum omni tempore fuisse in nostra sylloge
existimem — MUELLER.   non tamen novicium esse
puto octavum versum sed antiquis temporibus subscriptum
praecedenti carmini . . . nimirum anus 'cum futui vult, numerare
solet' (Martialis XI 62 et VII 75) — BUECHELER.

Another motif of CP 57 is that of *captatio* . . . offering oneself to
wealthy old women in return for monetary reward: cf Mart. 10.29
. . . Juv. 1.35 describes such *captatio* as one of the evils of the age
— O'CONNOR.

156

57

Priapus answers an old hag

> An old, decayed and corpse-like rotten crow,
> Who might have been a wet-nurse long ago
> To such as Tithon, Priam and Nestor,[1]
> If not an aged woman e'en before
> Their time, asks me that she may never lack
> A man — what if she asks her girlhood back?
> I'll tell her not to fret, nor be dismayed:
> If she can pay, they'll treat her as a maid.

[1]All three were often cited as examples of extreme old age.

This is yet another of those poems in which an old woman is vilified for remaining sexually passionate after becoming physically repellent (cp. Martial 10 67, Horace *epod.* 8, 12, etc.). We do not accept the view that the last line, "If she has money, she's a girl!" is spurious. It has impeccable manuscript credentials, and is pertinent. It is the answer to Priapus's question: "What am I to do if she expects me to make her a girl again?" — i.e. courted in the manner appropriate to a young woman? Then he answers his own question — or possibly a third party intervenes — with the reply: if she can pay there will be no difficulty in finding those prepared to treat her as a girl. Several other *Priapea* are of the question-and-answer type.

. . . du point de vue métrique, le vers en question [8] est tout à fait régulier; il faudrait donc supposer chez l'interpolateur une connaissance parfaite d'un mètre plutôt rare dans la poésie latine . . . l'explication la plus simple de cette régularité métrique semble être celle qui veut que le vers soit l'oeuvre du poète même — KNECHT.

LVIII

Priapus minatur pueris et maledicit puellis

Quicumque nostram fur fefellerit sedem,
effeminato verminet procul culo;
quaeque haec proterva carpserit manu poma
puella, nullum reperiat fututorem.

Inscriptio *P*   1 sedem *Muell. Ellis*: fidem *HLV et codd fere
omnes, edd. veteres, Clair.*, curam *A edd.recentiores praeter Clair.*   2
verminet *Voss. Muell. Pasc. Clair.*: marceat *Ald. 1534 Scal.*, imminet
AHLV, eminet *SWv et codd. deteriores*, emineat *Ald.* 1517, inane
pruriat *Baehr.*   procul] precor *Her. Pasc.*, puer *Ellis*   culo
SWv et codd. pauci Voss. Muell. Pasc.: dubio *codd. fere omnes Voll. Cazz.*,
lumbo *Baehr. ordo v. infra*   3 haec *HLV et cett. edd. veteres
Muell. Pasc.*: hic *A Buech. Baehr. Voll. Cazz. Clair.*   4 reperiat
AHPR edd. recentiores: reperiet *LVp*, inveniat *Wv et pauci minores*,
inveniet *h*, invenerit *Salmasius*

2. *effeminato imminet procul dubio* — codices A, H et L, editio
Parmensis 1482; *e. culo eminet procul* codices Wv et ceteri, editiones
Veneta 1475 et Vincentia 1476; *e. emineat procul culo* — ALDUS
1517; *e. marceat procul culo* — ALDUS 1534; *e. verminet procul culo* —
VOSSIUS; *e. inane pruriat lumbo* — BAEHRENS.

Die Verlesung des *culo* in *dubio* lässt sich noch rekonstruieren.
Zunächst ist wohl bei *procul culo* durch Haplographie *culo*
ausgefallen. Ein späterer Abschreiber hat den verkürzten Vers
bemerkt und ein *dubium* an den Rand geschrieben. Die Rand-
bemerkung ist sodann in den Text geraten. Dass *imminet* oder
eminet falsch sind, liegt auf der Hand. Es muss ein Konjunctiv
folgen, der aber bei diesen Verben (*-eat*) den Vers zerstörte. Is.
Voss hat somit glänzend ein *verminet* konjiziert, denn es ist nicht
nur paläographisch am einleuchtendsten, sondern es gibt auch
den hier erwarteten Sinn: "jucken, reizen" — BUCHHEIT.

58

Priapus wishes sexual deprivation upon the thieves

> The thief who robs this garden, may he feel
> For girlish boy unsatisfied desire;
> And any wench who comes in here to steal,
> May she no lover find t'assuage her fire.

This curse of sexual hunger pronounced upon thieves is a variation of that uttered by the god in **23**. There he wishes upon the male thief lack of both boy and girl; here he would deprive the man thief of boy and the woman thief of a man. It also recalls **47** where a similar curse is placed upon those who fail to bring verses to Priapus.

The text is badly corrupted, leaving room for conjecture as to what was originally written, but the general sense is quite clear.

LIX

Priapus ad fures

Praedictum tibi ne negare possis:
si fur veneris, inpudicus exis.

Inscriptio *g*   2 exis *Voss. Heins. edd. recentiores praeter Cazz.*: ibis
Ald. edd. veteres, eris *libri, ito Cazz.*

LX

Auctor facete in Priapum

Si quot habes versus, tot haberes poma, Priape,
    esses antiquo ditior Alcinoo.

Inscriptio *P*

"To give apples to Alcinous", i.e. "give food stamps to Rockefel-
ler", must have been proverbial; see Ov. *Pont.* 4.2.10: *quis poma det
Alcinoo?* — O'CONNOR.

59

Priapus gives a brief warning to the thief

> I warn you: come here as a thief barefaced,
> And surely you'll leave as man disgraced.

Here the watchman-god's warning to the thieves is short and sharp in contrast to the many more elaborate versions of the same motif. And the epigram speaks *obscure* rather than *simpliciter*, and lacks the blunt obscenity which Priapus all too often utters.

60

If apples were as plentiful as poems . . .

> Priapus, if as many apples as verses in store thou wert to
>   hold,
>   Thou wouldst then richer be than Alcinous of old!

One of several epigrams with the apple/fruit motif (*poma* generally means fruit, though sometimes more specifically, apples), joined on this occasion with the verses motif. Both fruit (cp. **16**, **21**) and verses (cp. **2**, **41**, **42**, **49**, **61**) were commonly consecrated to Priapus and placed respectively on the altar or the walls of his shrine.

LXI

Malus arbor excusat se colono et reddit causam sterilitatis suae

Quid frustra quereris, colone, mecum,
quod quondam bene fructuosa malus
autumnis sterilis duobus adstem?
non me praegravat, ut putas, senectus,
nec sum grandine verberata dura,   5
nec gemmas modo germine exeuntes
seri frigoris ustulavit aura,
nec venti pluviaeve siccitasve,
quod de se quererer, malum dederunt;
non sturnus mihi graculusve raptor   10
aut cornix anus aut aequosus anser
aut corvus nocuit siticulosus,
sed quod carmina pessimi poetae
ramis sustineo laboriosis.

Inscriptio *P*   6 modo *AHV et codd. fere omnes, edd. Mutin. &*
Parm., Avanc. edd.: mihi *v ed. Argent.*, meo *LSW et pauci, Ital.*   7
ustulavit] instillavit *LV*, afflavit *hm*   9 quererer *HR Ald. edd.*:
quereris *Wv edd. Mutin. & Parm., Avanc.*, queritis (quaer-) *S Ital.*,
querere *LV*, querer *A*   11 anser] auster *p*   12 corvus] corvos
Voll. Cazz.   13 quod] quia *p*

Mirum autem hoc Epigramma, quod Priapeium non est, huc
alieno loco immissum esset — SCALIGER.

162

61

Lament of a tree weighed down by poems

> It's no use, farmer, complaining about me,
> That once was known for a fruitful-yielding tree,
> Because two autumns I've nothing borne for thee.
> I know thou think'st it's because I've grown too old,
> Or hail has wounded me, or that late-spring cold
> Has nipped my buds; yet 'tis neither wind nor rain,
> Nor drought, has given me reason to complain.
> No daw nor starling dealt me a fatal blow;
> No water-living goose, nor yet an ancient crow,
> Nor thirsty raven, is cause that I seem dead,
> But that my branches are weighted down like lead
> By poet's verses, unworthy to be read.

This poem is not a *priapeum*. A moribund apple tree protests to the farmer, who has complained that it bears no fruit. It explains that it has been well-nigh killed by all the bad poems that have been hung upon it. There is no reference to Priapus, but the presumption is that the tree stands by a statue of the god, and has been used by poets as a convenient place to hang their tributes to him. It is very rare for Priapus to be represented in a picture or engraving without an accompanying tree.

This poem recalls the Pompeian inscription (*CIL* 4 1904):

> O wall! I wonder thou stayest in place:
> Such a weight of bad writing thou bear'st on thy face;

and also the poem *Nux*, attributed to Ovid, in which a nut-tree explains why it no longer bears fruit.

LXII

Priapus ad canes

Securi dormite, canes: custodiet hortum
cum sibi dilecta Sirius Erigone.

Inscriptio *g*   1 custodiet *AHLV et codd. optimi, Anton edd.*
recentiores: custodiat *Svz et pauci codd. minores, edd. veteres*   2 sibi]
tibi *A*, sua *L*

hoc epigramma calente sole diebus canicularibus factum putes:
vos canes non opus est vigilare; custodiet hortum Canis caelestis,
fidelis Virginis suae comes — BUECHELER.

hoc epigramma legi in Priapeis, iam miratus est Scal; mutilum
esse ego indicavi: puto Priapum loqui querentem se nimio aestu
vexari et officio se abdicare — VOLLMER.

recte iudicat Vollmer priorem partem carminis excidisse —
CAZZANIGA.

Die Hunde des Hausherrn können getrost schlafen, hier bewacht
ja ein anderer Hund den Garten, Sirius, d.h. die *mentula Priapi . . .*
Darauf spielt Erigone als 'sprechender Name' an. Es ist zweifellos
auf *mentulam erigere* hingewiesen — BUCHHEIT.

Erigone, das Muster einer virgo, steht in c.62 für ihr Gegenbild,
die mentula Priapi. Ein Paar, das sittlich beste Eigenschaften
verkörpert, steht fur den gar nicht sittenstrengen Priap und seine
mentula — EHLERS.

62

Priapus reassures the watchdogs

Sleep peacefully, dogs. For this orchard there's no need to
    fear
  When Sirius guards it with his own Erigone dear.

Erigone was led by a faithful dog, Sirius, to her father's grave,
where in sorrow, she hanged herself. Dog and Virgin were then
elevated to the heavens as stars. But what do they have to do with
Priapus?

It has been suggested — by Ehlers in 1971 — that Sirius stands
for Priapus and Erigone for his erect (cp. *erigere* = to arouse)
member, and if this is so, there could be no greater irony than
allowing a pair who personified the highest moral sense, to stand
for the lewd god and his obscene weapon. He also argues that, as
all *priapea* by definition must be spoken to or by Priapus, or be
about him, he must be the speaker. This being so, the probability
of Priapus = Sirius, and Erigone = his member, is greatly
enhanced.

But Buchheit (1962), relying on the identification of 'Erigone's
beast', i.e. Sirius, in a Greek epigram (*AP* 14 430) with the
membrum virile, took Sirius here also to stand for Priapus' member;
as for Erigone, she is there because the sound of her name
suggests 'erection': so the meaning would be "Priapus' member
with its well-loved tautness will guard the orchard".

Some such interpretation is essential if this couplet is to deserve
its place as a *priapeum*.

LXIII

Priapus conqueritur, quod impotens sit propter loci asperitatem

Parum est, quod hic cum fixerunt mihi sedem,
agente terra per caniculam rimas
siticulosam sustinemus aestatem?
parum, quod hiemis perfluunt sinus imbres,
et in capillos grandines cadunt nostros   5
rigetque duro barba vincta crystallo?
parum, quod acta sub laboribus luce
parem diebus pervigil traho noctem?
hoc adde, quod me vilem et e rudi fuste
manus sine arte rusticae dolaverunt.   10
interque cunctos ultimum deos numen
concurbitarum ligneus vocor custos.

Inscriptio *P*   1 quod hic cum fixerunt mihi sedum *Muell.*:
mihi, quod hic fixi sedem *libri Ital. Clair.*, amici, fixerim quod hic s.
Scal., mihi fixi quod hic miser s. *Sciop. Meyer*, miser, quod hic fixi s.
Ald. Burm., mihi quod hic cotidie fixi s. *Buech. 1863*, quod hic semel
pedem fixi *Buech. 1892*, mihi, quod hic, fixi ut semel s. *Pasc.*, quod,
hic ut fiximus semel s. *Lachmann, Baehr.*   sedem] fidem *HV ed.*
Mutin., pedem *Avanc.*   2 terra *AV ed. Mutin. Ald. edd.*: terram
HL et codd. plerique, Ital., terrae *Avanc.*   3 sustinemus (subst-)
AHLV ed. Parm. Ald. 1517 Muell. edd. recentiores: sustinens *C et codd.*
plerique deteriores, Ital., sustinens diu *Ald. 1534 Scal. Burm.*
Meyer   4 parum, quod *AH et cett. Ald. edd.*: parumque *LPV et*
codd. plerique, Ital., parumne *Scal.*   hiemis *Buech. Voll. Clair.*: imi
AV et codd. fere omnes Ald. Scal. Burm. Cazz., imos *g Meyer Muell.*
Baehr. Pasc., imis (immis) *Bgh*, nimis *ed. Mutin.*, uni *HVuxz Avanc.*,
udi *Heins.*, meos *p*   perfluunt *ANQR et cett. Avanc. Ald. edd.*
recentiores: superfluunt *CHLP et codd. plerique, Ital.*, perpluunt *Heins.*
ordo sinus superfluunt *v Ital.*   6 duro *p Heins. Meyer Buech.*
Muell.: dura *codd. fere omnes, edd. veteres Baehr. Pasc. Voll. Cazz. Clair.*,
uda *ed. Mutin.*   vincta *AHLV et codd. optimi Meyer edd. recentiores*:
iuncta *P plerique codd. deteriores*   7 parum, quod *AH et codd.*
plerique Ald. edd.: parumque *LV et codd. plerique, Ital.* luce] lucem *h et*
pauci, Ital.   9 adde, quod] addeque *pauci codd. deteriores*
Ital.   et e rudi fuste *Muell.*: terribilem fuste *AVh Ald. Clair.*,
terribiles fuste *CH et codd. plerique, Ital.*, terribiles fustem *L*, de rudi
levem f. *Buech.*, f. de rudi vilem *Scal.*, terribilem deum f. *Gabb.*,
terribilem deum e f. *Anton*, f. tetricum viles *Ellis*, de rude deum f.
Clausen-Schrader, perleven rudi f. *Büsche*   11 ultimum *HLV et*
codd. plerique ed. Mutin. Avanc. Meyer edd. recentiores: ultimos *Ital.*,
ultimo *A*, vilius *Ald. Scal. Burm.*

Priapus complains of his lot

Oh! is it not enough that to this spot I'm bound,
While with parched summer heat the Dog Star[1] cracks the
      ground?
And that my clothes in winter are soaked through with
      rains,
My beard ice-stiffened, my hair filled full of frozen grains?
Or that, day done, I have to work as guard all night?
Or that my weapon rude, a coarse and ugly sight,
Was chopped by rustic hand? That I am thought the last
Of all the gods — as wooden pumpkin-keeper cast?
To all this add the tension in that member mine
That pushes upward hard — of lechery a sign.
For which there comes a girl — I almost told her name —
Together with a man, and who — she has no shame —
Because all the positions in Philaenis'[2] guide
Portrayed, she hasn't tried, goes off unsatisfied.

[1] the rising of Canicula, the Dog Star, was associated with
excessive heat by the ancients.   [2] Philaenis: reputed author
of a Greek manual of modes of sexual intercourse.

This is a difficult epigram, because much of it has come down to
us so corrupted that many of its lines are either metrically or
gramatically unsound, or they lack sense. From the numerous
suggested emendations we have chosen those which seem to us to
be not only the most satisfactory as to metre, syntax and
meaning, but also reasonably close to the manuscript readings.

The most serious deficiency is that of the last line, since upon it
depends the point of the epigram, and therefore its interpretation.
What is clear is that a woman — whose name Priapus, in a
humorous aside, says he almost let out — goes off still hot with
unsatisfied desire. But why? According to some, it is because
Priapus himself, worn out by the hardships he so self-pityingly
describes, is unable to act out with her the various erotic
combinations portrayed in Philaenis' sex manual. The title over
the Latin text on p. 166, taken from a manuscript to which some

accedit istis impudentiae signum,
libidinoso tenta pyramis nervo.
ad hanc puella — paene nomen adieci—   15
solet venire cum suo fututore,
quae tot figuris, quot Philaenis enarrat,
non inventis, pruriosa discedit.

13 impudentiae] impudenti *V ed. Mutin.*   14 libidinoso *codd.*
optimi ed. Mutin. edd.: libidinosa *pauci codd. deteriores, Ital.*   15
hanc] haec *L Muell.*, hoc *Baehr.*   17 quae] quae ut *Scal.*, quo
Heins. Burm. Meyer Muell.   tot] parcit *H* figuris
CHLNVpvy Ital. Ald. 1517 Buech. Pasc. Clair.: figuras *APU Ald. 1534
Scal. Meyer Muell. Baehr. Voll. Cazz.*   quot *LWv et codd. plerique,*
edd. praeter Voll. Cazz.: quas *ACHPV et codd. plerique ed. Parm. Voll.*
Cazz., quod *ed. Argent.*   18 non inventis] novis inventis
Steading, non ad inventis *p ed. Rom.*, non invenit *u Ald. 1534*, n.
intultis *Avanc.*, n. admovente *Voss. Heins. Meyer*, n. adnuente *Muell.*,
n. adnuentis *Buech.*, n. admovetis *cod. Ubaldini Meyeri*, n. impetratis
Buech. 1863, novisque fictis *Her. Pasc. dubitanter*, conata veneris
Ellis, commenta bis *Baehr.*, noviens peractis *Iacobsius*, contenta non
est *Buech. 1892*   pruriosa *codd. fere omnes Meyer Muell. Pasc. Voll.*
Clair.: pruriginosa *Cz ed. Argent. Ald. 1534 Scal. Baehr.*, pruinosa *Vh,*
nos perosa *Buech. 1863*, pruriensque *Buech. 1892*   discedit *HV et*
codd. plerique Muell. Baehr. Buech. Pasc., Clair.: discedat *ALU et cett.*
Voll. Cazz.

1. ob rationes metricas certissime cum apareat et post *hic* et post
fixi esse lacunas, quas ita explevimus, ut aperte sensus flagitat —
MUELLER.

17. *Philaenis.* agitur de Philenidis libello graece conscripto —
PASCAL.

18. *Pruriosa* vocabulum non recte fictum . . . *pruriginosa* caesuram
versus reddit minus elegantem — BUECHELER.   das
auffälige *pruriosus* scheint ein vulgärform zu sein, da sich dasselbe
bei Caelius Aurelianus *chron. pass.* II 33 in der bemerkung *squilla,*
quam vulgo bulbum pruriosum vocant findet — STEUDING.   id
quod est *pruriosa*, omnibus firmatum codicibus, reliqui, cum
videatur poeta formam vulgi consuetudine breviatam in suum
usum convertisse . . . Nec tamen displicet quod Buechelerus
proposuit *nos perosa* — MUELLER.

copyist has added it, reads "Priapus complains that the harshness of the place [where he has been set up] has made him impotent".

Yet he refers to his erect member, and lists among his grievances the unbearable tension to which it is subject, a state difficult to reconcile with impotence. Also, he tells us that the woman comes to him *cum suo fututore* — "with her paramour". It is a fair assumption that this nymphomaniac has brought him with her in the hope that, in the god's presence, he will be enabled to excel himself and enact with her all the positions Philaenis describes. Women, virtuous and wanton alike, did see this as an important function of Priapus; they prayed to him accordingly, as witness these lines from the Tiburtine hymn:

> Priapus lord, of potency the friend,
> To whom chaste maidens fervent prayers oft send,
> That girdles, too long fastened, be untied.
> To thee prays too the newly-wedded bride
> Her husband's manliness may never fail.
> Priapus, holy father, lord, all hail!

LXIV

De puero avido pedicari

Quidam mollior anseris medulla
furatum venit huc amore poenae;
furetur licet usque: non videbo.

Inscriptio *P*   2 huc *HVW et codd. fere omnes, edd.*: hic *L.* hunc *A*

1. Cf. Catull. 25 1s: *Cinaede Thalle, mollior cuniculi capillo / vel anseris medullula* . . .

LXV

Quaedam litans Priapo

Hic tibi qui rostro crescentia lilia mersit,
    caeditur e tepida victima porcus hara.
ne tamen exanimum facias pecus omne, Priape,
    horti sit, facias, ianua clausa tui.

Inscriptio *g*   1 Hic] haec (hec) *HPV et codd. plerique*   mersit *libri edd. veteres Cazz.*: rosit *vel* rasit *vel* carpsit *Heins.*, rosit *Muell.*, morsit *Buech. Baehr. Voll. Clair. Pasc.*   3 ne] nec *libri*   exanimum *Scal. et edd. recentiores praeter Clair.*: extraneum *libri edd. veteres*, extinctum *Ald.*, externum *Clair.*   4 facias] posthac *Buech., Muell.*

1. It is incredibilis oscitantia to believe for forty years and more [as Buecheler did] that in the age of Ovid . . . they said *morsit* for *momordit* . . . The verb *mordere* is not even suitable . . . the devastation . . . is much better described by *mersit*— HOUSMAN.

2. Cf. Ov. *am.* 3 13 16: *ex humili victima porcus hara.*

170

64

Priapus turns a blind eye

> A soft smooth queer comes here to steal,
> Because he badly wants to feel
> The punishment he knows applies
> To garden thieves — I'll close my eyes!

In **51** Priapus wondered why thieves came to his garden when the produce was better elsewhere, and concluded that it was because they must actually want the punishment he gave them — here he refuses to co-operate.

65

A pig is sacrificed to Priapus

> Because its snout had rooted 'mongst the flowers,[1]
> From the warm sty a victim has been slain
> For thee. Please then, Priapus, in return
> Watch well the gate, lest we the whole herd lose!

[1]lilies in the original.

Another do ut des epigram (see p. 39). A pig that has strayed into the flower garden is sacrificed to Priapus in the hope that he will take better care of those that remain.

LXVI

Priapus ad quandam pudicam

Tu quae ne videas notam virilem
hinc averteris, ut decet pudicam:
nimirum, nisi quod times videre
intra viscera habere concupiscis.

Inscriptio *g*   3 nimirum] nil mirum *Muell. Pasc.*, a mirum
Buech. Voll. Clair.   videre *LQWpvz et codd. plerique, edd. praeter
Baehr.*: videri *AHPV et plerique Baehr.*

LXVII

Furibus poenam indicit Priapus per quoddam enygma

Penelopes primam Didonis prima sequatur
et primam Cadmi syllaba prima Remi,
quodque fit ex illis, tu mi deprensus in horto,
fur dabis: hac poena culpa luenda tua est.

Inscriptio *z*   1 Didonis *ALW edd.*: dido fac *HVghpy*, Didus fac
Heins. Muell.   2 Cadmi *p Scriverius edd. recentiores praeter Pasc.
Maggi*: Caci *Pasc. Maggi*, cani *libri edd. veteres*, canis *g*   3
quodque] quodcumque *L et cett. Heins. Meyer   ordo* quodcumque
ex illis fit *L et pauci Heins. Meyer*   tu mi (mihi) *AVWp ed. Mutin.
Baehr. Voll. Clair.*: mihi tu *Pv edd. veteres Buech. Muell. om.* mi (mihi)
codd. deteriores Meyer

2. *Cani* codd., quod servassem (a verbo *canus*), nisi nomen
proprium requiretur; *Caci* scripsi; acceperunt omnes Scriverii
coniecturam *Cadmi*, cuius tamen prior syllaba *Cad-* est, non *Ca* —
PASCAL.   Sed vide etiam GANDIGLIO.

172

66

Priapus addresses a bashful maid

You, who chastely turn away your eyes
From my manhood, as well befits a maid,
No doubt you long to have between your thighs
That thing on which to look you are afraid.

One is reminded of two earlier epigrams in which the modesty of
supposedly chaste women is cynically questioned — **8** and **10**, in
both of which the conclusion is also introduced by *nimirum* —
'without doubt', 'surely'. In line 3 the original has *intra viscera*,
'within your in'ards (or entrails)' rather than 'between your
thighs'. The sources agree on a female, and *intra viscera* probably
means no more than 'inside you'.

67

Priapus gives his warning in a word puzzle

From *Pe*nelope and from *Di*do the first two letters take,
    From *Ca*dmus, and *Re*mus too, and robber, what you make
From this will be the punishment you'll have deserved to
        feel,
    If in my garden here you should be found to steal.

This, as in **7**, is an elaborate way of achieving the word *pedicare*,
and at the same time threatening garden and orchard thieves
with the anal rape it implies.

LXVIII

Priapus ad rusticum quendam

Rusticus indocte si quid dixisse videbor,
    da veniam: libros non lego, poma lego.
sed rudis hic dominum totiens audire legentem
    cogor Homereas edidicique notas.
ille vocat, quod nos psolen, 'psoloenta keraunon'   5
    et quod nos culum, 'culeon' ille vocat.
merdaleon certe si res non munda vocatur,
    et pediconum mentula merdalea est.
quid? nisi Taenario placuisset Troica cunno
    mentula, quod caneret, non habuisset opus.   10
mentula Tantalidae bene si non nota fuisset,
    nil, senior Chryses, quod quereretur, erat.
haec eadem socium tenera spoliavit amica,
    quaeque erat Aeacidae, maluit esse suam.

Inscriptio *g*   4 cogor *Heins. edd. recentiores*: choris (coris) *AHP et codd. plerique*, constitui *CLWhzw Ital.*, constituique *p Ald. 1517*, constiti *Ald. 1534 Burm.*, institi *Scal.*, carpsi *V*   Homereas *Ald. 1534 Bentleius Meyer Voll. Clair.*: Homeriacas *Scal. Heins. Burm. Muell. Baehr. Pasc. Cazz.*, mericas *ed. Venet.*, meras *Avanc. Ald. 1517*, meracas (-achas, -archas) *AHLPQVWbg et cett.*   5 *ordo* ille vocat, quod nos psolon *Gronovius, Heins. Meyer*: psoleon ille vocat *edd. veteres*   vocat] vocamus *O Ald. Scal. Burm.* psolen *edd. recentt. fere omnes*: psoleon *libri*   psoloenta (ps-, s-) keraunon (ceraunon) *libri edd.veteres*: ψολόεντα κεραυνόν *edd. recentiores*   6 et *AL Buech. Baehr. Cazz. Clair.*: id *HPSVWvy et plerique, edd. veteres Muell. Pasc*   culeon *AHVW Ital. Ald. 1534*: coleon *Lpv ed. Mutin. Ald. 1517 Scal.*, kouleon *z*, κουλεὸν *edd. recentiores*   7 merdaleon (-ion) *libri Ital.*: Μερδαλέον *Muell. Baehr. Pasc. Voll. Clair.*, smerdaleon *p*, Σμερδαλέον *Heins. Anton Meyer Pasc.*, smerdaleos *Ald. Scal.*, σμερδάλεος *Burm.*, smerdalium *Avanc.*   si *Weber Muell. Pasc. Voll. Clair.*: nisi *codd. fere omnes Meyer Baehr.*, visa *V*, in se *Hy*, quasi *Buech.*   8 merdalea *LP ed. Rom. edd. recentiores*: smerdalea *Ald. Scal. Sciop. Burm. Meyer*, smerdaleum *p*, mendalea *AH ed. Mutin.*, mendalea *V*, est *om. ed. Rom.*   9 quid? *ed. Argent Sciop. Meyer Muell. Pasc.*: quid *S ed. Vincent. 1479 Scal. Burm.*, quod *libri edd. Rom. & Mutin. Ald. Voll.*, qui *Heins. Baehr.*, om. *z*   nisi] si *AGx*   11 nota] nata *Heusing Anton Scal. Muell.*

A lewd Priapus lampoons Homer

No scholard I, but country-bred, so pardon me
If I be crude: trees is my trade, not books, you see.
Yet I know this bloke Homer, for my master proud
Spends all his time out here a-reading him out loud.
I hear, for instance, what we rustics call a prick
Is 'psoloenta kheraunos' in that chap's Greek,[1]
And arse is 'khouleos', and 'merdaleos' — 'foul'
It means — what you'd expect of prick that's been in bowel.
If Trojan cock had not brought Grecian cunt such fun,[2]
This Homer fellow's book could not have been begun.
If bloody Agamemnon's prick had been less stout,
He'd given old Chryses damn nowt to moan about;[3]
Nor would he then have snatched the maiden from his
        friend,
And she'd have been Achilles' own until the end:[4]
Who now upon his Pelethronian lyre[5] must sing
A woeful tune, himself stretched tenser than its string.[6]
And so began the hero's noble rage,[7] the same
That's the chief matter of the Iliad's tale of fame.

---

[1]modern editors print these words in the Greek alphabet, but this seems inappropriate to a vulgar Priapus who disclaims literacy (line 2).   [2]i.e., if Helen had not been enamoured of Paris. Cp. Horace *sat.* 1 3 107f: *nam fuit ante Helenam cunnus taeterrima / belli causa.*   [3]Chryses was father of Chryseis, a Trojan girl carried off by the Greeks and given to Agamemnon, who was forced to release her because Chryses, a priest of Apollo, threatened the Greeks with a plague.   [4]Agamemnon then took her cousin Briseis, instead; but she had already been claimed by Achilles, who "sulked in his tent" at her loss.   [5]called Pelethronian because it was given to Achilles by the gifted centaur Chiron Pelethronius.   [6]the absence of Briseis, Priapus implies, made his member as taut as his lute string.   [7]the *Iliad* opens with the 'anger of Achilles', the very first word being Μῆνιν or wrath.

The Priapus of this poem is a coarse and foul-mouthed yokel who reduces the noble epics of the *Iliad* and *Odyssey* to tales of action motivated by lust alone.

ille Pelethroniam cecinit miserabile carmen   15
  ad citharam; cithara tensior ipse sua.
nobilis hinc nata nempe incipit Ilias ira,
  principium sacri carminis illa fuit.
altera materia est error fallentis Ulixei;
  si verum quaeras, hunc quoque movit amor.   20
hic legitur radix, de qua flos aureus exit,
  quem cum 'moly' vocat, mentula 'moly' fuit.
hic legimus Circen Atlantiademque Calypson
  grandia Dulichii vasa petisse viri.
huius et Alcinoi mirata est filia membrum   25
  frondenti ramo vix potuisse tegi.
ad vetulam tamen ille suam properabat, et omnis
  mens erat in cunno, Penelopea, tuo:
quae sic casta manes, ut iam convivia visas
  utque fututorum sit tua plena domus.   30

16 tensior] tentior *pauci codd. deteriores Ald.*   17 nobilis] nobis
A hinc] hic *HV et pauci ed. Venet. 1480*   nata *AL et codd. plerique
edd.*: nota *CHPV et plerique, Ital.*, mota *z Muell.*   18 princi-
pium] principiumque *Voll. Clair.*   illa] ile *Baehr.*, ille *L*   19
Ulixei *A et codd. plerique Baehr. Voll. Cazz. Clair.*: Ulyxi (Ulixi) *HLV
et plerique, Ital. Meyer Muell. Buech. Pasc.*, Ulyssei *Ald. ed. Argent. Scal.
Sciop.*, Ulyssi *C et pauci ed. Rom.*, ulixis *puw*   20 hunc *HV et
codd. plerique, edd. veteres Buech. Muell. Baehr. Clair.*: hanc *ALQ et
codd. plerique Ald. Burm. Voll. Cazz.*, hinc *V.*   21 hic *AHLV et
codd. optimi ed. Mutin. Ald. Heins. Baehr. Buech. Voll. Clair.*: hinc *codd.
deteriores plerique, Ital. Scal. Meyer Muell.*, haec (hec)
GNQpy   aureus] lacteus *Gyraldus*   22 quem] quam *Buech.
Baehr. Voll. Cazz.*, quae *v ed. Venet.*, qualem *ed. Mutin.* moly (*bis*) *OSc
et cett.*, *edd. veteres*: molly *ed. Vincent. 1479*, μῶλυ *Meyer edd. recentiores*,
moli *CHghx et cett.*, timoli (th-, tm- *et aliter*) *AHV et cett.*   23 hic
AHL et codd. fere omnes ed. Mutin. Ald. Heins. Baehr. Buech. Voll. Clair.:
hinc *CVW et pauci codd. deteriores, Ital. Scal. Meyer Muell.*   Calyp-
son] Calypso (-i-) *Cux edd. veteres*   24 vasa *AHLV et codd. optimi
ed. Mutin. Meyer edd. recentiores*: iussa (iusa) *Wpv et codd. deteriores,
Ital. Ald. Scal. Burm.*, iusta *ed. Florent.*, ista *ed. Nuremb.*   petisse]
tulisse *Cv et pauci codd. deteriores, edd. veteres*   27 tamen] vir
BVhg   28 mens] spes *BWgv Ital.- praeter edd. Mutin. &
Parm.*   29 sic] sit *HQR*   visas] quaeras *cod. Ubaldini Meyeri
Meyer*   30 utque] atque *Scal. Burm. Meyer*

The other book's about Ulysses and his treks,
And, truth to tell, here too the cause of all was sex.
You read about a beauteous blossom, 'molyhock',[8]
But when they speak of 'moly' they're really meaning
      'cock'.
What else we read? How Circe — and Calypso too —
Dulichian[9] Ulysses for his fine tool they woo.
Alcinous' daughter[10] wondered at it next: its size
Was such that leafy bough could not its bulk disguise.
Yet, all the same, to his old woman back he goes:
His mind is in your cunt, Penelope,[11] who chose
To remain true, yet you'd invited many a guest,
So with a crowd of would-be fuckers you were blessed;
The idea being, I dare say, to find out who
Was best at doing it of all that eager crew.
"To firmer member", says she, "no one could lay claim
Than Ulysses, in strength and skill a master at the game.
I need to know, now he has gone and left no trace,
Which one of you is man enough to take his place."

[8]'moly' is a herb described in the *Odyssey* (10 302) as having a black root and a milky flower (whence some have suggested *lacteus*, 'milky' instead of *aureus*, 'golden', 'beautiful', in the text); it has not been certainly identified. Priapus may have regarded it as symbolic of the penis.   [9]from Dulichium, an island in the Ionian Sea associated with Ulysses.   [10]Nausicaa, who came upon the naked, shipwrecked Ulysses; he covered himself with a tree branch.   [11]Ulysses' home was besieged, during his absence, by a crowd of suitors to his wife Penelope, the mythological model of the faithful wife; Priapus was not alone in his scepticism (see Roscher-Schmidt 1909–10).

22. The magic *moly* plant (μῶλυ) which Odysseus used to avert the power of Circe to unman him, is really his phallus — RANKIN

It is perhaps not surprising that the phallicentric Priapus should see the phallus as the prime mover in the two epics. In the *Iliad* it was the aggressive strength of Agamemnon's; here in the *Odyssey* it is the power of that of Ulysses to attract goddesses and women.

(LXVIII)

e quibus ut scires quicunque valentior esset,
   haec es ad arrectos verba locuta procos:
"nemo meo melius nervum tendebat Ulixe,
   sive illi laterum sive erat artis opus.
qui quoniam periit, vos nunc intendite, qualem   35
   esse virum sciero, vir sit ut ille meus."
hac ego, Penelope, potui tibi lege placere,
   illo sed nondum tempore factus eram.

31 quicunque] qui quoque *Muell. Pasc.*   32 arrectos] erectos
CLW ed. Mutin.   33 Ulixi] Ulysse (-i-) *edd. veteres*   34
sive (*bis*) *AHWv et ceteri Buech. edd. recentiores*: sive/seu *LV et codd.
plerique edd. veteres*   erat *AH Buech. edd. recentiores*: fuit *LVWvh et
plerique, edd. veteres*   artis] artus *cod. Vat. Chigianus HV 164,
Ital.*   35 vos nunc] modo vos *Wv et cett., Ital. Scal.*, vos modo
V   qualem] quem iam *Muell.*, quemquem Baehr.   37 lege]
parte hpz   38 factus] natus *Weber Muell. Baehr.*
Vide appendicem p. 205.

LXIX

Priapus monet et minatur furibus ne comedant ficus

Cum fici tibi suavitas subibit
et iam porrigere huc manum libebit,
ad me respice, fur, et aestimato,
quot pondo est tibi mentulam cacandum.

Inscriptio *P*   2 libebit] licebit *LW et cett., Ital*   4 quot
LWgv edd.: quod *AGHVy et cett. Muell.*   mentulam *HVWvg et
plerique*: mentula *A Ald. Scal. Burm.*   cacandum *AHLW et cett.,
edd.*: cacandam *PUvx ed. Nurem.*, cacanda *CGpz Ald. Scal. Burm.*
ordo mentula (-m) est cac. *Wv Ital. praeter Mutin. et Parm., Ald. Scal.
Burm.*

4. Cf. *CIL* 10 8145: *hanc* [mentulam supra pictam — Housman]
ego cacavi.

I should have been the one, Penelope, to fuck
In your mate's stead. But I was not yet made, worse luck.

He finishes with a coarse jest, which provides a fitting conclusion
to the poem which is about the historical importance of the
mighty members of heroes such as Paris, Agamemnon and
Odysseus. But Priapus implies that his own phallus is greater
than them all, for he alone could have replaced her husband to
Penelope's complete satisfaction. However, it is not really the god
Priapus, son of Venus and Bacchus, who is speaking, but a crude
wooden scarecrow priapus set up by some Homer-reading
gentleman in his garden. Gods do not have a 'master' as he does,
nor are they 'made' as he was. For this reason some have wanted
to read *natus*, 'born', for *factus*, 'made', in line 38. But if he had
been 'born' he would not have had a 'master'. This dual identity
allows the talking statue to be as lewd and coarse as he likes.

69

Priapus advises a thief to take a good look at him

Thief, when desire for fig's sweet taste you feel,
And stretching out your hand you think to steal,
Look first at me, and think how hard 'twill be
To rid your arse of that great bulk you see.[1]

[1]literally, "and think how heavy the weight of the prick you will
have to excrete". This interpretation, that of Housman, is rejected
by Buchheit and by O'Connor, who translates: "Estimate how
much my *mentula*, the one that will be smeared with your
excrement, weighs when I pedicate you". But, as Housman wrote,
cacandum male interpretantur concacandum — "those who translate 'to
excrete' as meaning 'to smear with excrement' are wrong".

Yet another variation of the threat of *pedicatio* levelled at orchard
thieves.

LXX

Priapus monet ne apponat aliquid comestibile ad mentulam

Illusit mihi pauper inquilinus:
cum libum dederat molaque fusa,
quorum partibus abditis in ignem,
sacro protinus hinc abit peracto.
vicini canis huc subinde venit   5
nidorem, puto, persecuta fumi,
quae libamine mentulae comeso
tota nocte mihi litat rigendo.
at vos amplius hoc loco cavete
quicquam ponere, ne famelicorum   10
ad me turba velit canum venire,
ne dum me colitis meumque numen,
custodes habeatis irrumatos.

Inscriptio *P*   1 illusit *Ald. 1534 edd.*: illa sit *GN*, illa fit
ACLQRyw, illa fuit *ed. Mutin.*, ille fit *V*, ira fit *H*, illo fit *Ald. 1517*, sit
pauper *Amg. Pmg. Wv ed. Rom. ordo* Sit pauper mihi sit et inq. *ed.
Venet. 1475 Ital.*, *om.* et *W*   2 cum *codd. fere omnes, edd. Mutin et
recentiores*: qui *SWv edd. veteres praeter ed. Mutin. Muell.*, qui cum
Buech. Pasc.   libum] libo *p Buech. 1863 Pasc.*, libido *Vhgy ed.
Mutin.*, verbum *ANQ*, ferctum *Baehr.*   dederat *HWvy edd.*:
dederit *AQRU*, deerat *CLV*, aderat *Buech. 1863 Pasc.*   molaque
fusa *libri Ital. Ald. Buech. 1892 Pasc. Voll. Clair.*: molamque fusam
Scal. Burm. Meyer Muell., molamque salsa *Buech. 1863*, molamque
tusam *Baehr. Clausen-Schrader*   3 quorum *Buech. 1863 Muell.
Baehr. Clair.*: quarum *codd. fere omnes ed. Mutin.*, quare *Rpv edd.
veteres Pasc.*, quadrae *Buech. 1892, Herter*, carnum *Voll.*   abditis
AHLV et codd. fere omnes ed. Mutin. Buech. Herter Pasc.: additis *Wvy
edd. veteres praeter ed. Mutin. Baehr. Voll. Cazz. Clair.*   ignem]
inguen *gy Muell. Pasc. Cazz.*   4 abit] abibit *HPghy ed.
Mutin.*   6 nidorem] odorem *gh*, nitorem *A Ital. praeter ed.
Mutin.*   persecuta *A Buech. Baehr. Voll.*: prosecuta *codd. omnes
praeter A edd. veteres Pasc. Clair.*   7 quae] qua *Sciop.*   8
rigendo] rigando *h*, rigenti *Muell.*, ligendo *pro* lingendo *vel* hirnendo
Her., ligurriendo *fortasse Buech.*   10 famelicorum *codd. fere
omnes, edd. veteres Buech. Voll. Cazz. Clair.*: famelicarum *Muell. Baehr.
Pasc.*   12 ne] neu *Muell. fortasse Baehr.*

3. *mola fusa* (sc. *effusa* recte Pacal) . . . in ignem, si libi partes
aliquas flammis abdidisse putamus inquilinum, cum Buechelero
quadrae restituamus suadeo — HERTER.

70

Priapus tells of an offering that went wrong

A paltry tenant played me a dirty trick:
After he'd scattered some wafer on my prick,
Carelessly some of it on the fire he spilled;
Off then he went, his sacrifice fulfilled.
Soon comes next-door's bitch, her appetite awoke
By the aroma of the burnt food's drifting smoke,
And greedily licks the offering off my cock;
All night she worships thus: it's rigid as a rock.
So please take care with offerings you bring here:
Else will a crowd of famished dogs appear,
And while your sacrifice to me you consecrate,
Your watchdogs will, I fear, by me be irrumate.

An extraordinarily original and wittily-conceived epigram, despite its obscenity. A carelessly applied offering has brought a dog to the scene, leading to the excessive stimulation of the garden god's member. He warns that, unless greater care is taken, more dogs will appear and behave in the same way; he will not be responsible for the consequences: they will get it in their mouths — *irrumatio* instead of the more usual *pedicatio* threatened to thieves.

Parts of the text have come down to us badly corrupt, making the meaning difficult to determine. But the above rendering gives the most likely interpretation.

LXXI

Priapus cum furibus iocat

Si commissa meae carpes pomaria curae,
dulcia qui doleam perdere, doctus eris.

Inscriptio *z* 2 qui *P Heins. Dorvillius Muell. Baehr. Voll. Cazz.:*
quid *codd. fere omnes, edd. veteres Buech. Pasc. Clair.*, quia *h*

2. forte *dulcia* hic capi possunt eo sensu, quo *dulce* et *dulcia* in rebus
amoris dicuntur — BURMANNUS.

LXXII

Villicus ad Priapum ut bene custodiat hortum

(A) Tutelam pomarii, diligens Priape, facito:
rubricato furibus minare mutino.

(B) Quod monear non est, quia si furaberis ipse
grandia mala, tibi, 'bracchia macra' dabo.

Inscriptio *P* 1 Tutelam *AHL et codd. optimi, edd.:* curam *Wv et
codd. plerique Ital.*, cura *ed. Argent. Scal. Burm.* 2 rubricato
furibus] furi rubricato *ed. Argent. Anton. Burm. Meyer* mutino
HLmg. v et cett., edd. veteres Muell. Baehr. Pasc.: Mutino *Clair.*;
mutinio *AL Voll. Cazz.*, mutonio *Anton.* 3 monear *Buech. Voll.
Clair.*, moneat *A et codd. plerique*, movear *RWv et cett., edd. veteres
Muell. Baehr. Pasc.*, moveat *H*, moneam *Lu*, moneas *Avanc.
Cazz.* 4 bracchia *APQR edd. recentiores:* brachia *HLWh Ital.*,
brachica *Ald. Anton. Meyer* macra] mala *w Ald.* μαϰρὰ βραχὲια
Gabbema Hadr. Burm.

Quest'epigramma consta di due parte ben destinte: i primi due
versi, che sono sbagliati o corrotti perchè fuori d'ogni metro,
contengono una preghiera a Priapo perchè minacci i ladri,
mentre il disticho che segue è una delle solite minacce di Priapo
contra i ladri — MAGGI.

182

71

Priapus warns that it upsets him to lose sweet fruit

If from this orchard, committed to my care, you thieve,
    You'll learn that if I lose sweet things, I grieve.

Although this couplet is not, on the face of it obscene, it has been
suggested that *dulcia* could mean sexual favours as well as sweet
fruit. But such would not be the *dulcia* he would lose if visited by a
thief.

Priapus is told to do his duty

"Watch well my orchard, Priapus", he said,
    "Scare off the thieves with penis red."
Don't worry, sir! If you yourself should steal,
    For apples, evils you'll soon feel![1]

[1] or possibly, My trouser-apples [i.e. balls] you'll soon feel.

Nearly all manuscripts and the early editors have lines 1 and 2
and 3 and 4 as separate epigrams, and they are distinct metrically
— lines 1 and 2 have no regular metre. But editors from
Burmannus onwards have taken them together, though often
doubting their coherence. If the four lines do form a single poem,
then it is a question-and-answer epigram as rendered above, but
doubt remains about the meaning of line 4. We have accepted
Piero Vettori's interpretation (1553): Priapus is playing on the
fact that *mala* with a long *a* means 'apples', and with a short,
'evils'; he says, if you steal my apples, I will make your 'longs'
(macra), i.e. *māla* or 'apples', 'shorts' (bracheia), i.e. *mǎla*, 'evils'
or 'punishments'.

LXXIII

Priapus in puellas pathicas deridentes mentulam ligneam

Obliquis quid me, pathicae, spectatis ocellis?
non stat in inguinibus mentula tenta meis.
quae tamen exanimis nunc est et inutile lignum,
utilis haec, aram si dederitis erit.

Inscriptio *P*   quid me pathicae] pathicae quid me *plerique codd. deteriores, edd. veteres praeter edd. Mutin. & Parm., Muell. Pasc.*   2 non stat] stat non *W et plerique deteriores, Ital. praeter edd. Mutin. & Parm.*   in *om. LP et plerique, Ital.* 3 est] stat *A et cett.*   4 haec] esca *Cazz.*   aram] arram *Uuvx,* arvum *Anton Muell.* arrham *Lessing,* arae *Sciop. Goethe,* erucam *Burm.*

4. Aram enim puellarum cunnum esse vult, ad quem veluti ad aram Priapi solet mentula facere libamenta — MEYERUS.

Priapus addresses a group of *pathicae puellae*, asking them to bring life to his wooden *mentula* by providing an *ara* (i.e. a *culus*) — O'CONNOR.

LXXIV

Indignatio Priapi in barbatos senes

Per medios ibit pueros mediasque puellas
mentula, barbatis non nisi summa petet.

Inscriptio *w*   2 petet *Wv edd.*: petit *AHL et codd. plerique,* petat *Bhp et cett. ed. Mutin.*

2. Cf. Mart. 11 46 6: *summa petas.*

73

Priapus tells some wenches that they could revive his lifeless member

> Now, wanton girls, why are you looking at me so askance?
> I know my prick doth not from midst my loins upward
>   prance,
> And seems a lifeless piece of wood, unfit to do the deed:
> Yet, if you give it sanctuary, you'll find it meets your need.

Priapus's organ *non stat tenta*, "is not standing erect". This is most unusual. But he reassures the girls about its potency. They are described as *pathicae*, 'pathic', which can mean 'practising anal intercourse' (see O'Connor opposite), but it can also mean 'lascivious', 'wanton', and most commentators, by identifying the *aram* of line 4 with the *cunnus*, accept this more general meaning.

74

Priapus threatens rape according to age and sex

> Into the middle of boys and girls goes my pole:
>   With bearded adults it seeks a higher hole.

The last of three brief epigrams dealing with the 'three-fold punishment': *pedicatio* for boys, *fututio* for girls, and *irrumatio*, for grown males. They could be punishments for orchard thefts, or — as there is no reference to stealing here — merely the lewd god's boastings. Compare with **13** and **22**.

LXXV

Priapus enarrat loca sacrata deis atque deabus

Dodone tibi, Iuppiter sacrata est,
Iunoni Samos et Mycena dites,
undae Taenaros aequorisque regi;
Pallas Cecropias tuetur arces,
Delphos Pythius orbis umbilicum;   5
Creten Delia Cynthiosque colles,
Faunus Maenalon Arcadumque silvas;
tutela Rhodos est beata Solis,
Gades Herculis umidumque Tibur;
Cyllene celeri deo nivosa,   10
tardo gratior aestuosa Lemnos;
Hennaeae Cererem nurus frequentant,
raptam Cyzicos ostreosa divam,
formosam Venerem Gnidos Pathosque.
mortales tibi Lampsacum dicarunt.   15

Inscriptio *g*   1 Dodone *OR Meyer edd. recentiores*: Dodona *codd.
fere omnes, edd. veteres*   est *post* Dodona *Pz Avanc. Ald. 1534
Scal.*   2 Mycena *Ald. 1534 edd. recentiores*: Mycenae (-ne) *libri
edd. veteres*   dites *ALH et codd. fere omnes, edd. veteres Suess Cazz.
Clair.*: ditis *W Pierius Buech. Muell. Baehr. Pasc. Voll.*, dives *Ald. 1534*,
diti *Gabbema Anton. Meyer*   3 undae] unda est *Burm.*, uda
Dorvillius   Taenaros *R Avanc. ed.*: Tenedos *codd. fere omnes
Ital.*   et *post* undae *Anton*   aequorisque *Wv edd. veteres Buech.
Muell. Clair.*: aequoreoque (eq-) *HLV et codd. plerique*, aequorumque
AR et pauci Baehr. Pasc. Cazz.   7 Maenalon *edd.*: Maenalos
libri   silvas] silva *v Ital.*   8 tutela Rhodos est] est tutela
Rh. *Vat. Chigianus HV 169 Scal. Burm. Meyer*   9 umidumque]
uvidumque *Cazz.*   12 Hennaeae *Scal. edd. recentiores*: Enee *A*,
Aetneae (*et fere*) *codd. fere omnes, edd. veteres*   13 Cyzicos *Ald.
edd.*: cocytos (-ythos) *libri Ital.*   15 deest *codd. fere omnes, edd.
Mutin. et Parm. Ald. edd. recentiores*: adest *Wp Harleianus 2578 edd.
veteres*   mortales] et patres *p*   tibi *Ital.*: mihi *p Burm.*

3. *dites, ditis.* Vide Buechelerum, Suess, Cazzaniga, p. xiv.

5. Cf. Liv. 38 48 2: *Delphos . . . umbilicum orbis terrarum.*

75

Priapus has his own place, just as other gods do

Dodona is a sacred place, O Jove, to thee:
To Juno — Samos town and richest Mycenae.[1]
Among Taenarian waves the sea-god's cavern lies;
Athenian forts protection find with Pallas wise.
At central Delphi great Apollo has his rites;
Diana watches Creta and the Cynthian heights.
Faun Pan has Maenalos and the Acadian hill;
Fair Rhodes is blessed and guarded by the sun-god's will,
By Hercules Gades and Tibur (damp, they say),
Cyllene by the god that's swift upon his way;[2]
Lemnos by him of gods who's tardy, slow or lame;[3]
And Henna's women celebrate their Ceres' fame.
Cyzicos, rich in shells, worships the raped goddess.[4]
And Pathos and Gnidos both praise Venus' loveliness.
And our Priapus too, is not without his town:
Lampsacus in the Hellespont guards his renown.

[1]however, as we have adopted the plural form *dites* in the text, both Samos and Mycenae should be described as wealthy. [2]Hermes/Mercury. [3]Hephaistos/Vulcan. [4]Persephone/Proserpina.

This is the last of the cycle in which Priapus is compared with other gods or goddesses, and lists the largest number — fourteen, with one line for each.

In most manuscripts the poem ends abruptly with *Pathosque* in the fourteenth line, omitting the obvious conclusion, a reference to Priapus and *his* place, Lampsacus. It is generally supposed that one or two lines have been lost, and modern editors add a row of dots. But a few manuscripts do have a concluding line, and this was added to several of the others which do not have it in the original hand. The early editors accepted this, and rather than give an unfinished version, we have done the same.

LXXVI

Priapus dicit de sua potentia

> Quod sim iam senior meumque canis
> cum barba caput albicet capillis:
> deprensos ego perforare possum
> Tithonum Priamumque Nestoremque.

Inscriptio *g*   1 sim iam] iam sim *Vat.Chigianus HV 164 ed.*
Rom.   sim *HVWv*: sum *CLpux et pauci deteriores*, si *A et*
pauci   2 albicet *LHVv edd. Mutin. et recentiores*: albicat *hv Burm.*,
albica *SW ed.Rom.*   3 deprensos *ALW et codd. plerique, edd.*:
deprehensos *HNVgþ*

Hiare in principio patet . . . Desideratur in principio tale aliquid:
Heus vos notite mihi cavere — PASCAL.

76

Priapus claims that, though old, he is still formidable

> Though I am old, and white my beard and thatch,
> I still can penetrate all those I catch,
> E'en be they such heroic men of yore
> As Tithonus and Priam and Nestor.

Why does Priapus choose three ancient heroes as examples of those he, though aged himself, is able to 'penetrate'? In **57** they were instanced as examples of great age, but what credit can Priapus possibly expect in claiming to be able to humiliate them? Or is it their pristine valour rather than their age that he is thinking of? This seems more likely. Most commentators follow Buecheler in believing a line or lines to be missing at the beginning, but we agree with Shackleton Bailey that "the four lines make an acceptable whole as they stand".

LXXVII

Priapus iratus ad villicos saepientes hortum

Immanem stomachum mihi videtis,
qui densam facitis subinde saepem
et fures prohibetis huc adire.
hoc est laedere, dum iuvatis; hoc est
non admittere ad aucupem volucres.   5
obstructa est via, nec licet iacenti
iactura natis expiare culpam.
ergo qui prius usque et usque et usque
furum scindere podices solebam,
per noctes aliquot diesque cesso.   10
poenas do quoque, quot satis superque est,
in semenque abeo salaxque quondam
nunc vitam perago — quis hoc putaret?
ut clusus citharoedus abstinentem.
at vos, ne peream situ senili,   15
quaeso desinite esse diligentes,
neve imponite fibulam Priapo.

Inscriptio *P*   1 immanem *HLVW et codd. plerique, edd.*:
immane *AC et pauci*   stomachum mihi *codd. optimi, ed. Mutin.*
edd.: mihi stomachum *AC et pauci Ital.*   videtis *libri edd. veteres*
Voll. Clair.: movetis *Burm. Buech. Pasc.*, cietis *Muell. Baehr.*
Cazz.   2 qui] quid *L et pauci*   5 admittere] admittetur *h,*
amittere *Q,* admictere *pauci*   11 poenas] poenae *Heins.*   quot
W Buech. edd. recentiores: quod *codd. fere omnes, edd. veteres*   14
clusus *A Buech. edd. recentt.*: lusus *CHLVW et codd. fere omnes, Ital.,*
lusu *px Ald. Scal.*, elusus *NQ*   abstine(n)tem *H Buech. edd.*
recentt.: abstinerem *AVR et codd. plerique ed. Mutin. Ald. Clair.*,
abstineret *LWv et codd. plerique, Ital. Scal.*, abstinacem
Baehr.   17 *om. A et pauci*

17. Fibulam cantorum atque aliorum iuvenum quorum libidinem
continere voluerunt membro virili et quidem ut apparet praepu-
tio impositam fuisse non ignoramus — GOETHE.

190

77

Priapus claims that a fence denies him his natural outlet

I'm angry you should build a fence so stout
To keep the robbers from this garden out.
I know you mean to help, but have a care:
You'll keep the birds from entering the snare.
The way is blocked, and so I cannot make
Thieves punishment between their buttocks take;
And I, who have grown used up them to thrust,
Up, up and up, their in'ards splitting, must
Myself be punished now, beyond belief:
Whole nights and days without getting relief.
I'm getting weak, and though with lust once blessed,
I now exist just like — who would have guessed? —
Some fibulated player of the lyre,
And fated, like an old man, to expire.
Be not so keen the access to restrict;
Or on Priapus fetters[1] you'll inflict.

[1] in the text a *fibula*, a device attached to the penis to prevent copulation. Singers were 'fibulated' to preserve their voices (line 13).

Many *priapea* parody the belief that the setting up of a wooden priapus would, through the deterrent supernatural power of its member, ward off evil, which for the owner of an orchard or market garden usually meant theft of his produce. The poet converts the magic of an apotropaic charm into an actual physical assault upon the interloper, usually anal rape. Sometimes, however, the owner considers it prudent also to hire a watchman (**17**) or dogs (**62**, **70**), or, in this case, to erect a fence. Priapus's complaint is a witty commentary upon this, developing three motifs: first, the violence of the punishment, hammered home by the repetitive *usque et usque et usque* (line 8) — 'up, up and up'; then the strain upon him of being denied this outlet; and lastly, his likely demise as a result.

LXXVIII

Priapus maledicit cuidam cunnilingo

At di deaeque dentibus tuis escam
negent amicae cunnilinge vicinae,
per quem puella fortis ante nec mendax
et quae solebat impigro celer passu
ad nos venire, nunc misella landicae   5
vix posse iurat ambulare prae fossis.

1 At] Ah *Anton*   di *edd. recentiores*: dii *libri edd. veteres*   escam
AHLW et codd. fere omnes Ital. Buech. edd. recentiores: escas *Vp Ald.
Scal.*   2 amicae *Avanc. Ald. edd. recentt.*: amicas *codd. fere omnes,
edd. veteres,* amicos *V* cunnilinge *Avanc. Ald. edd.*: cunnilingi *LSWvx
et pauci, Ital.,* cunniligni (cunni ligni) *AH et codd. plerique ed.
Mutin.*   3 fortis *edd. Rom. & Mutin. Ald.*: foris *libri Ital.*   4
celer *Wc edd. Venet. & Rom. edd.*: celerique *codd. fere omnes*   5
landicae *Munckerus Buech. edd. recentiores*: landice *Az et pauci,*
landices *HV et codd. plerique,* landacae (landace) *Wv et cett. edd.
veteres,* laudices *LQU ed. Mutin.,* Labdace *Scal. Sciop. Burm.*

5. Lego Labdace . . . dictum a Labda litera . . . quia Lesbia ea
infamia flagrarunt Ausonius quoque allusit: Cur ipse linguam
quum deit suam, Labda est. Huiusce modi quoque detestandae
libidinis homines Labdas vocat Margopoli — SCALIGER.

landicae . . . eius memoriam Munckerus . . . excitavit e Philoxeni
glossa . . . non extat hoc verbum nisi in glande Perusina C.I.L.
1507: *peto landicam Fulviae* et in epistulis quas homo Italus . . .
finxit Sorani de priapismo Cleopatrae . . . ubi cunnus describitur:
"intus vero quod a superiore parte discendit in medio, dicta est
landica." . . . verum certum est eodem Ciceronem spectare in
epistula ad Paetum IX 22.2: ". . . memini in senatu disertum
consularem ita eloqui *hanc culpam maiorem* an illam dicam? [an-*il-
landicam*] potuit obscenius?" — BUECHELER.

78

Priapus curses a rival

> Because down there he licks and bites my love,
> See that his teeth go hungry, Gods above!
> The girl who once was healthy, full of pep,
> And used to come to me with eager step,
> Now swears that she, poor wretch, can walk no more,
> Her cunt and clitoris are bit so sore.

The last of the maledictory or 'cursing' cycle of epigrams within the *Priapea*, and the only poem in the book to mention, at least directly, *cunnilinctio*. It also contains one of the very few direct references to the *landica* or clitoris in the ancient languages.

Because this poem is in the *Priapea*, one assumes that Priapus is the speaker, but O'Connor pertinently asks: "If the speaker is actually Priapus, why should he not invoke his own power rather than the *di deaeque*?"

In the original, the girl is described as not only *fortis*, 'strong and healthy', but also as *non mendax*, i.e. 'reliable': she would have come to him if she could. Horace (*sat.* 1 5 82) writes of a *mendacem puellam* who failed to visit him as she had promised.

LXXIX

Poeta hortatur Priapum ne erubescat propter mentulam sibi tentam

Priape, quod sis fascino gravis tento,
quod exprobravit hanc tibi suo versu
poeta noster, erubescere hoc noli:
non es poeta sarcinosior nostro.

1 tento *Pmg. Vmg. Avanc. Ald. edd.*: tenero *HLVW et codd. fere omnes,
Ital.*, mero *A*　　2 exprobravit *LW Ald. edd.*: exprobavit *AHV et
codd. fere omnes, Ital.*　　hanc tibi] tibi hanc *P* hanc *AHLPV et codd.
plerique Her. Voll. Cazz. Clair.*: hic *GWpv et codd. plerique, edd. veteres,
Buech. Muell. Pasc.*, hoc *Vat. Reginens. Lat. 1803 Baehr.*, hac *P*, hacne
h　　3 poeta noster] noster poeta *L*　　4 es *Scal. edd.
recentiores*: est *libri edd. veteres*　　sarcinosior (*vel* similia) *libri Ital.
Ald. 1517 Her. Clair.*: fascinosior *Ald. 1534 Scal. Burm. Meyer omnes
edd. recentiores praeter Clair.*

. . . die einzige Aussage des Poeten über sich selbst und seine
Person . . .; hatte er eingangs über seine Verse gesprochen und sie
entschuldigt, so sprechen diese nun abschliessend ihrerseits über
ihren Dichter sonst in eigener Person abzuleugnen pflegten: dass
er selbst dem Gotte Priap in priapischer Weise dient und dem
verehrten Numen nicht nachgestellt zu werden braucht, was
dessen eigentliche, das heisst sexuelle Aktivität anbelangt —
KYTZLER.

79

Don't feel ashamed, Priapus, of your large member — the poet's is even bigger

There is no need, Priapus, to feel shy
Because your member stretches up so high,
For which our poet has chosen you to mock:
He has himself an even bigger cock!

There is irony here, as Priapus was hardly one to blush for the size of his member, nor to find consolation in the poet's being just as big. Indeed, a Greek epigram (*AP* 16 224) runs:

When our lad Cimon's prick stand up, Priapus did espy,
He cried, "A mortal's bigger there than am immortal I!"

O'Connor points out, however, that to call someone "a big prick" was an insult then as now.

LXXX

Votum unius Priapo pro mentula flaccida

At non longa bene est, non stat bene mentula crassa,
    et quam si tractes, crescere posse putes?
me miserum! cupidas fallit mensura puellas:
    non habet haec aliud mentula maius eo.
utilior Tydeus qui, si quid credis Homero,   5
    ingenio pugnax, corpore parvus erat.
sed potuit damno nobis novitasque pudorque
    esse, repellendus saepius iste mihi.
dum vivis, sperare decet: tu, rustice custos,
    huc ades et nervis, tente Priape, fave.   10

1 *ordo*: *v. appendicem*   At] Ut *Sv et pauci codd. deteriores, Ital. praeter ed. Mutin.*   bene est *Muell. et edd. recentiores praeter Pasc.*: satis *Wv et pauci, Ital. Scal.*, *om.* est *libri Pasc.*   add. at *ante* non *edd. recentiores*   non stat bene] bene non stat *S Muell.*, bene stat non *p*   stat *om. Baehr. Buech. 92 Voll. Cazz. Clair.* (*cp. Ov. am. 3 7 1s*: at non bene culta puella)   bene *om. Cg Scal.*   2 et] sed *Hy*   4 haec] hoc *RWhv et cett., Ital.*   aliud] aliquid *H Baehr.*   maius eo] materiae *Buech.* 1863   maius] mancus *Voll.* eo] ea (*sc.* mensura) *Barth. Anton Housman*, ero *Baehr. Castiglioni*   7 novitasque] gravitasque *Vp*   8 repellendus] repetendum *A*   9 sperare *A et ceteri, edd.*: spectare *HLVW et plerique*   decet *codd. fere omnes, edd. veteres Muell.*: licet *duo codd. Burmanni, in Petronii Satyrico, edd. recentiores*

1. *mentula* non Priapi, sed aegroti precantis — VOLLMER. *Vide etiam p. 206.*

9–10. Hoc distichon est singulare Epigramma et seorsum separandum est — SCALIGER.   A Scaligero vero separatum editum, quia in Petronii Satyrico c. 131 legitur. Sed totum epigramma Petronii esse iudico — MEYER.   Hos versus miror Scaligerum a prioribus segregasse, cum quibus apertissime cohaerent — MUELLER.   Wenn man aber erkennt, dass nicht Priap der Sprecher in diesem Gedicht ist . . . sondern ein wegen seiner Impotenz zu dem Gott um Hilfe Flehender, so bleibt von der These zweier Gedichte kaum noch etwas übrig — BUCHHEIT.   Clearly these two verses do not belong to CP 80 — O'CONNOR.

80

The poet laments the size of his member

> My prick is neither long enough, nor thick enough doth
> > stand:
> > Think'st thou 'twill grow, e'en if thou work'st it with thy
> > > hand?
> Alack, it does not satisfy the wenches' wantonness:
> > And if a prick's not big, what worth does it possess?
> Why now, if Homer thou believ'st, Tydeus[1] could do more,
> > For though he was a small man, brave he was in war.
> But this, I fear, could ruin me: the strangeness, the
> > > disgrace;
> > Again, and yet again, it's what I have to face.
> But, orchard guard, while yet there's life there's always
> > > hope, they say:
> > Priapus, hard of member, bless my tool, I pray.

[1] in the *Iliad* (5 801) Homer says "Tydeus was small in body, but a
warrior". In fact, few mythological heroes slew more enemies than
he.

Two main difficulties here are the meaning of the first couplet
and the status of the last; another is the interpretation of line 4.
The problem is not merely a corrupt text, but knowing how to
take the Latin — literally? ironically? interrogatively, etc.?
According to how the text is read and how construed, the opening
couplet can be rendered in several ways, besides that given —
diffidently — above:

> But isn't it a good long prick, but isn't it a good thick one,
> And one which, if you'd handle it, you'd think could grow?
> — RICHLIN

> Which do you think the more desirable, a long or a thick
> > penis,
> And which of the two will swell the more when you work it
> > with your hand? — FISCHER (trans.)

For further commentary on this epigram, *see Appendix, p. 206.*

197

REFERENCES

I Burmannus, P. (ed.) *Anthologia veterum Latinorum epigrammatum et poematum*, 2 (Amsterdam, 1773), 478–9; Barthius, C. *Adversarii* (Frankfurt, 1624), 44 6 1997.

II Burmannus *Anthologia* 2, 480; Buchheit, V. *Zetemata* 28 (1962), 10.

III Burmannus *Anthologia* 2, 480–2.

IV Scioppius, C. (ed.) *Priapea* (Frankfurt, 1606), 32: Buecheler, F. *Rh.Mus.* 18 (1863), 385.

V Menagius, A. *Laertii Diogenis de vitis dogmatis* (London, 1664), 61; Burmannus *Anthologia* 1 (Amsterdam, 1759), 696–7; 2 (Amsterdam, . 1773), 411–12; Huebner (ed.) *Menagius* 2 (Leipzig, 1833), 441.

VI Buecheler *Rh.Mus.* 18, 385.

VIII Buchheit *Zetemata* 28, 40; Marquardt, qu. in *Fiedlaender*, L. (ed.) *M. Valerii Martialis epigrammaton* 1 (1886), 319 fn. 8; Isaac, H.J. *Martial épigrammes* 1 (Paris, 1930), 254; Schilling, R. *Études et commentaires* 92 (1979), 149–51.

IX Buecheler *Rh.Mus.* 18, 386; Scaligerus, J. (ed.) *Publii Virgilii Maronis Appendix* (Leyden, 1595), 187.

XI Buecheler *Rh.Mus.* 18, 386.

XII Buchheit *Zetemata* 28, 132–6; Cazzaniga, E. *Carmina ludicra Romanorum* (Turin, 1959), 27; Buecheler *Rh.Mus.* 18, 387.

XIII Lindenbruchius, F. *In appendicem P. Virgilii Maronis* (Leyden, 1595), 306.

XIV Buecheler *Rh.Mus.* 387.

XVI Clairmont, R.E. *Carmina Priapea* (Diss. Loyola Univ., Chicago, 1983), 161; Lessing, G.E. *Sämtliche Schriften* 8 (Berlin, 1855), 490; Buecheler *Rh.Mus.* 18, 388.

XIX Holland, R. *Phil.Wochenschr.* 39 (1925), 143; Buchheit *Zetemata* 28, 136–7.

XX Buecheler *Rh.Mus.* 18, 389; Avancius, H. *In Valerium Catullum et in Priapea emendationes* (Venice, 1495), n.p.

XXI Scaliger *Appendix*, 190; Barthius *Adversarii* 27, 8; Mueller, L. *Catulli, Tibulli, Propertii carmina* (Leipzig, 1872), xlix–l; Buecheler *Rh.Mus.* 18, 389–90; Housman, A.E. *Hermes* 66 (1931), 402–3; Buchheit, *Zetemata* 28, 137.

XXIV Mueller *Catulli*, 1; Buchheit, *Zetemata* 28, 107 fn.1; Richlin, A. *The Garden of Priapus* (New Haven & London, 1983), 142.

XXV Buecheler *Rh.Mus.* 18, 390; O'Connor, E.M. *Dominant themes in Greco-Roman Priapic poetry* (diss. Univ. Calif. Santa Barbara, 1984), 289.

XXVI Maggi, A. *I Priapea* (Naples, 1923), 29; Pascal, C. *Carmina ludicra Romanorum* (Rome, 1918), 47; *Anthologia Palatina* 16, 239.

XXXI Buecheler *Rh.Mus.* 18, 391; Pascal, *Carmina ludicra*, 48.

XXXIII Buecheler *Rh.Mus.* 18, 394; Pascal, *Carmina ludicra*, 48.

XXXIV Payne Knight, R. *A discourse on the worship of Priapus* (London, 1786), 178.

References

XXXV Richlin, *Garden of Priapus*, 26.

XXXVI Buchheit, V. *Gnomon* 35 (1963), 36–7; Lindenbruch, *Appendix*, 307; Buecheler *Rh.Mus.* 18, 394; Mueller *Catulli*, li.

XXXVII Buchheit *Zetemata* 28, 78.

XL Riese, A. (ed.) *Historia Apollonii Regis Tyri* (Leipzig, 1893), 67–8 (cap.33).

XLII Burmannus *Anthologia* 2, 514–5.

XLIII Mariotti in Terzoghi, N. *Lanx Satura* (Genoa, 1963), 261–2; Lactantius *Opera* (ed. Fritzsche) 1 Institutionum divinorum (Leipzig, 1842), 50 (cap.20).

XLV Scaliger *Appendix*, 197; Goethe qu. in Grumach, E. *Goethe und die Antike* (Berlin, 1949), 386; Buecheler *Rh.Mus.* 18, 396; Vollmer, F. *Poetae latini minores* 2 2 (1923), 56; Bailey, D.R.S. *Phoenix* 32 (1978), 315; Cazzaniga *Carmina*, 37; Burton, R. ('Outidanos') in Neaniskos *Priapea* (Cosmopoli, 1890), 43.

XLVI Vossius qu. in Meyer, H *Anthologia Latina* 2 (Leipzig, 1835), 144; Alciatus qu. in Meyer *Anthologia* 2, 144; Scaliger *Appendix*, 197; Dorvillius qu. in Burmannus *Anthologia* 2, 517–19; Buecheler *Rh.Mus.* 18, 396–7; Mueller *Catulli*, li; Baehrens, Ae. *Poetae latini minores* 1 (Leipzig, 1879), 72; Vollmer *PLM* 2, 2, 56; Ellis, R. *Rh.Mus.* 43 (1888), 264; Holland *Phil.Wochenschr.* 39, 144; Bailey *Phoenix* 32, 315. See also Gandiglio, A. *Boll.Fil.Class.* 31 (1925), 130.

XLVII Burmannus *Anthologia* 2, 517–19; Columella *de re rustica* 108–9; Petronius *Satyricon* 60; Gandiglio *Boll.Fil.Class.* 31, 130.

XLIX Scaliger, *Appendix*, 198; O'Connor, *Priapic poetry*, 324.

L Buecheler *Rh.Mus.* 18, 397–8; Haupt, M. *Hermes* 8 (1874), 241; Ellis *Rh.Mus.* 43, 264; Hallett, J. *Rh.Mus.* 124 (1981), 344.

LI Burmannus *Anthologia* 2, 523.

LII Scaliger *Appendix*, 200; Buecheler *Rh.Mus.* 18, 400–1; Süss, W. *Philologus* 23 (1910), 445–6.

LIII O'Connor, *Priapic poetry*, 331.

LIV Burmannus, *Anthologia* 2, 527; O'Connor *Priapic poetry*, 332; Buecheler *Rh.Mus.* 18, 401–2; Scioppius, *Priapea*, 90.

LV Anton, G.C. *Diversorum poetarum veterum in Priapum* (Leipzig, 1781), ad carm. 55.

LVI O'Connor, *Priapic poetry*, 335.

LVII Scaliger *Appendix*, 201; Mueller *Catulli*, lii; Buecheler *Rh.Mus.* 18, 402–3; O'Connor, *Priapic poetry*, 336; Knecht, D. *Antiquité classique* 35 (1916), 213.

LVIII Buchheit *Zetemata* 28, 143–4.

LX O'Connor, *Priapic poetry*, 340.

LXII Buecheler *Rh.Mus.* 18, 403; Vollmer *PLM* 2, 2, 62; Cazzaniga *Carmina*, 44; Buchheit, *Zetemata* 28, 126; Ehlers, W.W. *Rh.Mus.* 114 (1971), 96.

LXIII Mueller *Catulli*, liii–iv; Pascal *Carmina*, 53; Buecheler *Rh.Mus.* 18, 405; Steuding, H. *Jb.class.phil.* 35 (1889), 600; Büsche, K. *Phil. Wochenschr.* 45 (1925), 1103.

LXV Housman, A.E. *CR* 29 (1915), 173–4.

LXVII Pascal *Carmina*, 53.

LXVIII Rankin, H.D. *Petronius the artist* (The Hague, 1971), 64.

References

LXIX Housman *Hermes* 66, 404–5; Buchheit *Zetemata* 28, 144–6; O'Connor, *Priapic poetry*, 353–6.

LXX Herter, H. *De Priapo* (Giessen, 1932), 274–5.

LXXI Burmannus *Anthologia* 2, 542.

LXXII Maggi I *Priapea*, 77; Victorius, P. *Variarum lectionum* (Florence, 1553), 167.

LXXIII Meyer *Anthologia* 2, 152; O'Connor, *Priapic poetry*, 361; on *aram* see also Grumach, *Goethe und die Antike* 1, 387; Lessing, *Sämtliche Schriften* 8, 489.

LXXV Buecheler *Rh.Mus.* 18, 411; Suess *Philologus* 23, 444.

LXXVI Buecheler *Rh.Mus.* 18, 412; Bailey *Phoenix* 32, 317.

LXXVII Goethe in Grumach *Goethe und die Antike* 1, 387.

LXXVIII Scaliger *Appendix*, 208; Buecheler *Rh.Mus.* 18, 413; O'Connor, *Priapic poetry*, 369; Fay, E.W. *CQ* 1 (1907) 13–14 (and editor's postscript); Pascal, C. *Riv.Fil.* 50 (1922), 172–6; *Thesaurus Linguae Latinae* 7, 2 (1970–79), 920 landica; Hallett, J.P. *AJAnc.Hist.* 2 (1977), 152.

LXXIX Kytzler, B. in Fischer, C. *Priapea* (Salzburg, 1969), 134; O'Connor, *Priapic poetry*, 371.

LXXX Scaliger *Appendix*, 209; Meyer *Anthologia* 2, 153; Mueller, *Catulli*, lvi; Buchheit *Zetemata* 28, 147; O'Connor, *Priapic poetry*, 374; Richlin *Garden of Priapus*, 117; Burton, R. ('Outidanos') in 'Neaniskos', *Priapea* (1890), No. lxxxi; Fischer *Priapea* (1969), 117.

Appendices

Appendix A Carmen XIX (continued from p. 98)

extis satius altiusve motat — *A*
extis satius altiusve movet — *HL ed. Mutin. 1475*
extis altius altiusve movet — *V*
extis aptius altiusque movit — *W ed. Rom. 1473*
extis aptius altiusque movet — *edd. Vincent. 1476 & Venet. 1475*
extis aptius altiusque motat — *Ald. Scal.*
exsertam aptius altiusque movit — *Heins.*
sistris aptius altiusque movit — *Buech. 1863*
sistris aptius acriusque motat — *Mueller*
aestu latius altiusque motat — *Baehr.*
festis acrius altiusve movit — *Ellis*
extis latius altiusque movit — *Pasc.*
exos altius altiusque motat — *Voll.*
extis scitius altiusve motat — *Cazz.*
exossem aptius altiusque movit — *Forberg*
extis latius altiusque motat — *Clair.*

Appendix B Carmen XXI (continued from p. 103)

The early commentators believed the master of a 'priapus' to be
speaking, asking it not to betray the fact that he has so few of his
own apples that he has had to buy some in order to make his
offering, e.g.

> The master speaks to his priapus. The sense is obscure, but this is
> what it seems to mean. Because I have made myself rich, or
> pretended to be so, I am almost reduced to poverty because I am
> ever compelled to give; when, therefore, they come to you asking
> about my wealth, this I ask of you: do not betray my poverty, of
> which you are aware, to them. And to make it easier for you, say
> that these apples that I have given you, and which I bought on the
> Sacred Way, came from my own estate — SCIOPPIUS.

Scaliger and Barthius gave similar explanations, but they had to
tinker with the opening words to add plausibility to them.
Burmannus (1773) quoted Tollius' view that the owner of a poor
orchard, which is for sale, hopes to deceive potential buyers by
giving a false impression of its productivity. We have accepted
Buecheler's opinion (1863):

A thief, who has made off with a large quantity of apples from the Sacred Way, is speaking. He has dedicated some of them to Priapus, partly to reduce the excessive burden, but also to conciliate the god, whose function it is to prevent the theft of fruit (*trans.*).

Pascal (1918), Vollmer (1923), Maggi (1923), Herter (1936) and Buchheit (1962) have also endorsed the view that a thief is speaking, but Mueller (1874) rejected it:

> It is most unlikely that the author, an able and liberally-educated man, would demean himself by assuming the role of a thief; nor would a thief have dedicated stolen apples to Priapus, the bitterest enemy and castigator of thieves (*trans.*).

Housman (1931) gave an obscene meaning to the poem: the salacious owner of the 'priapus' is complaining that so many thieves have taken apples in exchange for sexual favours (in accordance with Priapus' 'rule' as enunciated in **5** and **38**), that he has none left. O'Connor (1984) has an original explanation: apples were 'love tokens' given to prostitutes. One who has gained plenty, offers some to Priapus, but asks him not to reveal their shameful source — the *Via Sacra*. For the Sacred Way was known as a 'red-light' district, as is attested by Martial (2 63 2) and Propertius (2 23 15); this being so, it seems not unlikely that its occurrence in a *priapeum* would be linked with this association. And whores were prominent among those who made offerings to the phallic god. The *perdit* in line 1 remains to be accounted for, however.

Appendix C Carmen XXXII (continued from p. 119)

13–14. Most commentators, since and including Burman (1773), have taken *ductor ferreus* to mean an 'iron worker', and have changed *insularis aeque* — although all the mss. have it — to *insulariusque*, so adding to the ironworker the slave who looked after an *insula* or apartment block, a caretaker. Thus Buecheler (1863): "Well may I think myself an ironworker or the servant who thrusts the lantern to and fro" (trans.). Cazzaniga (1959), assuming *ductor* to be a mistake for *custos*, writes: "the caretaker is an iron priapus who holds up the street lantern on his iron penis" (trans.). Buchheit (1962), accepting the ms. reading (though adding a necessary *et* at the end of line 13, whence it may well have dropped off), reads *ductor* as 'lampholder', and renders the couplet: "Just like the iron holder of a house lantern, I seem to scrape against the horn" (trans.). He agrees with Cazzaniga that such a holder may have taken the form of a phallus, for just such a one was discovered at Pompeii. O'Connor has recently communicated to us another interesting 'conjecture: he reads *insulariaeque*, "taking *ductor* as the present passive of *ductare*, with *insulariae* now describing *lanternae* in the line below. The idea is that Priapus is being 'handled', though he can't feel a thing (*ferreus*) and appears to rub an apartment house lantern's 'sheet of horn'".

Appendix D Carmen XLIII (continued from pp. 134–5)

Augustine (5th cent. AD) exclaimed: "What can I say, when the all-too-masculine Priapus is here, and when the newly-wedded bride was told by the chastest and most religious of the matrons to sit on his huge and most shameful member?" An ancient engraving on cornelian stone illustrated in the *Monuments du culte secret des dames romaines* (1784), by Hugues d'Ancarville, shows a woman so seating herself.

The chief difficulties in the way of a perfect understanding of this epigram are its punctuation (how much speech is to be attributed to the girl, how much to Priapus), and the ms. reading of line 4 (*utetur veris usibus*) which Buecheler described as "not to be tolerated". The usual variety of conjectures exist to solve the latter, some changing *utetur*, some *veris*, and some *usibus*.

Dixit ergo puella. Haec rudis hasta in me veris usibus utetur, et in me inibit. Hic sensus est epigrammatis — SCIOP-PIUS.   in tertio versu *mihi credite* dubites num Priapo tribuendum an includendum sit in verba puellae. ego in exemplari meo adsignavi illa Priapo, nunc coniungi cum puellae oratione malo. nam praeterquam quod eiusmodi affirmatio magis decere videtur puellam quae prior elocuta est incredibilia, quam Priapum qui eadem narrat posterior, valde molestum est *me* et *mihi* ad diversos referre — BUECHELER.   A me *veris usibus* sembra appropriato ed efficace e preferei toccare *utetur* (corotto anche per influenza di *usibus*?) sostituendovi un congiuntivo, *aptetur* — MARIOTTI.

Appendix E Carmen LII (continued from p.150)

6. ... unter den beiden Assistenten niemand anders als die testiculi zu verstehen ist ... Diese naheliegende Deutung wäre auch gewiss ausgesprochen worden ohne den Schluss des Gedichts ...

> cum tantum sciet esse mentularum

Wenn man aber sich vergegenwärtigt, dass dieser Vers eine Parodie von Catull V ist

> cum tantum sciat esse basiorum

und die oben angedeute groteske Erfindung des Dichters bedenkt, wird man gewiss auch in dieser Schlusswendung nicht ein Instanz gegen unsere Auffassung sehen — SUESS.

10. *nilo.* Ita scripsi pro nihilo ... nihil *et.al.* nam metrum requirit duas syllabas longas — ANTON. *nihilo* ... bisyllabum est *nihilo* — MEYER.

Appendix F Carmen LIV (continued from pp. 152–3)

Hoc dicit. Si scribas E D et temonem in medio addas hoc modo: E—D tum mentula erit quodam modo depicta quae te medium scindere volt, sive quae te suprare volt. Ambiguitas est in D in pronunciatione: Te enim intelligit — SCIOPPIUS ...
colligatae uno ductu CD exprimunt scroti et temo superne additus rigentis mentulae imaginem: scito autem in arte antiqua 'nullum phallum sine scroto esse' — BUECHELER.
And even if this poem is not worth the labour of interpretation, my duty demands that I finish what I have begun. This is what it says: if you write ED and a hyphen in between, thus E—D, then the penis, which wishes to cleave your middle, will be shown — SCIOPPIUS (trans.). It is to be understood in this way. If you write ED and add a bar, with the thick line drawn so that it cuts the middle of the D, then a phallus will be shown: E———D. And indeed, children and the uneducated draw pictures in this way. For children draw the arms and legs of men by the same method by which here we have represented the neck of the phallus — GOETHE (trans.). If you believe the mss. Ed ..., if me, CD ..., for if drawn as one, CD shows the scrotum, and the "bar added above" represents the erect *mentula*: for, in the

art of the ancients, there was "no phallus without a scrotum" —
BUECHELER.

Appendix G Carmen LXVIII (continued from p. 178)

totum hoc quoque Epigramma, variis in locis mendosum et
depravasum — BURMANNUS.   Coniunxi carmen 69 et
70 auctoritate ductus Fauriani [*p*] — MEYER.

4. Homerum cuius carmina omnes, pueri senes, docti indocti
noverant, veteres multi ridiculis parodiis atque sordidis vexabant
— BUECHELER.

5. Psoleon ille vocat quod nos psolenta ceraunon — *libri*
   Psoleon ille vocat quod nos psoloenta vocamus — *edd. veteres*
   ille vocat. quod nos psolon, psoloenta ceraunon — *Gronovius, Heins.*
   ille vocat. quod nos ψωλήν, ψολόεντα κεραυνόν — *Buech.*
   ille vocat. quod nos psolen/psolon, ψολόεντα κεραυνόν — *Burm.*

7. certe nisi res non munda — *codd. fere omnes*
   certe in se res non munda — *H*
   certe visa res non munda — *V*
   certe merda huic inmunda — *Heins.*
   certe res huic non munda — *Francius*
   certe si res non munda — *Weber edd. recentiores*
   certe sti res non munda — *Lachmann*
   certe quasi res non munda — *Buech. 1893*

9. Cf. Hor. *sat*.1 3 170f: *nam fuit ante Helenam cunnus taeterrima / belli
causa.*   Ab hoc versu vulgo carmen 70 incipit — MEYER.

11. *non nota*. Dunque da *non nota* conviene ricavare una sola
parola, e questa parola è *morata*: "Se la *mentula* di Agamennone
fosse stata ben custumata, se non fosse stata troppo avida, Crise
non avrebbe avuto di che lamentarsi" — MARIOTTI.

20. non debebam ex Burmanni codicibus *hanc* recipere . . . repono
igitur quod alii libri habent *hunc* id est errorem Ulixi —
BUECHELER.

21. Cf. Ov. *met.* 14 291: *huic dederat florem Cyllenius album, / moly
vocant superi, nigra radice tenetur.*   lectione miror alios legere
solitos, flos aureus exit, cum flos lacteus legendum sit, tum ex fide
ipsius moly naturae ac carminis Homerici, tum propter obsce-
num sensum, quo humanum semen significatur; huius modi
tamen obscena libentius tegerem, quam scriberem — GYRAL-
DUS.

31. Neque *quicumque* praebet ullum sensum nec vero *valentior*. Nam valentissimus omnium a Penelope expetebatur. Itaque haud cunctanter reponendum *qui quoque*. quod librarii per neglegentiam acceperunt, quasi esset *quiquomque* — MUELLER.

35. Illud *qualem* omni sensu carere consentiunt docti, ex quo lenissima mutatione fecimus *quem iam* — MUELLER. At intellige: "ut ille vir meus sit talis, qualem sciero esse virum (scil. virile robore praeditum)" — PASCAL.   Baehrens proposed *quemquam* for *qualem*, thus committing Penelope to polyandry. I incline to let *qualem* stand as due to the idea *qualem quemque virum sciero, ita iudicabo*. But the possibility that two lines are missing after 35 is not excluded — BAILEY.

Appendix H Carmen LXXX (continued from pp. 196–7)

1. At non longa bene non stat bene mentula crassa — *AHLPV*
    At non longa mihi non stat bene mentula crassa — *z*
    At non longa bene, bene stat non mentula crassa — *Q*
    At non longa bene, bene non stat mentula crassa — *S*
    At non longa satis, bene non stat mentula crassa — *W*
    At non longa satis, non stat bene mentula crassa — *ed. Mutin. Ald.*
    Ut non longa satis, bene non stat mentula crassa — *Ital.*
    At nunc longa satis, nunc stat mentula crassa — *Tollius*
    At non longa benest, bene non stat mentula crassa — *Muell.*
    At non longa bene, at non stat bene mentula crassa — *Buech.* 1863
         Pasc.
    At non longa bene est, at non bene mentula crassa — *Baehr. edd.*
         recentiores

Der Sprecher redet von Vorwürfen, die ihm wegen seiner non bene longa, non bene crassa mentula gemacht werden. Die Mädchen urteilen nur nach der mensura. Aber gibt es denn nicht noch etwas Wichtigeres? — SUESS.

> Know that this crass coarse yard nor lengthens nor stands as becomes it;
> Though as thou handle the same unto fair growth will it grow. — BURTON

Goethe saw it as a Priapus speaking, and telling how girls, finding his member neither long nor stout enough, had tried to increase its size by manipulation, but had failed.

A point at issue is, does the poet mean to tell Priapus that, although his prick is of perfectly normal size and behaviour, it still will not satisfy the girls (O'Connor), or that it is "too large for some" (Richlin), or that he is impotent — as most critics have taken it (e.g. Herter)? The similarity of the final couplet to one in the *Satyricon* (131) supports the third interpretation. These last two lines are ignored by Clairmont, despite their presence in the mss.

REFERENCES

B (XXI) Scioppius *Priapea* (Frankfurt, 1606), 57; Barthius *Adversarii* (Frankfurt, 1624), 27 8; Burmannus *Anthologia* 2 (Amsterdam, 1773), 497; Buecheler, F. *Rh.Mus.* 18 (1863), 389–90; Pascal *Carmina ludicra Romanorum* (Rome, 1918), 46–7; Maggi, A. *I Priapea* (Naples, 1923), 24–5; Herter *De Priapo* (Giessen, 1932), 211; Buchheit, V. *Zetemata* 28 (1962), 137–9; Mueller, L. *Catulli Tibulli Propertii carmina* (Leipzig, 1872), xlix–l; Housman, A.E. *Hermes* 66 (1931), 402–3; O'Connor, E.M. *Dominant themes in Priapic poetry* (diss. Univ. of Calif. Santa Barbara, 1984), 281–5.

C (XXXII) Burmannus *Anthologia* 2, 505–8; Buecheler, *Rh.Mus.* 18, 392–3; Cazzaniga. E. *Carmina ludicra Romanorum* (Turin, 1959); Buchheit *Zetemata* 28, 139–42.

D (XLIII) Augustinus, A. *De civitate dei* 6 9; Hugues, P.F. *Monuments du culte secret* (Capri, 1784), 43, pl. xxii; Scioppius *Priapea*, 79; Buecheler *Rh.Mus.* 18, 395–6; Mariotti, S. in Terzaghi, N., *Lanx Satura* (Genoa, 1963), 261–2.

E (LII) Anton, G.C, *Diversorum poetarum veterum in Priapum* (Leipzig, 1781), carm. 52, v.10; Meyer, H. *Anthologia Latina* 2 (Leipzig, 1835), 146; Suess, W. *Philologus* 23 (1910), 446.

F (LIV) Scioppius *Priapea*, 90; Goethe in Grumach. E. *Goethe und die Antike* (Berlin, 1949), 386; Buecheler *Rh.Mus.* 18, 402.

G (LXVIII) Burmannus *Anthologia* 2, 536–41; Meyer *Anthologia* 2, 149; Buecheler *Rh.Mus.* 18, 408; Gyraldus, L. Diologismus XIV in Gruterus, J. *Lampas* (Frankfurt, 1604), 2, 422; Mueller *Catulli*, xliv–v; Pascal *Carmina ludicra*, 54; Bailey, D.R.S. *Phoenix* 32 (1978), 317; Mariotti in Terzaghi, *Lanx Satura*, 264.

H (LXXX) Suess *Philologus* 23, 444–5; O'Connor, *Priapic poetry*, 373; Richlin *Garden of Priapus*, 123; Herter *De Priapo*, 224; Clairmont *Carmina Priapea* 377–80.

Index

Index

Index

Martial
and *Priapea* 38
arrangement 38–9
author of *Priapea*? 33–7, 44
Epigrams 3 68 27, 38, 78–9, *10 92*
11
his *priapea* 25–8, 37, 38
masturbation in 121
metre 37, 46–7
obscenity in 41–2
Priapus in 27
refers to Elephantis 73
Sacred Way in 204
Telethusa in 131
uses *pone supercilium* 67
Martianus Capella 25
masturbation 43, 99, 120–1
Melissus, Paul 35
Menagius 35, 74
Mercury 81, 125, 128–9, 187
metre
caesura 46, 47
choliambic 39, 45, 46, 47–8, 124
double glyconic 1
elegiac distichs 19, 39, 45, 46–7
hendecasyllabic 37, 39, 45, 46, 114
iambic 14, 21
priapean 1, 12, 14
scazons *see* choliambic
see also under Priapea
Meyer, H.
arrangement of *Priapea* 57
cited 184 (**73**), 196 (**80**), 206
(**52**), 207 (**68**)
his *Anthologia Latina* 55
Minerva 100–1, 124–5
moly 176–7
Mommsen, T. 19
Mt Olympus 127
Mueller, L.
cited 102 (**21**), 106 (**24**), 156
(**57**), 168 (**63**), 196 (**80**), 204
(**21**), 208 (**68**)
edition of *Priapea* 34, 55, 57
on authorship 34
Murbach library catalogue 32
Muses 69
Mutinus Tutinus 135
Mycenae 186–7
mythology 21, 38, *see also under Priapea*

Naiads 120–1
Nausicaa 94–5, 149, 176–7
Neptune 81, 100–1, 186–7
Nestor 156–7

nymphs
addressed in Tivoli hymn 29
Flora 28
have disappeared 120–1
Lotis 21–2
Priapus chases 21, 27
Priapus friend of 23

obscenity *see under Priapea, priapea*
O'Connor, E.M.
cited 108 (**25**), 132–3 (**41**), 143
(**49**), 152 (**53, 54**), 155 (**56**), 156
(**57**), 160 (**60**), 179 (**69**), 184–5
(**73**), 193 (**78**), 195 (**79**), 196
(**80**), 204 (**21**), 205 (**32**), 208–9
(**80**)
his Priapic poetry 56
on authorship 36
on date 37
Odysseus 176–9
Odyssey 24, 95, 149, 174–9
Ovid
and *Priapea* 38
and unchaste verse 42
Ars. Am. 2 265–6 102–3
author of the *Priapea*? 33–6, 44–5
cited 121
Fasti 1 21, *6* 22–3
Hippolytus in 99
his *Nux* 103
his Priapus 21
Metamorphoses 22, 23
metre 46–7
priapic poetry by 21–3
3 ascribed to 34, 36, 70–1

Pallas *see* Athene
Pan 2, 29, 186–7
parody 11, 24, 25, 41, 42, 44, *see also
under Priapea*
Pascal
cited 88 (**13**), 110 (**26**), 116 (**31**),
120 (**33**), 136 (**35**), 168 (**63**), 172
(**67**), 188 (**76**), 204 (**21**), 208 (**68**)
edition of *Priapea* 55
on authorship 34
Pathos 186–7
Pausanias 78
Payne-Knight, R. 123
pedicare
in letter and word games 76–7,
172–3
Priapus' battlecry 71, 122, 128–9
variations on 48
pedicatio
as aggression 50
as punishment for thieves 10, 42,

211

Index

Index

threatens *irrumatio* 112–13, 114–15, 122–3, 134–5, 154–5, 180–1, 184–5

threatens *pedicatio* 6, 10, 25, 42, 43, 44, 84–5, 88–9, 96–7, 108–9, 112–13, 116–17, 122–3, 150–1, 172–3, 184–5

threatens thieves 24, 96–3, 104–5, 106–7, 160–1, 178–9, 182–3 *see also* threatens *pedicatio*

vessels shaped like 28

where found 9

witty 50

Propertius 46–7, 204

Proserpina 187

prostitutes 2, 3–4, 43, 50, 98–9, 122–3, 130–1, 204

Prudentius 30

Quid hoc novi est? (What have we here?) 19–21, 54

Quintia 113

Quintilian 49

Radford, R.S. 34, 35, 36, 45, 47

Rand, E.K. 34, 35

Rankin, H.D. 45

Rhodes 186–7

Richlin, A. 45, 107, 197, 209

Roman male 43, 44, 49–51

Roman matrons 78–9

Rome 15, 17, 102–3, 130–1

Rubrius of Samos 9

Sabinus, Floridus 33

Sacred Way 103, 203–4

Samos 186–7

Satyricon 10, 23, 141, 209

Scaliger

cited 115 (**30**), 132 (**42**), 136–7 (**45**), 138 (**46**), 142 (**49**), 150–1 (**52**), 156 (**57**), 162 (**61**), 192 (**78**),196 (**80**), 203 (**21**)

commentary by 54

edition of *Priapea* 54

on authorship of *Priapea* 33

priapea assigned to Tibullus by 19

Schilling, R.

Schönberger, H.K. 48

Scioppius

cited 72 (**4**), 132 (**41**), 138 (**46**), 153 (**54**), 203 (**21**), 205 (**43**), 206 (**54**)

edition of *Priapea* 54

on authorship of *Priapea* 33

Scopas 82–3

Seneca 34, 36, 71

Servius 32, 35

Sibyl of Cumae 86–7

Sidonius Apollinaris 24

Silenus 21–2

Sirius 164–5

slave-owning 50–1

sodomy *see* anal rape and *pedicatio*

Steele, R. 34

Steuding, H. 168

Strabo 1

Strato 37, 37–8, 67, 69

Suess, W. 151, 186, 206, 208

Suetonius 1, 12, 32, 35, 73

Tatian 49

Telethusa 38, 98–9, 130–1

Terpsichore 79

testes 92–3

Tharsia 131

Thasos 23

Theocritus 2, 4, 19

Thera 1

Theseus 86–7, 99

Thetis 127

Thomason, R.F., 34

Thyrreum 1

thyrsus 80–1, 100–1

Tiberius 73

Tibullus

asks Priapus for help 17

author of *Priapea*? 33, 44

Elegy 1 1 19, *1 4* 17–19

priapea attributed to 19–21

Tibur *see* Tivoli

Tiburtine hymn *see* Tivoli hymn

Tisiphone 16

Tithon 156–7, 188–9

Tivoli 10, 28, 57, 186–7

Tivoli hymn 10, 11, 28–30, 57, 169

tree, poems hung upon 41, 162–3

Trimalchion's feast 27, 141

t'Serstevens, A. 56

Tydeus 196–7

Ulysses 24, 176–7

Vanggaard, T. 49

Venus 27, 29, 124–5, 186–7

verses

asked for Priapus 132–3

hung on tree 162–3

obscene 142–3

on temple walls 33, 46, 69, 142–3

Vesperi, A. 56

Vesta 22, 67, 103, 116–17